PRAISE FOR *88 GREAT MBA APPLICATION TIPS AND S* YOU INTO A TOP BUSINESS SCHOOL

"Other MBA application books provide 'guidance', but Royal's 88 Tips and Strategies gives you hands-on, usable knowledge to really get the job done right. It removes the intentional mystery and confusion of this very important first step to getting one of the most valuable professional degrees."
Steve Silbiger
Author of The Ten-Day MBA: A Step-By Step Guide to Mastering The Skills Taught in America's Top Business Schools

"Every candidate has gone to university, has at least a couple of years of work experience, and has a certain amount of life experience. One part of the application process involves simply restating your academic, professional, and personal accomplishments. Another part is about how to interpret these experiences in a meaningful way. This is the trickier but more interesting and rewarding part of applying to b-school. Read this book and gain insights into how other candidates have done it."
Brian Li
MBA Graduate, Class of 2002
Stanford Business School

"There are no guarantees when it comes to MBA admissions. However, as in the business world, effective communicators always come out ahead. Successful applicants know how to turn even a generic B-school application into a showcase of their own talents and accomplishments. Mr. Royal's publication is valuable in that it shows applicants how to do just that."
Yukiko Asada, Director of Admissions
Graduate School of International Management
International University of Japan

"Applying to a top business school is hard work. My first application package took me around 40 hours to complete. It gets easier after that but the most important thing is to develop the ability to constantly boil everything down, especially when writing the application essays. Brandon's approach helps you combine 'who you are' and 'what you've done' with 'where you're going' in order to present a complete and distinguished picture of yourself."
Jeremy Cheung
MBA Graduate, Class of 2000
Harvard Business School

"Mr. Royal clearly knows how to combine academic expectations with real-world competence. Even if the applicant went no further in his or her application, the advice on how to assemble and present appropriate information is a life-skill well worth acquiring. Anyone considering an MBA at some point in their careers would be well advised to use this book; not only will it improve their application chances, it provides a model of effective communication that is worth emulating."
Dr Ailsa Stewart-Smith
Director of Admissions, Graduate School of Business
University of Cape Town, South Africa

"Brandon Royal's 88 Great MBA Application Tips and Strategies is an excellent, comprehensive and easy-to-use guidebook for anyone considering an MBA education. It is also one of the few resources which addresses business schools in Europe and Asia."
Brook Hardwick
Associate Director, MBA Admissions
IESE Business School

張
佳
子

"This book helped me to prepare my B-school application with a newfound perspective, without which, my application will have been duller and more disorganised if left to my own accord. I never knew writing application essays could be that fun, till I came across the 'creative structure' concept used to write the 'who are you?' type essay. With this inspiration, I came up with my creative essay using tarot cards as the subject matter in describing who I am as a person.

Moreover, this book also demonstrates how to put the standard information, i.e. resume, employment history, extracurricular activities, etc in an organised and outstanding manner. It clearly helped me in distinguishing my application from others."

Nancy Chan
MBA Graduate, Class of 2002
London Business School

"Applying to MBA programs can be a daunting task, and this book helps ease that process by providing excellent guidance for the prospective MBA student. The advice included here is very much in line with the feedback and counseling we provide to our applicants at the University of Michigan Business School, and it is presented in an easy-to-use format. The FAQs and the tips are really helpful."

Kris Nebel
Director of Admissions
University of Michigan Business School

"88 Great MBA Application Tips and Strategies is a fantastic resource for any person applying to business schools. Brandon's publication helped me to organize my application and refine my strategy to enhance my chances of being admitted to a top-choice business school. I would recommend this book to be read and re-read before and during the application process."

Jesse Friedlander
MA/MBA Graduate, Class of 2001
SAIS/Wharton

"It is said, 'You cannot judge a book by its cover'; however people still tend to do so. This is also true when it comes to reading MBA applications. The reader relies heavily on what the applicant reveals in writing. Admissions committee members will read your application like a book so why not make it the best one possible? You only have one shot at making a good first impression. The best read applications are those with hours of well thought out planning and preparation behind them. Brandon Royal's book, 88 Great MBA Application Tips and Strategies to Get You into a Top Business School will be instrumental in assisting you to get it right the first time."

Joann Pitteloud
Former MBA Director of Admissions
IMD

"Getting into a top MBA program is more competitive than ever. Show your leadership skills early and get this book."

Tom Fischgrund
Former Senior Marketing Manager, Coca Cola
Harvard Business School Graduate
Author, The Insider's Guide to the Top Ten Business Schools

88 Great
MBA
Application Tips
and Strategies
to Get You into a
Top Business School

Second Edition

Brandon Royal

Singapore   London   New York   Toronto   Sydney   Tokyo   Madrid
Mexico City   Munich   Paris   Capetown   Hong Kong   Montreal

Published in 2004 by
Prentice Hall
Pearson Education South Asia Pte Ltd
23/25 First Lok Yang Road
Singapore 629733

Pearson Education offices in Asia: *Bangkok, Beijing, Hong Kong, Kuala Lumpur, Manila, New Delhi, Seoul, Singapore, Taipei, Tokyo, Shanghai*

Printed in Singapore

5 4 3 2
08 07 06

ISBN 981-244-587-0

National Library Board (Singapore) Cataloguing in Publication Data

Royal, Brandon.
  88 great MBA application tips and strategies to get you into a top business school/Brandon Royal. – 2nd ed. – Singapore : Prentice Hall, 2003.
  p. cm.
  ISBN : 981-244-587-0

1. Master of business administration degree.   2. Business education.
3. Business schools.   I. Title.

HF1111
650.0711 — dc21   SLS2003030991

Contents

Foreword: From One of America's Leading Admissions Spokespersons

Pursuing graduate education in business has grown in popularity in the past five years. Applications have increased at many business schools worldwide, making the competition to get in stiffer than ever.

Having worked in the graduate admissions and financial aid field for over 15 years now, I have had the privilege of working with many prospective students. Perhaps the best part of my job, and the most humbling, is that of being in a position to help very talented and motivated individuals accomplish their educational and career goals.

Over the years, I have found that students who benefit most from their graduate business education tend to approach the subject systematically. Therefore, I would advise you to do the following:

1. Plan ahead. Giving serious thought to what you are planning to do and how to get there may seem elementary to some. But it often happens that prospective students wait until the last minute to start preparing their applications. Advanced planning is crucial if you are going to have time to contact various business schools, read the information they send, apply, and evaluate options if you get more than one admission offer.

2. Do your homework. A lot of time is spent preparing written materials on graduate schools—most take great pains to ensure that they present as accurate a picture as possible about what they have to offer in terms of curriculum, faculty, students, facilities, extracurriculars, financial aid, career options, etc. You will get a wealth of information if you simply take time to read this information. Admissions officers can be less than impressed when a prospective student asks questions that are readily answered in the brochure or application.

3. Visit the campus. It is well worth the investment to experience first hand the "real" environment of those schools in which you are most interested. Word-of-mouth is helpful, as are written materials. But "being there" allows you to formulate your own perceptions of academic and student life.

4. Attend an MBA event if possible. MBA forums, admissions receptions, or other informational-type programs can provide additional information on the business schools you are thinking about. In some cases the alumni will assist the admissions office at these events—meeting them can provide another source of "inside" information.

5. Spend time on your application. Do not wait until the last minute to start preparing your application materials. In addition, make sure you follow directions. Do not send in a handwritten application, essays or recommendations letters that are for another business school. You should ensure that what you

send in to the admissions office is your best effort at preparing a first class application.

6. Apply early rather than late. You will probably have a list of first and second choice business schools. Be sure to submit your application of your top choices early in the process. This usually means you hear sooner about admission and, if you are admitted, your chances of being considered for scholarship dollars are greater.

7. If admitted, consider your options carefully. Perhaps you were somewhat reluctant to ask certain questions about certain schools while in the application process for fear you might hurt your chances of being admitted. Now that you have been accepted, you are in the position of making a choice, and you should make sure all of your questions are answered so that you are able to make an informed decision about enrollment.

8. If denied, try to remember that this is not a personal rejection. Admissions committees at most business schools must make very difficult decisions, often choosing among excellent candidates who are best qualified for their program. A decision to deny is almost never a judgment about someone's ability to do graduate study in business. It is more often than not based on the number of openings a school has for its incoming class versus the number of applicants. If you are turned down by a particular business school you really want to attend, you might consider re-applying the following year.

9. If waitlisted, take the initiative to provide additional information to the admissions committee. Being placed on the waiting list is usually something about which you should be encouraged. It means that the admissions committee sees something in your application that they want to come back and review at a future date. It is very important that you respond if placed on the waiting list. By doing so you demonstrate that you are genuinely interested in that school— this could make a difference when your application is re-visited.

10. Remember that just as you evaluate the treatment you receive in the admissions process, so will your behavior be evaluated. Neither the admissions staff nor the applicant gets a second chance to make a first impression. Be sure that you are courteous and handle frustration graciously.

Best wishes as you make plans for the future!

Donald C. Martin, PhD
(Donald Martin is currently the Associate Dean for Enrollment at the University of Chicago's Graduate School of Business. He was Director of Admissions for the GSB from 1993–1998.)

Introduction

The MBA degree is the world's most versatile advanced education credential. With it you can rise in the ranks of the corporate world, start your own business, or go into government or non-profit work. An MBA is a highly transferable degree, and unlike law, medicine, accounting, or engineering which may place quotas on the number of professionals that practice in a given region or country, there are no restrictions placed on the number of practicing businesspersons holding graduate business degrees.

The business school student marketplace is both a buyer's market and a seller's market. With some 1,500 programs currently existing worldwide, and with more institutions offering an MBA degree every year, the good news is that if you just want to get "an MBA" you can invariably do so. There are a number of less competitive schools and you can also pursue the degree in a variety of ways including full-time, part-time, or executive MBA programs. You can even do an MBA by correspondence.

However, competition to get into the best full-time business schools is significant. For the top 20 or so of the world's leading business schools the acceptance rate is low—20 percent or less. The vast majority of applicants reading this book desire, and in some respects insist on, going to a "top" full-time MBA program. This alters the equation because there are about 10 to 15 full-time business schools worldwide that are extremely popular these days and you will not be alone in applying. Knowledge of as many tricks and tips is needed to help master the process.

Who would you bet on to win a game of chess—an elementary school chess champion or a top ranking PhD candidate who knows little about the game but is familiar with the general rules? Answer: the elementary school chess champion. Why? Because personal savvy is more important than unfocused intelligence. Individuals who know the intimate rules and workings of a game can wipe out the uninitiated. Every game has its general rules, as well as its insider rules. The MBA admissions process is no exception. It is important to try to understand as many of these insider rules as you can to maximize your chances for acceptance. The admissions process is not perfectly fair. Sometimes individuals who are not entirely deserving get accepted to schools; other times individuals who deserve to be accepted get rejected. That having been said, if you believe you are a serious candidate bent on a place at a top school, this book will help you to play the admissions game and stand the best chance of winning.

This book summarizes the best, most up-to-date techniques used to help university graduates and young professionals get into today's leading business schools. It is a compilation of real-life experiences and a distillation of hundreds of hours of one-on-one personal tutoring sessions with prospective MBA students who have succeeded in gaining acceptance to one or more of the world's leading business schools. It not only offers an insider's guide to the MBA admissions process, as opposed to a factual description of MBA programs, but also supplies a distinctive admissions philosophy. This book differs from any other MBA book of its kind in at least three crucial ways:

1. A practical, detailed approach. This book is written with the informed candidate in mind. Today's informed candidate is smart, determined, and resourceful. He or she is looking for more than generalities. The details in this book, coupled with its easy-to-follow 88 tips, make it the ultimate "how to" book in the marketplace in terms of MBA application books.

2. A focus on the application essay. As essays are arguably the most important element in the admissions process, this book is the first of its kind to provide a detailed framework of how to actually write MBA essays, in addition to providing sample essays. All ten types of essay questions are covered as well as common mistakes and winning approaches.

3. An international perspective. This book draws on numerous examples presented from an international viewpoint. Not only do international applicants represent the largest growing segment of the applicant pool, but more and more domestic candidates increasingly secure international experience prior to attending business school. This book is a gold mine for any candidate who plans to truly maximize his or her international experience.

A DETAILED APPROACH AND A DISTINCTIVE PHILOSOPHY

This book is written foremost for the candidate who insists on getting into a "top" business school; it is not designed for the person still trying to answer the question: "Should I or should I not go to business school?" One primary goal is to go beyond generalities and supply concrete examples of how to win acceptance through your admissions essays. Other materials in the marketplace commonly suffer from superficiality. Many books follow a shotgun approach and try to cover essay writing as it applies to getting into graduate school in general, including law, medicine, engineering and business.

WRITING UNIQUE APPLICATION ESSAYS

The philosophy contained herein is that everyone is a potentially unique candidate who must first identify this uniqueness before going the extra distance to make his or her application stand out. "Do what your competitors would not do, and go the extra mile." Where is the best place to do this? Answer: Throughout all parts of your application, but especially through your application essays. Essays are perhaps the most important single component of your application. It is the subjective nature of essays that creates an edge for you in the admissions process. With the possible exception of an actual interview, the reading of your essays is the closest the admissions committee will get to meeting you. In a number of universities, no interviews are given. In this respect, your essays are probably the admissions committee's only introduction to the "real" you.

This book seeks to do what no other book on the market has succeeded in doing so far on the topic of MBA admissions. It will actually show you how to write your essays.

Some books compile sample essays (of which only a few are distinctive) but fail to explain how to write similar essays. The candidate will read these samples and nod in general agreement but will still have no real idea of how to write his or her own essays when the time comes. The year 2003 and beyond will continue to be hectic times for applicants. The MBA marketplace has to keep pace with the increased demands of top applicants who seek to put together better and better applications. It is hoped that this book can expand the mindset and degree of mental toughness needed when applying to the most selective business programs.

BUILDING A WINNING APPLICATION IS LIKE BUILDING A HOUSE

Putting together a good application is like building a house. In terms of building a house, 25 percent of your time is spent planning and designing the house including drawing blueprints. Fifty percent of your time is spent actually building the house, including digging the foundation, framing the walls, and putting in the wiring and plumbing—getting the work done and grinding it out. Twenty-five percent of your time is spent painting walls and ceilings, putting in carpets and wallpaper, decorating, making everything look visually pleasing, making last minute changes, and getting ready to move in or readying it for resale.

The application process may be broken down as follows:

1.   Planning. Twenty-five percent of your time and effort is spent on collecting and reading information and creating a strategy that will work to get you into a top school. The key question to ask is, "What makes me a special candidate?"
2.   Execution. Fifty percent of your time and effort is spent getting the Graduate Management Admissions Test (GMAT) done, revamping your resume, getting your letters of recommendation, completing your interviews, drafting your application essays, and filling in the application forms.
3.   Marketing. Twenty-five percent of your time and effort is spent completing interviews, finalizing your essays and application, and ensuring that all pieces of the application are coordinated.

YOUR KEY TO APPLYING TO BUSINESS SCHOOL

What would you pick as the major reason for rejection by a top business school?

(A) A candidate applies late rather than early.
(B) A candidate has minimal work experience.
(C) A candidate makes a number of grammatical errors in his or her application essays.
(D) A candidate has a poor admissions interview.
(E) A candidate has a "low" GMAT score.

This is a trick question. The answer is really all of the above and none of the above. It is all of the above in that the admissions process is holistic and it is difficult to isolate one particular factor as the key for rejection. It is none of the above in so far as none of the answers are likely correct in terms of the *major* reason for rejection. For example, there are many misconceptions about the admissions process and these answer choices play upon them. Students who assume Choice A is correct make the assumption that their application is a "winner", but just late. This is a big assumption. Choice B might be true in some cases, but certainly not true in the majority of cases where applicants have sufficient work experience, usually two to five years.

Candidates who choose Choice C are likely to confuse grammatical accuracy with the more important topic of essay content. Strategically correct writing combines what you write (content) and the order in which you write it (structure), which is more important than grammar, particularly for international candidates where English is not their first language. Choice D, a poor admissions interview, is also less likely to be the major reason. The trend in interviews is to make cuts based on an initial review of business school applications, and then to offer interviews to a select number of applicants. Since most candidates will not make this cut, the interview will not be the major reason for rejection. Students choosing Choice E probably underestimate the range of GMAT scores accepted at top schools. It is true that the average GMAT score of successful candidates applying to top schools has increased significantly in the last decade, but you may want to review the answer to the most frequently asked admissions question, no. 13 in Chapter 2, for an insight into the range of scores accepted.

The answer to this question is also none of the above as there is another choice not presented, which is more likely to be the major reason most individuals get rejected by top business schools. Approximately 50 percent of all candidates applying to top business schools fail because they cannot communicate concrete or well-defined career goals, in particular, as demanded by the "career goals" application essay. Business schools are impressed by candidates who know where they are going and have a clear idea of how they are going to get there. Consequently, this area is of paramount importance and is addressed specifically in Chapter 3 under the topic of *goal* and *vision statements*.

A WORD ABOUT DIVERSITY

One of the biggest areas of interest for the international applicant is how to leverage international experience—professional and educational—in the application process. Business schools seek international applicants and prize applicants with international experience. Geographically diverse backgrounds or unusual personal and professional experiences are often a key to getting accepted by a top business school. This book provides many tips on how you can use your background to make yourself appear as a "one-of-a-kind" applicant. Moreover, today's leading business schools make a real effort to try to support under-represented groups in the admissions process. Minority programs at major universities exist to recruit minority students and it is worth looking into such programs in the event that you fall into one of these categories. Twenty-five to thirty percent of a typical MBA class is female, and because of this fact, female applicants have a slight advantage over male counterparts in the admissions process. Certain ethnic groups, such as Hispanics, make up two to three percent of the typical incoming class at major U.S. business schools and admissions officers would like to see a higher percentage of these candidates represented. It would also seem evident, based on world population statistics, that candidates native to Africa are under-represented in the entering classes of major business schools.

However, rather than endorse specific strategies aimed at minority or international candidates, this book resolves to look at all candidates as unique in themselves and thus on equal footing. The words "international" or "minority" are slowly losing their significance because we live in a world that is increasingly multicultural. In the U.S., for example, international students comprise 30 percent of a typical high-profile business school class. That does not, however, imply that the other 70 percent of a typical U.S. business school class is homogeneous in makeup. Although 70 percent might be American, this could include Asian-Americans, African-Americans, Hispanic-Americans, native American Indians, or newly-arrived U.S. immigrants from every conceivable geographical location. The same is true of international students, who although holding foreign passports, might represent a cross-section of different ethnic backgrounds.

The playing field for international applicants is being leveled. This means that it is mattering less, not more, where you come from. The days are disappearing when you could bet on an acceptance letter just because of your country of citizenship, your ethnic background, or your international travel experience. In the mid-1980s, for example, if you were an applicant who had graduated from Moscow State University or Beijing University, you could bet on acceptance at most top business schools. Nowadays, admissions officers are seeing many applicants from places considered unusual in the past. It is much harder to play the "Take me—I'm from a strange and unusual place" card. Every candidate should first think in terms of presenting himself or herself on the basis of his or her own merits, including intelligence, passion, personality, hard work, ingenuity, and dedication.

WHAT DOES THIS BOOK COVER?

MBA admissions is a process that covers the interplay of seven primary application components: (1) GMAT, (2) college transcripts, (3) employment record, (4) letters of recommendation, (5) interviews, (6) extracurricular activities, and (7) application essays. Visualize the seven application components as divided between quantitative and qualitative elements. Whereas Grade Point Average (GPA) and GMAT are considered to be the "number side" of the admissions process, the resume, letters of recommendation, interviews, essays, and extracurricular involvement are the other qualitative side of the process. Although this book covers all of the seven application components, only light coverage is given to the "numbers" side of the admissions process. The GMAT is an intensive but completely separate undertaking. GPA, as reflected by college transcripts, is generally set before a person applies to business school and cannot be changed.

In short, MBA admissions strategies are focused on the "qualitative" aspects of the MBA admissions process—the ones over which you exercise significant control in terms of content and presentation. These strategies are aimed at helping each candidate write excellent application essays, present a strong employment record, get good letters of recommendation, embellish extracurricular involvement or community service, and prepare for interviews, if required.

The thrust of this book addresses the qualitative side of the MBA admissions process, with a focus on application essays. Chapter 3, *Essay Writing Part I: The Classic MBA Essays* is an anchor chapter for addressing the four classic essays and highlighting common weaknesses and winning approaches for completing each of these four essay types. This chapter follows up with sample essays to show how to apply the winning approaches in practice. Chapter 4, *Essay Writing Part II: The Other MBA Essays* presents a discussion of the *other* commonly encountered MBA essay types and, again, includes sample essays for each type.

The ability to write optional essays, as covered in Chapter 5, *Essay Writing Part III: Optional Essay Entries* could be a deciding factor in your being accepted by a business school. The answer to the question: "Is there anything else you would like the admissions committee to know?" lends itself to five separate strategies as covered under the five uses of the optional or "blank" question. Make no mistake—very few prospective candidates are so stellar that they are without anticipated weaknesses. The secret is not only how to neutralize your weaknesses but also to emphasize your strengths and diverse background. Writing optional essays can be a key step in doing both of these things. Finally, the employment record, letters of recommendation, interview, and extracurricular activities are each covered in separate chapters.

This book is a compilation of real-life experiences of students applying to top business schools. The road to building an exceptional business school application can be exhausting but it can also be energizing. Once you master one application, it is easier to cut and paste your previous work to complete similar parts of other MBA applications. The time spent on applications will repay itself by getting you accepted by a "top" business school—the business school of your choice—and by taking you to the next stage of your career.

Please feel free to write in this book while you are making your review. When you get an idea, pencil your comments in the margin, and you will be less likely to forget them when sitting down to complete your essays and application package. Lastly, your suggestions are welcome and invited. Please send them care of the author:

Brandon Royal
G.P.O. Box 440
Central, Hong Kong
Tel: (852) 2559-8054
Fax: (852) 2559-8047
Email: brandonroyal@attglobal.net
Internet: www.brandonroyal.com

Acknowledgments

This book is dedicated to all of my former GMAT and MBA admissions students, many of whom have gone on to attend leading MBA programs throughout the world. I would especially like to thank a few of those students who have contributed material to this book—Allegra McNeally, Alice Tsui, Amar Reganti, Angel Wan, Angelina Lee, Audrey Tse, Ben Desollar, Brian Frisby, Bryant Lu, Camilla Deichmann, Cedric Gouliardon, Claire-Louise Nightingale, Elena Borovsky, Gary Clemenson, Jeremy Cheung, John Floto, Josephine Lee, K.K. Mak, Karina Lo, Lori Lai, Mark Cho, Niels Thomsen, Peter Chiang, Priyanka Dhaul, Sameer Sopori, Shannon Gill, Steve Chan, Veronica Poon, Vivian Soren, William Fung, and Yen Shiau Sin.

Thanks also go to current and former members of the Kaplan Center Hong Kong including Lee and Miltinnie Yih, Colin Cha Fong, Erika Archer, Ivan Chan, Kacinee Suthipongchai, Kerstin Hall, Laura Ho, Melba Hui, Patrick Graham, Paul Lundquist, and Regina Pei.

Don Martin, Associate Dean for Enrollment at the University of Chicago's Graduate School of Business and Bill Kooser, Associate Dean for Part-time MBA Programs at the University of Chicago both provided me with some helpful hints. Their professionalism, dedication, and compassion for admissions work are noteworthy.

I am equally indebted to key members of the publishing arm of Pearson Education in Singapore: Chua Hong Koon (Publishing Director), Pauline Chua (Editorial Executive), Irene Yeow (Senior Editor), and Angela Chew (Production Editor), Lee Meng Hui (Cover Designer).

CHAPTER 1

What are Schools *Really* Looking For?

*"I would never join any club that would have me as a
member."*

Groucho Marx

OVERVIEW

The goal of the admissions committee is to recruit the best students. Every school defines "best" a little differently, but in general, the following three things hold true. Business schools look for:

1. Applicants with the best career potential and leadership ability.
2. Applicants with the best background and preparation (including academic, professional, and personal experience).
3. Applicants with the greatest need for getting an MBA including the most compelling reasons for attending a particular school's graduate business program.

The admissions committee has an enormous responsibility with regard to selecting its students. Ideally, every committee hopes to get students who are leadership minded and technically skilled, personable, outgoing, and articulate, perseverant yet responsive, career minded but good team players, and who will contribute to their schools as students and alumni, as well as give something back to their communities and societies.

To evaluate these things, admissions officers are said to summarize your candidacy by looking at "who you are" and "what you have done" and "where you are going" with your career, as well as "why you want an MBA", and "why you want to attend a particular MBA program". Who you are likely translates to your being a person of good character with an interesting personality. What you have done translates to solid academic and professional achievements including your accomplishments, awards, and recognition. Where you are going with your career translates into having reasonably clear career goals and, hopefully, a vision of where your chosen industry is headed.

Another way to think about what schools are looking for is to view your background as a triumvirate of academic, professional, and personal experiences. Your academic background may be presented through your college transcripts, academic recommendation(s) (if applicable), and GMAT score. Your professional background may be presented through your resume and professional letters of recommendation. Your personal qualities and background may be seen in all parts of the admissions process but particularly through your interviews and application essays.

This might be the place to mention that although top schools are hoping to find ideal candidates, the perfect candidate does not really exist. Most candidates are weak in one or more areas. This is where the game of admissions begins—you will try to emphasize your strengths while minimizing your weaknesses. The admissions committee will try to pick the best candidates in the light of knowing it cannot find "perfect" candidates.

Obviously your primary goal as an applicant is to get accepted to the business school of your choice. To do this, you must show at a minimum that:

1. You have a noble goal and a real need for an MBA.

2.   You can explain in a clear and logical way how you will accomplish your career goal and how your background and experiences act as stepping stones toward this goal.

3.   You have sufficient experience, intellect, and passion to compete for your goal.

What is the ultimate goal for an applicant to achieve in the process of applying to a business school? Answer: To present an application that is so compelling that the admissions committee would believe that failure to accept you would cause the incoming class to be something less than what it would otherwise be. However, the reality is that so few applicants fall into this category that it is not worth worrying about. Most successful applicants do not even meet this criterion; successful candidates are likely to have shown only that they are well-prepared and well-focused individuals.

The first goal of the applicant: "To reveal a noble goal and a need for an MBA."

What is a "noble" goal? A noble goal is essentially any goal that you deem worthwhile to pursue. Do not worry so much what your career goal is as much as your ability to support your goal throughout your application. Thus, the goal of becoming an investment banker is deemed to be equal to the goal of becoming a missionary doctor in Thailand who needs business skills to advance his or her goals. However, the following is not a noble goal: "My goal is to work for the Mafia to assist in their expanding international role." This is not deemed to be a noble goal and will lead to rejection even if the applicant is otherwise well qualified.

What does it mean to have a *need* for an MBA? You must show that an MBA is a necessary stepping stone toward your future goal. Often an MBA degree can be viewed as a missing piece to your career puzzle. An otherwise well-focused and qualified applicant might get rejected if his or her goal is already included in his or her background, and an MBA would not be needed to reach it. For example, "I work as a stockbroker and want an MBA to continue to work as a stockbroker." The admissions committee will likely wonder how an MBA will help you or, more precisely, if you really need an MBA as much as the other applicants. The MBA must be perceived as having value-added quality and/or a greater value-added component relative to other competing candidates.

The second goal of the applicant: "To explain how your background and experience act as stepping stones to your future career goals."

Although you may have an interesting background, it is best that your future be a logical extension of this background. If a person's background and previous training differ greatly from his or her intended career goal, the impression will be that the future goal is not realistic. That is, the goal will not be impossible but arguably implausible. Naturally, your goal should be "bigger" than your background, or else you would not have the need to go to a top business school to gain the knowledge, credential, and contacts. The feeling that an admissions person should come away with after reviewing your application is that of transition. There should be a sense that the applicant is reaching, perhaps straining, but not unduly leaping toward his or her future goal.

The third goal of the applicant: "To show sufficient experience, intellect, and passion to compete for your goal."

The committee is concerned with getting students who can do their best, contribute the most, and not unduly burden themselves, professors, or classmates while doing so. "Numbers" (GPA and GMAT) are important but, beyond given thresholds, numerical comparisons become fruitless. In general, business schools reject students not because they think students cannot do the work but because competition for entering places forces business schools to make choices. In fact, most applicants applying to business school would make it through an MBA program, albeit not all with excellent records. One piece of evidence to support this fact is how few students actually flunk out of business school despite significant variations in GPA and GMAT scores among the entering students. Note that business schools also have a vested interest in helping students succeed and generally do everything in their power to help enrolled business school students pass and graduate.

On another level, admissions personnel want to attract those people who aim to be leaders in their chosen fields. This will likely require skills beyond those required to get through business school. Having sufficient experience and intellect to compete for your career goals involves not only getting through business school but also reaching your mid- to long-term career goals. The higher, more difficult your goal, the more experience and intellect you will require to reach it.

THE ADMISSIONS PROCESS

Exhibit 1–1 is a sample flowchart of the admissions process at the University of Chicago's Graduate School of Business.

THE SEVEN MBA APPLICATION COMPONENTS – AN OUTLINE

Basically there are seven components from the applicant's standpoint (see Table 1–1).

HOW ARE THE APPLICATION COMPONENTS REVIEWED?

Let's look at the hypothetical order in which application components are reviewed. What does the likely order in which they are reviewed tell us about their probable importance?

The seven application components are (in alphabetical order):

Exhibit 1–1   Flowchart of the admissions process

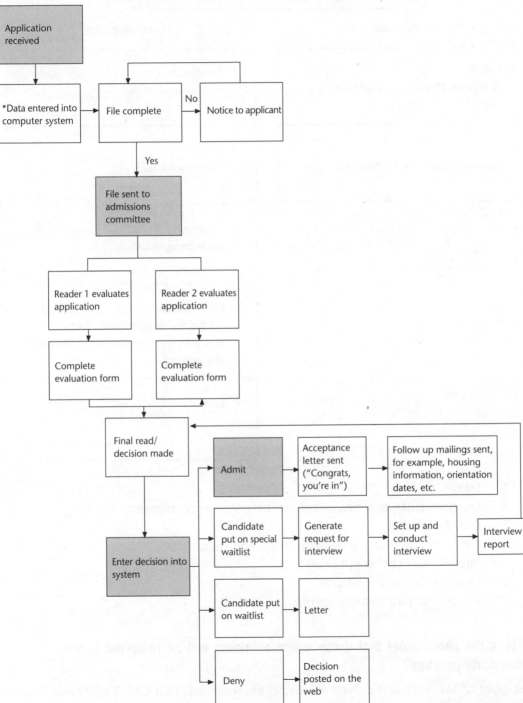

* Data entered into the computer includes biographical information, GMAT score, undergraduate GPA, interview request, round applying for, etc.

Table 1–1 The seven MBA application components

"Numbers side"   "Qualitative side"

1. GMAT (Graduate Management Admissions Test)	3. Resume or employment record
2. GPA (Undergraduate Grade Point Average)	4. Letters of recommendation
	5. Interviews (may be optional)
	6. Extracurriculars (including extracurricular collegiate activities, awards and recognition, and community service)
	7. Essays

1. Essays
2. Extracurricular activities/awards and recognition/community service
3. GMAT
4. GPA – Grade Point Average from college transcripts
5. Interviews (may be optional)
6. Letters of recommendation
7. Resume or employment record

What is the likely order that these seven elements will be reviewed in the admissions process?

First, your GMAT score and college transcripts are reviewed. Your GMAT score and GPA are easily quantifiable components that show up on the data input sheet, which is the first page or two of your application. Second, your resume or employment record is reviewed.

It is after all "business school". The reviewer will be curious to see where you have worked and the caliber of your work experience. Professional letters of recommendation will be perused after a review of your resume because of the complementary nature of these two application components. Admissions officers will first seek to understand the nature of your work experience before going on to interpret what your recommenders have said about this experience. The same is true for academic letters of recommendation (when applicable) in which college transcripts are reviewed first before going on to interpret what your teacher or professor has said about you.

Interview results, if applicable, will be reviewed next. Interview appraisals are short documents, usually one page in length, and will be reviewed before your essays are read. Extracurriculars come next and essays are reviewed last. Essays are both longer and more subjective than other components but will give the reviewer a more holistic picture of who you are as a person and where you are going professionally. The following is a most revealing statement. It is said that unless your numbers are incredibly high or abysmally low, the committee must read your essays to decide whether you will be accepted or rejected. *Put another way, your offer of acceptance or notice of rejection will generally always come down to the reading of your application essays.* This is precisely the reason that so much emphasis is given to essay writing in this book.

In summary, the seven application components are often reviewed in the following order:

1. GMAT
2. College transcripts (GPA)
3. Resume
4. Letters of recommendation
5. Interview results (if applicable)
6. Extracurricular activities
7. Application essays

HOW DO ACCEPTANCE RATES AFFECT A CANDIDATE'S ADMISSIONS CHANCES?

Let's look at a few hypothetical scenarios in order to understand the probable reasons why applicants get accepted and rejected by business schools as a function of falling acceptance rates. Table 1–2 is probably the closest we can come up to actually quantifying the admissions process.

FROM THE NUMBERS SIDE – GMAT

Naturally, the higher your combined GMAT score the better, but generally, a scaled score of 680 (680 out of 800 corresponds to the 90th percentile) is what most candidates aim

Table 1–2 Reasons for acceptance or rejection by business schools

Acceptance rate	Reasons for acceptance or rejection
50% One in two applicants gets accepted.	A candidate who fails to get accepted by a business school with a 50 percent acceptance rate generally has *three* or *more* weak areas in his or her application. For example, a low GPA and minimal work experience are further weakened by writing mediocre application essays. A likely reason that essays are mediocre commonly includes lack of a career focus or an inability on the part of the candidate to give adequate support using specific examples.
25% One in four applicants gets accepted.	A candidate who succeeds in getting accepted by a business school with a 25 percent acceptance rate generally has *two* or *fewer* weak areas in his or her application. For example, a low GPA and weak letters of recommendation are nonetheless combined with a high GMAT score, a good resume, a good interview record, as well as with well-written application essays, and evidence of extracurricular activities.
12% One in eight applicants gets accepted.	A candidate who succeeds in getting accepted by a business school with a 12 percent acceptance rate generally has *one* or *fewer* weak areas in his or her application. For example, a low GPA is overshadowed by a high GMAT score, good resume, strong letters of recommendation, a good interview, and solid application essays, including evidence of extracurricular activities and community service.
<12% Fewer than one in eight applicants gets accepted.	A candidate who succeeds in getting accepted by a business school with a less than 12 percent acceptance rate generally has *no* major application weak point and a couple of outstanding application areas. For example, competitive GPA and GMAT scores are complemented by a particularly strong resume and set of application essays. It is not necessarily correct to say, however, that the applicant is *outstanding* in all areas.

for if applying to top business schools. Although a high GMAT score does not guarantee acceptance and a low score does not preclude it, there is some credence given to the idea that everyone applying to a top business school is equal in the admissions process after scoring 680 or above. In other words, if you get rejected with a score of 680 or above, the problem lies not with your GMAT score but with another part of your application. In terms of applying to business school, particularly top business schools, admissions officers typically view combined GMAT scores as if divided into four arbitrary categories.

Score:	What this likely means:
Less than 500	Not acceptable; take the test over again.
Between 500 to 600	Marginal; low for a top business school, although you could still get accepted.
Between 600 to 700	Below average/average; in the "ball park" for a top business school.
Greater than 700	Above average/excellent!

What type of scores do you get when you take the GMAT?

You actually receive four scores from taking the GMAT exam:
(1) total score, (2) quantitative score, (3) verbal score, and (4) AWA (Analytical Writing Assessment) score. Your total score ranges from 200 to 800. Scores on individual quantitative and verbal sections range from 0 to 60 and are accompanied by a corresponding percentile rank. Your AWA score ranges from 0.0 to 6.0 and is totally independent of your quantitative or verbal and/or total score.

What is on the GMAT?

GMAT quantitative sections are divided into two types of problems: Problem Solving and Data Sufficiency. GMAT verbal sections are divided into three types of problems: Reading Comprehension, Critical Reasoning, and Sentence Correction. In addition, the GMAT contains two short writing exercises called Analytical Writing Assessment (AWA). One assessment is called "analysis of an issue" and the other is called "analysis of an argument". The basic difference between these two exercises is that to analyze the issue, you are required to take a stand and "build" an issue essay whereas to analyze an argument, you are required to critique or breakdown an argument. The AWA samples were added to the GMAT (October 1994) to reflect the growing importance of writing skills both in business school and on the job. Do not confuse the AWA essays that appear on the GMAT with your application essays required in the actual application packages of each school and which are the focus of this book.

You will get an overall or combined score on a scale of 200 to 800 and a corresponding percentile ranking on a scale of 0 to the 99.9th percentile (see Exhibit 1–2). Scores on the GMAT, like other standardized tests, increase geometrically as a given test-taker scores better than the average test-taker. For example, it only takes a scaled score of 630 to score in the 80th percentile, and a scaled score of 680 puts you in the 90th percentile. In layperson's terms, small differences in test performance can lead to relatively big increases in test scoring. This is one argument in favor of preparing for the test including taking a GMAT test preparation course.

Exhibit 1–2 GMAT combined test scores

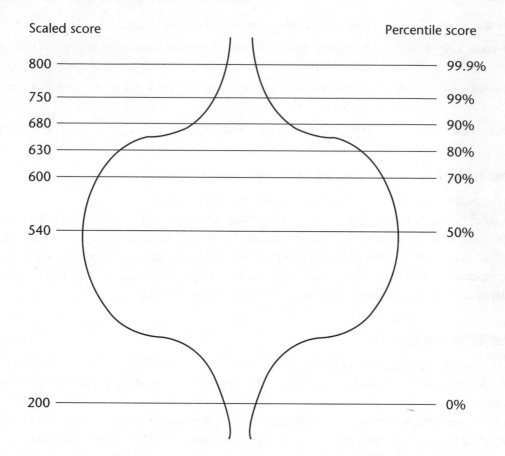

Scaled score

Percentile score

Scaled score	Percentile score
800	99.9%
750	99%
680	90%
630	80%
600	70%
540	50%
200	0%

Did you know?

Although once upon a time it was rare that MBA candidates took the GMAT test more than a single time, nowadays it is a common occurrence. Approximately 50 percent of the incoming students accepted at top business schools have taken the GMAT more than once. Here is one quick tip regarding taking the GMAT multiple times. Say that you have taken the exam once and scored a 650—a pretty good score. But you think you could score higher and want to gamble. In this case, release your first score to all schools that you are applying to. When taking the test for the second time, do not initially request (at the start of the exam) that ETS send your score to any schools. Upon seeing your score (at the end of the exam), you will then know whether you want to send it. If your score is significantly higher than your first score, then contact ETS and get your score sent. If your score is equal or lower than your first score, then don't request ETS to send it. This will protect you against a bad score. It is true that ETS sends all scores on file at the time of a request. But ETS does not send scores unless you tell them to. Such scores remain in the data bank and no one except you will ever know you took the test twice. This strategy is identical for a candidate who has taken the test two times and is attempting a third try.

FROM THE NUMBERS SIDE – GPA

GPA stands for Grade Point Average which should be immediately contrasted with PGA, which stands for the Professional Golf Association! Most U.S. schools grade on a 0.0 to 4.0 scale and will require the grades of students who have studied in international locations to be converted to a comparable scale. Academic transcripts are evaluated on three fronts:

- Reputation of your undergraduate institution.
- Academic difficulty of your undergraduate major.
- GPA.

In other words, think of your academic transcripts as evaluated based on "where you studied, what you took, and what you got." *Where you studied* refers to the general strength and reputation of your undergraduate institution. *What you took* refers to the difficulty of the subject matter studied. Certain majors such as molecular biology are considered more academically difficult than majors such as international relations. In addition to depth or intensity of your academic work, your breadth or variety of academic work (e.g., dual majors, honors courses, special research, etc.) is taken into account. *What you got* refers to your overall GPA. Generally more emphasis is given to the GPA in your major, and/or your GPA trend (e.g., it's better if third and fourth year GPA is higher than first and second year GPA).

How is your GPA looked at?

In terms of applying to business school, admissions officers view GPAs as if divided into four arbitrary categories:

- Below 3.0—marginal.
- Between 3.0 and 3.4—below average/average; in the running for top business schools.
- 3.5 or higher—above average/excellent; includes honors standing, Phi Beta Kappa.
- 3.8 to 4.0—highest standing (*magna cum laude*). However, it is not necessary to have a GPA this high in order to get into a top business school.

For candidates whose undergraduate institutions do not have GPAs, some method of conversion must be done in order to express your GPA on a rough 0.0 to 4.0 scale. International applicants may want to contact the "academic transcript evaluator" at the school they are applying to. Basically, an A grade is considered 4.0, a B grade is considered 3.0, a C grade is considered 2.0. For international applicants applying to the U.S. whose undergraduate degrees last three years instead of four years, a problem may arise. You may want to cite an education report to substantiate your claim that a three-year degree is substitutable for a four-year degree. Refer to the optional essay entry covering this topic contained in Chapter 5. In both of the above situations, you may need to contact the school you are applying to and determine what is needed to resolve the matter.

GMAT SCORES VERSUS GPA

A trade-off appears to exist between GMAT scores and a candidate's GPA as obtained through undergraduate study (see Table 1–3). This analysis is hypothetical. In practice, admissions decisions are not based merely on comparing GMAT scores with GPA. But these two factors do give an indication of the strength of a candidate from the numbers side of the admissions process. The higher a candidate's GPA, the lower his or her GMAT score may be and still gain acceptance. Conversely, the higher a candidate's GMAT score, the lower his or her GPA may be and still gain acceptance. It is unclear whether business schools place more weight on the GMAT score relative to GPA or vice-versa.

GMAT SCORES VERSUS QUALITY OF MBA APPLICATION ESSAYS

A trade-off is also believed to exist between GMAT scores and the quality of MBA application essays (Table 1–4). In practice, essays cannot be contrasted merely with GMAT scores. GMAT scores are likely to be reviewed along with college transcripts for a "quantitative" measure of ability. Essays are likely to be reviewed along with employment record (resume), letters of recommendation, extracurricular activities and/or interviews for a "qualitative" measure of ability. There appears to be empirical evidence to support the idea that application essays carry more weight than the GMAT score in the admissions process. Assuming this to be true, an excellent set of essays with a low GMAT score (**MAYBE) is closer to a "yes" than a high GMAT score with a mediocre set of application essays (*MAYBE).

SEVEN IMPORTANT APPLICATION TIPS

Tip #1: Plan your attack—make a map and chart your progress.

Applying to business school is not for the slothful; it takes a great deal of organization. If you are applying to five or six schools, you will have many items to keep track of. It is recommended that you think of either labeling a large piece of paper or creating two or three separate sheets and labeling these sheets accordingly. The formats shown in Tables 1–5 and 1–6 have been used by successful applicants. Duplicate forms are included for your convenience: see Appendix V, *Application Tracking Sheets*. Alternatively, candidates can use computer spreadsheet programs to create their own forms employing either a "portrait" (vertical) or "landscape" (horizontal) format.

Table 1–5 can help you keep track of the schools you are applying to and applicable application deadlines.

The chart in Table 1–6 can be used to keep track of your college transcript requests, interviews, GMAT scores, letters of recommendation, data information forms, and application essays.

Table 1–3 Trade-off of GMAT scores and GPA for top business schools

GMAT scores	GPA		
	Below 3.0 (marginal)	3.0 to 3.4 (below average/average)	3.5 and Above (above average/excellent)
500 to 590 (marginal)	No	No	Maybe
600 to 690 (below average/average)	No	Maybe	Yes
700 and above (above average/excellent)	Maybe	Yes	Yes

Table 1–4 Trade-off of GMAT scores and quality of MBA application essays

GMAT scores	Application essays		
	Marginal	Below Average/Average	Above Average/Excellent
500 to 590 (marginal)	No	No	**Maybe
600 to 690 (below average/average)	No	Maybe	Yes
700 and above (above average/excellent)	*Maybe	Yes	Yes

✍ Tip #2: Submit applications to "lesser" schools first.

Try to first complete the applications for those schools that are not your first or second choices. Candidates invariably improve on their ability to put together applications, including their ability to write effective essays, as the application process moves forward. You want to match your best applications with your most competitive schools. Too often in practice, most candidates write and submit the essays of their first choice schools right away, which often leaves the less competitive schools with a given candidate's best appli-

Table 1–5 Application tracking sheets — Selected schools and deadlines

Universities	Berkeley	Chicago	Cornell	Dartmouth	Harvard	INSEAD	McGill
Rank	15	5	19	11	2	6	37
App. pckg. downloaded	✓	✓				✓	
Fin. aid. info.							
1st round	rolling	Nov 1	Dec 1	Dec 3	Nov 13	Sep 11	rolling
Reply	–	Dec 13	Jan 31	Jan 14	Jan 15	Nov 6	–
2nd round	–	Dec 2	Jan 15	Jan 17	Jan 8	Nov 27	–
Reply	Jun 1	May 2	May 15	May 19	May 14	all year	Apr 15
Deposit req'd. by							

Table 1–6 Application tracking sheets — Selected schools and deadlines

Universities	Berkeley	Chicago	Cornell	Dartmouth	Harvard	INSEAD	McGill
Transcripts sent	Nov 7					Dec 5	
GMAT taken	✓	✓	✓	✓	✓	✓	✓
1st recom.							
Rec'd.							
2nd recom.							
Rec'd.							
Essays Ok							
Interviews scheduled							

cations. Former applicants tell a similar story each year, "If I had to do it again, I would have applied to AAA school after first applying to BBB school...." This situation can be nullified if you start the application process early enough so that you finish all of your applications before sending off the first one, thus, ensuring that you have time to go back and incorporate changes into your previously completed applications. An alternative (and more realistic) approach is to send out your applications in batches of three. This way you can complete applications in "groups" and can incorporate positive changes in all applications before sending them out.

Tip #3: Supply goals and vision.

Resolve to complete your goal and vision statements before you write your essays or do anything else, including interviewing, if that is an option. You may want to refer to Chapter 3, *Essay Writing Part I: The Classic MBA Essays* for clarification on the specifics of writing good *goal statements* and *vision statements*. Your goal and vision statements will directly affect the quality of your essays, and will indirectly affect all parts of your application, including your interviews and letters of recommendation. In short: A "goal statement" summarizes your career objectives. A "vision statement" summarizes where you think your chosen industry is headed and the special ideas you have on doing business in your chosen field. You may want to ask other people currently working in your company where they believe your chosen industry is headed. It never hurts to take a stroll past the magazine stand to see what trade magazines are available to help sharpen your insights. Lastly, on-line search services, (e.g., Lexis-Nexis, Google, Hotmail, Yahoo, AOL, etc.) are usually excellent resources to use to locate up-to-date information including newspaper and magazine articles that indicate what is going on in your industry.

Tip #4: Create optional or "blank question" entries.

Are you familiar with the question: "Is there anything else you would like the admissions committee to know?" Almost every business school has this question. Do not leave this area blank. Plan to have one or two items which can be included in this section as extra materials at the back of your application. The optional or "blank" question entry may be anything from a clarification of an anticipated weakness to a sample of your creative writing to a sample business document you have worked on. Refer to Chapter 5, *Essay Writing Part III: Optional Essay Entries* for examples of the wide range of topics to write about.

Tip #5: Build your application around a theme.

Think of your application as tied to a theme. A theme may be used to link your work experience, as presented by your resume or employment record, with your application essays and record of extracurricular activities. A theme is one way to express your uniqueness. It may assist the admissions committee in understanding why you are a person who is not only different, but who will make a difference.

The most likely place to build a theme is around your chosen career path. Will you be an entrepreneur, consultant, banker, or marketer? Perhaps there is a general overall theme that characterizes your past, present, and future. A theme may be tied to your background, skills, or talents. Are you a star pianist, baseball aficionado, sports person, or fiction writer? Examine your background and find something that means a lot to you, or a topic you are an expert on, around which you can build a theme. It is said that the admissions committees of major business schools enjoy being able to refer to a candidate in terms of a short captivating phrase. For example, "that's the pianist who wants to work in the music industry", or "the mathematics whiz who likes finance", or the "volunteer junkie who wants to do fashion merchandising." Think of yourself as a label or theme.

Tip #6: Reality check—boil down the whole MBA process.

The MBA admissions process may be thought of as boiling down to: (1) who you are, (2) what you have done, (3) where you are going, and (4) why a particular business program is right for you. Candidates sometimes get lost in the *game* of applying to business school. Certainly there are a number of valued tips of which you want to be aware and take advantage when putting together your application, but there is also a good deal of reality to the admissions process. The most important thing is to ask yourself: "Is the career goal I set for myself really what I want?" Say for example that you strive to be a venture capitalist. Stop and ask yourself: "Does my application feel like that of a venture capitalist?" Is this goal coming like sweat out of my pores? If not, then maybe you should choose another goal. In other words, often the problem with a person's application is not with the writing of essays but rather with the person as he or she defines himself or herself. The sure-fire approach to setting up a winning application is for you to become one with the goal you seek. If you are not already like the person who would naturally succeed in a long-term career position, then start moving in this direction. Talk to people, join the clubs, read the magazines, and start thinking like the type of person who would be a leader in this field. Concentrate on *your* goal, not the one you think a business school would like to hear. Keep drawing a link between who you are, what you have done, and where you are going.

Tip #7: Think of your target audience.

Admissions staff members are your target audience and they are people persons. They are not necessarily businesspersons in the strict sense of the word. Besides being very good at the job they do, they look at things from a personal, human interest perspective. They are especially moved by candidates whom they believe to be interesting and personable. Your ability to express the unique aspects of your candidacy will enhance your overall application.

THREE BLOOPERS TO AVOID

✘ Blooper #1: Switching school names.

Every year admissions officers receive application essays which read perfectly except that they are written to the wrong business school. For example, a person completing a London Business School application states, "This is why I want to apply to INSEAD." Obviously, this is not going to do wonders for your application chances.

✘ Blooper #2: Saying you cannot learn business from books.

If you write in your application essays that businesspersons cannot learn from books, or that entrepreneurship cannot be taught, you should stop and think about what you are saying. The admissions reviewers will likely want to respond by asking why you want to go to business *school*. Of course, nearly everyone would agree that effective and efficient business practices are a combination of theory and practice. However, if you say you cannot learn from books (notwithstanding the fact that books are not the only tool you can learn from in business school), you are belittling the role of business schools and the lives of business school professors. Professors are likely to believe that knowledge or theory is important to help you avoid making basic business mistakes. Saying that books or theories do not "count" is a blooper from the admissions side of the equation.

✘ Blooper #3: Referring to your second choice schools as "backup schools".

Can you imagine going to a job interview and telling the interviewer that the only reason you are interviewing with their company is that you couldn't find a job elsewhere? Likewise, if you mention that your main reason for applying to a given business school is to give you a "backup" option in the event you do not get into any other business schools, this will not help your admission chances. You do not need to state that every school you are applying to is your first choice, but you should not say that a given business school is your last choice.

CHAPTER 2

Most Frequently Asked MBA Admissions Questions

"My job is not to worry about insulting any of you. It is to worry about insulting each of you equally."

Professor Minlind M. Lele, University of Chicago, in his opening course lecture for Strategic Management. He refers humorously to the need to call on students at random to answer case study questions.

THE MOST FREQUENTLY ASKED MBA ADMISSIONS QUESTIONS

1. Is it better to apply early rather than late?

"The rule of thumb is that it is better to apply earlier rather than later."

As a rule, it is better to apply early rather than late. Applying earlier means that you gain some advantage over other candidates because a large number of applicants either procrastinate or underestimate the effort required to make the first round. Should you apply early and get accepted, there is one less spot for someone else. Most admissions officers recommend somewhat equally the first round or second round but urge candidates to avoid the third round. In the old days, more applicants would end up applying in the third round compared with either the first or second rounds. In fact, as many applicants would apply in the third round as in rounds one and two combined. Schools have now "scared" applicants into applying earlier which has effectively moved third round to second round. That is, there are now as many applicants in the second round as in rounds one and three combined.

Let's review the theory behind the rounds and the theoretical advantages and disadvantages of applying in each. This helps explain why it is not categorically correct to say that it is better to apply early.

- **Early.** This theory is based on the simple idea of vacancy. In the beginning of the admissions process, there are more places available than at the end. There is some truth to the idea that schools tend to over-accept in earlier rounds. Other reasons for applying early may include the advantage gained, if accepted, of having more time to arrange for finances, including applying for financial aid. Furthermore, if accepted at the school of your choice, you may want to stop applying and save your time, money in terms of application fees, and energy. The theoretical disadvantage of the first round is the idea that it has a disproportional number of "eager beavers" or overachievers. According to some, the toughest and most prepared candidates apply early, which makes the first round most competitive. Also, some people believe admissions officers take fewer chances in earlier rounds. Certainly this helps explain why first round statistics (i.e., average GMAT scores and GPA) are usually slightly higher than they are for the second or third round.
- **Middle.** There is a second theory that says that it is best to apply in the middle round. The rationale follows that not only does the first round have a disproportionate number of "eager beavers" but the last round is too competitive because it has too few spots. Thus, middle is best.
- **Late.** There is a third theory that says apply in the last round. This theory is much more unorthodox than the previous two. But it is grounded in the idea that if a candidate believes that the true strengths of his or her application is one of diversity, then he or she may be advantaged in applying at the very end. It is at the end of the admissions process, more than at any other time, that the

admissions committee looks for a well-rounded class. In looking for diverse candidates, admissions personnel may favor a unique last-round applicant more so than in earlier rounds. This may be particularly true if the "diverse" candidate has significant weaknesses in other areas of his or her application. The clear disadvantage of this round is that most spots are gone. In a typical top-tier business school scenario it is not unlikely that there are only ten percent of spots available in the final round.

A candidate might avoid applying early should he or she feel that a significant future promotion or salary increase is probable. In practice, such a reason for applying late is unwarranted. If you feel that a significant promotion or salary increase is imminent, you may mention it in your application (and the basis for your assessment) and apply in an earlier round.

Realistically, there will always be some element of chance associated with the admissions process, regardless of whether one applies early or late. The admissions process is an imprecise science with a human element. There is an on-going mystery question: "Would the same candidate with the same application get accepted (or rejected) at different times in the admissions process just because of vagaries, human or otherwise, inherent in the admissions process?" The answer to this question is not known. But this having been said, full-time admissions committee members at top schools are trained professionals who seek to reduce admission vagaries to a minimum.

2. Which of the seven application components is the most important? How is each of these weighted in the admissions process?

"With the possible exception of an interview, the essay is the closest the admissions committee will get to knowing the 'real' you."

The application components include: (1) GMAT, (2) GPA, (3) employment record or resume, (4) letters of recommendation, (5) interviews, (6) extracurriculars, and (7) application essays. Your essays are arguably the most important component. Whereas your GMAT score and GPA give an indication of your quantitative ability, the strength of your essays lie in their subjective, qualitative nature. For example, it is in your essays that you talk about yourself, your career goals, your accomplishments, your need for an MBA, and why a particular school is right for you. In addition, essays include not only "standard" essays, but also optional essays should you plan to include them.

The question of how application components are weighted is very difficult to answer because every school evaluates applicants a little differently and virtually no business school uses a "simple" weighted average system that assigns values to each application component, e.g., 25 percent to GMAT and 25 percent to GPA and 50 percent to resume, recommendation letters, essays, and/or interviews. In practice, it is extremely difficult to associate a percent or specific value with any individual application component. Not only does each school have its own admissions criteria, but, in general, the admissions process is holistic, not piecemeal.

3. Will the admissions committee start reviewing my application as soon as they receive it even if my application is not complete?

"The burden of making sure your application is complete rests with you."

The admissions committee will not review your application until it is complete. In most cases, the admissions committee will not even see your application until the school's clerical assistants check to verify that everything in your application is complete and pass it to the committee members. The burden of making sure your application is complete rests with you. Schools follow the "one-package" rule. Make sure your official college/university transcripts and GMAT score have been sent, and recommenders have submitted their recommendations. By requiring you, the applicant, to collect and send all application materials to a business school at approximately the same time, the admissions committee actually assists you in getting your application complete and ready for review.

4. When asked in my application, should I mention that I am applying to more than one school?

"Admissions committee members will not favor an applicant simply because he or she is applying to only one school."

It makes little difference whether a candidate states he or she is applying to just one school versus a whole number of schools. Some candidates believe that by stating that they are applying to only one particular business school, the admissions committee will be impressed and this will work in their favor. Admissions committee members will not favor an applicant simply because he or she is applying to only one school. The goal of the admissions committee is to get the best candidates it can. Also, unless you have well-articulated and specific reasons for applying to just one school, committee members might be a little skeptical about why you cannot apply to a variety of top business schools and still gain much from these alternative programs. All in all, it makes little difference whether you mention that you are applying to one school or a number of top schools. It is best to be honest and fill in this information exactly as it applies to you.

5. I have heard that business schools look for evidence of teamwork and leadership ability. How can I show this in my application?

"In the workplace ... through extracurricular involvement ... during the interview."

There are a number of ways to show this. Firstly, the workplace is replete with opportunities for teamwork and leadership. Secondly, opportunities often stem from involvement in extracurricular collegiate activities, membership, or community service. Since many of these activities and organizations require working with people in groups, you will naturally have opportunities to mention teamwork or leadership. Rather than simply listing such activities or memberships and placing dates beside each of them, you need to elaborate a little and say what these activities mean to you. See Chapter 9: *Presenting Your Extracurricular Activities/Awards and Recognition/Community Service* for more discussion and illustrated examples on how to enhance this area of your application. Thirdly, interviews may also provide an opportunity for you to talk about evidence of teamwork and leadership ability. You can also mention some of these things when speaking face-to-face with alumni, admission committee members, or current students.

6. Is it necessary to write anything when asked in the application: "Is there anything else you would like to tell the admissions committee?"

"The optional question should be thought of as an opportunity to emphasize your strengths, not just address your weaknesses."

The question is optional and therefore you are not required to write anything. However, it is likely that the standard essay questions will not give you sufficient space to elaborate on all-important aspects of your candidacy. In particular, should you anticipate a weak point in your application, you need to address it. Common examples of application weaknesses include low GPA or low GMAT scores. Clarification is needed if you have an undergraduate degree from an international location which you feel the admissions committee may have trouble recognizing. In line with strengths, it is highly recommended that you talk about special aspects of your personal and professional background to ensure that you come across as a unique candidate. The optional or blank question should be thought of as an opportunity to emphasize your strengths, not just address your weaknesses. For information on the uses of optional essays, as well as sample essays for each of these uses, refer to Chapter 5, *Essay Writing Part III: Optional Essay Entries.*

7. If I take the GMAT more than once, will schools recognize the higher score?

"It is hard to argue that a candidate received a much higher GMAT score than he or she is ultimately capable of. But it is much easier to say that a candidate scored below his or her true level of ability."

Rather than average scores, schools consistently claim to take your highest GMAT score. You may, however, want to check the application brochure of the school you are planning on applying to for the official word. In practice the highest score is almost always used.

The reasons for this have to do with a general philosophy in admissions of wanting candidates to present themselves in the best light possible. In other words, admissions officers want candidates to look as good as they can before being judged. This may be contrary to what many prospective MBA students think—that admissions people are just looking for reasons to find flaws in their applications.

The GMAT is viewed as a representation of your academic potential. Here there is a good argument behind the practice of looking to the highest score: it is hard to argue that a candidate got a higher score than he or she is ultimately capable of; however, it is much easier to say that a candidate scored below his or her true level of ability. Moreover, admissions officers prefer to look at the higher score since the highest score is what schools will report for the purposes of business school rankings. It would not make a lot of sense for schools to evaluate you based on your lowest score, but upon acceptance, switch to reporting your highest score for ranking purposes.

8. What can I do to address application weaknesses?

"When weaknesses are properly addressed there is a feeling that they are strengths in disguise."

First, think of doing something with the optional question—"Is there anything else you would like the admissions committee to know?" This is one place where weaknesses can be addressed. You may also mention a potential weakness during the interview but it is generally best to do so through an essay question.

Specific explanations of weak points should not appear in your main essays, unless you are specifically talking about strengths and weaknesses, particularly as part of a "Strengths and Weaknesses" type essay question (see Chapter 4). When addressing a weakness, try to do so in a positive, candid way, without glossing over it. Concentrate on seeing the seeds of greater benefit in your past failure or underachievement. When weaknesses are properly addressed there is a feeling that they are strengths in disguise.

The most common anticipated weaknesses are low GMAT scores and low GPA. If you have a low GMAT or GPA, you need to communicate a sense of rigor to meet the academic challenge of business school. In looking at your GMAT score, determine whether one side (quantitative or verbal) is significantly lower than the other side. Next, analyze your college transcripts. Separating your undergraduate courses into technical and non-technical courses, again analyze which type of course resulted in higher overall achievement.

Assuming your GMAT score is problematic, start with the GMAT and work toward your college transcripts. If, for example, your quantitative GMAT score is low, then search through your college courses and find examples of quantitative classes, e.g., economics, accounting, statistics, computer science, etc. in which you received decent grades and make the case to help off-set your weak math score on the GMAT exam. If your GMAT verbal score is low, then search through your college courses and find examples of liberal art type courses, e.g., English, speech, philosophy, law, etc. in which you received decent grades to help off-set your weak verbal score on the GMAT exam. Of course, if your college grades are shaky but your GMAT scores on both quantitative and verbal sides of the GMAT are strong then this analysis works in reverse. The GMAT serves as "proof" that your basic skills are strong.

Applicants generally think of weaknesses as being one of low GPA or low GMAT score because these are numerical in nature and less subjective. But weaknesses may also include having a weak resume, weak recommendation letters, a mediocre interview, poorly constructed essays, or not having much in the way of extracurricular activities. Possible application weaknesses stemming from these latter qualitative application components are typically less able to be judged by the applicant as good or bad prior to actually applying to business school. Furthermore, in the case of recommendation letters and interview results, the candidate is unlikely to know what has been written. One major goal of this book is to proactively strengthen qualitative application areas.

If you do get rejected by a business school and plan to apply again, you should request from the admissions office a possible reason for your rejection. The admissions office may refer to one of these qualitative application components and this will greatly help you plan a new strategy to strengthen the cited weakness, should you reapply the following year.

9. How do I highlight my diverse international study or work experience?

"You will have a chance to mention your international experience when completing your resume/employment record, application essays, extracurricular activities, and/or when performing interviews. However, in order to highlight a diverse experience, it is recommended you use an optional essay."

Most business schools appreciate candidates who have diverse backgrounds including international work or study experience. Some business schools even think of themselves as International Business Schools or at least business schools with a specialty in international business. The optional question in the application is one place to embellish your strong points and highlight your international experience. Another place to make mention of your international work and study experience is in your main application essays. In the "career goals" type essay, for example, you are likely to talk about aspects of your background and preparation leading up to your career goals. Your background can be broken down into professional, educational, cultural/international, and personal components. Refer to Chapter 3, *Essay Writing Part I: The Classic MBA Essays* for coverage on how to summarize your background and experiences in essay writing.

As with other areas of writing, the impact is greater if you state why you feel certain experiences are important or relevant. The same is true with international experience. Do not merely mention in passing that you worked for a summer in the Middle East—state why this is important to your future, or why there are things you have learned that make this an invaluable experience.

10. How do I handle a waiting list situation?

"A waiting list situation is no time to sit back."

A waitlist is used by a business school to keep track of candidates whom the admissions committee feels may be admitted in the near future pending availability of places. Some candidates on the waiting list get accepted; a number always get rejected. Rather than just wait it out, this is a chance to further your candidacy. It is important that you think about what additional pieces of information you may want to send to the school. A letter to the director of admissions expressing your continued interest in the school and/or current employment update are two such ideas. You want to give the impression that you are energetic and moving closer to your goals. Express your hunger—most candidates just sit back and wait for a decision.

Try to ascertain why you might be short-listed. Can you anticipate some sort of application weakness? If so, you might want to send a note to your interested school to specifically address this point. Addressing your anticipated weakness(es) may help to dispel possible doubts the committee has about your candidacy. For the names of all admissions directors, refer to Appendix VII, *Contact Information for the World's Leading Business Schools.*

The trend among business schools is to waitlist more candidates than in the past (even though class size at most business school has remained roughly unchanged). In other words, a candidate is not as close to acceptance upon receiving notification of a waitlist, as he or she might have been in the past. One explanation for why schools place more candidates on the waitlist is to increase their "yields". From a candidate's standpoint, the most important number is "acceptance rate"—what percentage of the people who apply get accepted. But to a business school, the magic number is "yield". This is the number of people who accept the school's offer of admission. The higher the yield the better.

Candidates placed on the waitlist must, for all intensive purposes, signal to the school that they are still interested, otherwise they will be dropped from consideration. This helps a school increase its yield because it does not have to gamble as much with sending acceptance letters to candidates who might in turn "reject" the school.

11. If I get rejected one year, should I reapply the very next year? What are my chances as a reapplicant?

"Your chances as a reapplicant are better only if you submit an improved application."

Generally, business schools welcome reapplications. When you are reapplying the very next year, it is important to show that you are an improved candidate. To have a better chance for admission, an improved application must be received. Some schools do not encourage, and may not even accept a reapplication from a candidate, in the very next year following his or her unsuccessful try. Check with the particular school.

Your ability to reapply to business school the very next year following an unsuccessful first attempt is dependent in part on the reasons for initial rejection. If you can find out why, it will help you in forming a strategy for reapplication. For example, it is easier to reapply if your weakness was lack of sufficient work experience. An extra year's worth of work experience might spell the difference. Likewise, if you were rejected because you showed no evidence of extracurricular activities, you may get the hint that it is time to join a professional or service organization to bolster your application. On the other hand, if the reason for rejection was because you lacked a clear career focus (refer to Chapter 3, *Essay Writing Part I: The Classic MBA Essays* for the goal statements segment) then this is arguably a harder deficiency to overcome. You must carefully map out a plan for why you have chosen a different career path. Schools generally keep applications on file for two years. After this time they throw out all materials. If you plan on reapplying you will want to update schools so that they will be sure to keep your materials on file. On the other hand, if you want business schools to get rid of all the materials in your file, just wait a couple of years and come back with a new application. But this means you will also have to get a new or additional set of recommendations because these will also be discarded.

12. How do I know if my application is good enough to send in?

"When you have a 50 percent chance, you are essentially saying that you have twice the chance of the average applicant—it is time to send your application in."

Is your application ready? Your application is ready when you have completed all required forms, requested copies of GMAT scores and academic transcripts, and received confirmation that recommendation letters have been sent. The last thing you will likely be working on are your application essays, and readying yourself for interviews. Your essays are finished when they "sit still" and no more major rewrites or changes are required. Ideally, this process requires letting your essays sit for a week or two before rereading them and making final changes.

Is your application good enough to send in? You should apply to a top school whenever you figure you have a 50–50 shot. The rationale is that if you have a 50–50 shot and are applying to two top business schools, you are likely to be admitted to one of them. Think of tossing a coin. You may be thinking, "Wow, how can I apply with only a 50 percent chance of acceptance?" but the reality is that "good" candidates usually do not have better than a 50 percent chance of acceptance in applying to a top school. The acceptance rate at top schools is on average about 20 to 25 percent. When you have a 50 percent chance, you are saying that you have effectively twice the chance of the average applicant. Thus, having a 50–50 shot is *not* insignificant. The trick is knowing how to judge when you have a 50–50 shot. This unfortunately requires a good deal of knowledge about MBA admissions (and current trends in MBA admissions), and is one reason for seeking MBA admissions help in applying to business schools.

13. Do business schools have GMAT or GPA cut-off points? Do schools use quotas to limit the number of applicants accepted from one region of the country or world?

"Admissions personnel point out that the diversity of an entering class (e.g., geography, race, gender, age, academic, or work background) is largely a direct reflection of the diversity present in the applicant population as a whole."

There is no evidence to support the claim that secret cut-off points or quotas are used by today's top business schools. Cut-off points imply that a given school has rigid admissions criteria whereby the admissions committee would not even read an application unless a certain quantitative threshold were exceeded. For example, if a GPA cut-off point were set at 3.0, then no admissions person would read your application unless your GPA were 3.0 or above. Likewise, if a GMAT cut-off point were set at 600, then no one would even read your application unless your GMAT score were 600 or above. Not only do admissions personnel claim that cut-offs do not exist, there is concrete evidence which supports the complete absence of cut-off points. One such piece of evidence is the entering class profiles compiled and published by many leading business schools. Obviously, if cut-off points really existed, certain categories listed in the profile would not exist.

For example, the highly ranked University of Virginia, Darden Graduate School of Business Administration, listed the following admissions profile for its 2002 entering class (Table 2–1).

Table 2–1 Admissions profile of Darden Graduate School of Business Administration, 2002

GMAT distribution		GPA distribution	
500–590	5%	Not calculated	21%
600–690	49%	Less than 2.5	1%
Above 700	46%	2.5–2.99	8%
Middle 80%	620–740	3.0–3.49	43%
Median	690	3.5–4.0	27%
Mean	683	Mean	3.4

The use of quotas would serve to limit the number of candidates that could apply from a given region, industry, or functional work area. Some individuals conclude that because top MBA programs seem to have a particularly diverse makeup this somehow implies quotas are in place. Whenever admissions persons are asked to respond to the question of whether quotas exist, they claim that quotas do not exist. Admissions personnel point out that the diversity of an entering class (e.g., geography, race, gender, age, academic, or work background) is largely a direct reflection of the diversity present in the applicant population as a whole. That is, in terms of geography, there are fewer people from say, Madrid, who apply each year as compared with people from New York; hence there will be correspondingly fewer people accepted from Madrid compared with New York. Likewise, because there are fewer people from Stockholm who apply for admissions as compared with London, there is a corresponding smaller representation of students accepted from Stockholm.

14. What if I do not know what I want to do with my career but I still want to apply to a good business school?

"It is best to come across as goal-oriented; any career focus is better than no career focus."

Perhaps the most important thing to know in preparing for business school is knowing what you want to do with your MBA. Your career depends on it. And while in business school, your ability to know what you want to do after business school will also help you make better use of your time in terms of course selections, clubs, summer internships, etc. For the purpose of getting accepted to business school, it is paramount that you come across as a person who knows what you want to do before starting the program. In other words, admissions people want to be confident that you have a good idea of why you need an MBA.

If you do not know what you want to do and you still want to go to a good business school, you must above all else, concentrate on choosing a career focus. Any career focus is better than no career focus. In reality many people go to business school uncertain of exactly what they want to do but, hopefully, exit their programs with a sufficiently clear career direction. Business schools have a serious aversion toward people who have no idea of what they want to do with their careers. Generally speaking, the admissions committee will always be preferential toward a candidate who knows what he or she wants to do with an MBA as opposed to the person who is undecided or cannot articulate a reason. If you are still undecided about what you want to do with your career, the best advice is to pick a plausible goal based on your current background and experience and try to support that career goal or vision. Goals and vision are of paramount importance. They are the main focus of Chapter 3 and the writing of "classic" MBA essays.

15. Can I exceed the length limits of application essays and, if so, by how much?

"Don't exceed length limits by more than 10 percent."

Acceptably exceeding limits—sounds like a paradox. But in the same way that a driver may marginally exceed the speed limit without fear of getting a ticket, an applicant can arguably exceed the word length limit without being penalized. Almost all business schools assign length limits to the writing of application essays. Usually the length is stated in terms of words but it may also be stated in terms of pages. Some schools even ask you to put the number of words in brackets at the bottom of an essay to insure that you have stayed within the prescribed limits. In this case, exceeding limits is a slightly trickier proposition.

The rule of thumb is that you should not go over by more than ten percent. If the essay states 500 words, keep it to 550 words. One top admissions director commented that the limits are guidelines and that if you need another couple of paragraphs to explain your point then do so. There is a general belief that if what you are writing is good stuff then the reviewer will not object to reading.

Many candidates complain that business school essays with limits of 200 to 500 words are too short to use to adequately address points. However, consider two facts: (1) If business schools didn't think it was possible to answer within such limits, then they wouldn't have set such limits, and (2) Any essay question can in theory be answered in a single sentence, so 200 to 500 hundred words should give sufficient opportunity to add relevant detail.

The vast majority of applicants claim to be better writers as a result of having gone through the application process. This is invariably the by-product of three processes. The first process is distillation. Relatively short essays require you to write in a forceful, straightforward way, culling out the unnecessary. The second process is resourcefulness. You will not always have the perfect answer (based on your background) to answer every essay question. This requires that you be creative and strategic. The third process is introspection. In thinking about your past experiences, you will be forced to glean meaning from them. Why were they important? What did you learn from them? How do they fit into the grand scheme?

CHAPTER 3

Essay Writing Part I: The Classic MBA Essays

"The MBA is the BA degree of the investment banking and management consultancy world."

The Author

INTRODUCTION

Of all the admissions components, it is probably a good bet to say that application essays are the most important component. This is even more true if we conveniently lump together with essays, an individual's record of awards, extracurricular involvement, and community service. Essays are subjective by their very nature but it is their subjective nature that gives them that extra weight in the admissions process. Here is your chance to tell your story and interpret events in your own way. Essays are sometimes referred to as interviews on paper. With the possible exception of the interview, essays are the closest that the admissions committee can get to knowing the "real" you.

WHAT TYPES OF ESSAYS ARE THERE?

Business school essays are subject to considerable variety. They may vary based on the *number* of required essays, the *length* of a given essay, and the *type* of essay question asked. The number of essays may vary from two to eight depending on the school while the length of essays may vary from half a page to seven or more pages. There are ten different types of essays and these include:

1. Who are you?
2. Career goals
3. Why an MBA?
4. Why XYZ school?
5. Background and diversity
6. Strengths and weaknesses
7. Greatest accomplishments or leadership
8. Overcoming difficult situations
9. Wildcard questions
10. Analyze a business situation

In short, there are essentially two broad classifications of essay questions. The first is the "who are you?" type question, which seeks to pinpoint your personal character, motivations, and diversity. Often other essay types are used which mimic the "who are you?" type essay and these include: "background and diversity", "strengths and weaknesses", "greatest accomplishments or leadership", "overcoming difficult situations", and "wildcard" type essay questions.

The second major essay type is the "career goals" essay. The "career goals" essay is ubiquitous and found in every business school application. The primary purpose in asking this type of question is to find out what you are planning on doing with your future and to capture important elements of your professional background. Often the "career goals" type essay question is combined, for practical reasons, with the third and fourth essay questions—"why an MBA?" and "why XYZ school?"

There are four classic MBA essay types:

1. Who are you?
2. Career goals
3. Why an MBA?
4. Why XYZ school?

The best example of the classic MBA essays can be seen in the former Stanford Business School Essays A and B. These two application essay questions contain all four of the classic MBA essay types and lend themselves well to the study of the classic essay types. And we can learn about the approaches and techniques to be applied when answering the essays of other business schools. Former Stanford Essay A is an example of the classic "who are you?" type essay question. Former Stanford Essay B is an example of the classic "career goals" type essay question combined with the "why an MBA?" and "why XYZ school?" type essay questions. In summary, the purpose of these four essays is to find out what kind of person you are, where your career is headed, why you want an MBA, and why a particular business school is the right choice for you.

The following are excerpts of the two Stanford essay questions which were asked year after year by the Stanford Business School. Although these two questions have been changed as per fall 1999, they remain excellent essay questions for our purpose of study. You can feel confident that at least some other business schools will be asking similar questions either now or in the near future.

Stanford Business School Essays – Please answer question A and question B

Please double space your essays and make sure that they are easy to read. We suggest at least a ten-point font. The length of your responses is up to you. While you should feel free to take the space you need to answer the questions fully, most applicants find that three to seven pages per essay is appropriate.

Essay A: Each of us has been influenced by the people, events, and situations in our lives. How have these influences shaped who you are today? (Our goal is to get a sense of who you are, rather than what you have done.)

Essay B: How do you see your career developing? How will an MBA further that development? Why are you applying to Stanford? (Dual degree applicants: Please also discuss the relevance and applicability to the dual degree you are seeking.)

Why were these essays regarded as the toughest of all business school admissions essays? Prospective business school applicants have had and continue to have more problems with the Stanford Business School essays than with those of other business schools. Some of the reasons for this include:

- The essays can be long, making the task of writing them psychologically difficult.
- Stanford dedicates one entire essay to cover the "who are you?" question which, from a content and structure standpoint, is arguably the most difficult type of essay to write.

WRITING THE "WHO ARE YOU?" ESSAY

Let's take a look at how to answer perhaps the most classic example of a "who are you?" essay question.

"Each of us has been influenced by the people, events, and situations in our lives. How have these influences shaped who you are today?" (former Stanford Business School question)

Common mistakes

There are a number of common mistakes that candidates make when answering this type of question, including:

- Not using a clear and simple structure to help organize and signpost your discussion of who you are.
- Not supplying specific concrete examples to support what is said; in short, superficiality.
- Not describing who you are but rather what you have done.

Other common mistakes include making the "introduction" too long. If you spend the first two pages talking about your parents, brothers, or sisters, the admissions committee may wonder if it is not your parents, brothers, or sisters, who should be applying for admission instead of you. The best approach is to center the essay on you and use information about your parents, etc. to support the kind of person you have become. Another mistake lies in using a shopping list of traits to describe yourself. For example, one actual candidate put the following sentence in her essay: "I am an energetic, loyal, creative, diligent, honest, strict, humorous, responsible, flexible, and ambitious person." Giving adequate support for all of these traits is practically impossible. The better approach is to choose two or three of these traits and develop each in more detail.

Winning approaches

The following is a summary and follow-up discussion of how best to write a "who are you?" essay.

- Use a clear structure to organize your essay. One way of looking at a "who are you?" essay is to consider breaking it down into one or more of these categories: people who have influenced you; places visited or lived in; events or situations that have influenced you; personal traits you possess; personal strengths and weaknesses; other relevant categories, including hobbies which have had an impact on you.

  Once you have decided what categories you want to include in your discussion, create an outline. Consider using a *lead* or summary sentence to break your essay or essay section into major parts. A lead sentence is like a topic sentence but whereas a topic sentence summarizes the contents of a single paragraph within an essay or report, a lead sentence is used to summarize the contents of an entire essay or report or its major sections. Each topic in the lead sentence should be developed into a separate paragraph in the body of the essay. For example, when introducing personal traits you may use the following summary or lead sentence: "Who I am as a person can be seen in the three personal traits that best describe me, namely my courage, empathy, and practicality. In terms of courage ... (one paragraph) ... In terms of empathy ... (one paragraph) ... In terms of practicality ... (another paragraph)."

- Supply specific, concrete examples to support what you say. If you are writing about your personal traits and you say that you have an analytical mindset and work with numbers, you must give examples to support the idea that you really do have an analytical mindset or at least a facility with numbers. You must clarify these statements. Show the reader exactly what the significance or benefit of having an analytical mind or working with numbers is. You cannot assume that the reader knows.

- Talk about the kind of person you are and not only about what you have done. Say you are writing about your personal traits and you state that you ran a marathon. This is an example of something you have done, not necessarily who you are. The following is better: "I am a person of great perseverance and generally finish the things that I start. Running a marathon in under three hours is one example of my ability to...." In this latter example, you are strategically mentioning the kind of person you are (i.e., persevering) and using your accomplishments (i.e., running a marathon) as examples to support the kind of person you are.

SEVEN TIPS FOR WRITING THE "WHO ARE YOU?" ESSAY

✍ Tip #8: Make an outline for your "who are you?" essay.

The first challenge you are likely to face when writing a "who are you?" essay is deciding *what* to include in your essay. This is a content issue. The second challenge is *how* to organize your essay. This is a structure issue. Incidentally, readability (in addition to grammar) is the only other major issue, and this entails making your writing look presentable. This latter concern is the focus of Chapter 10, *Packaging Your MBA Essays and Application*.

The ability to write an outline for your essay, reducing it to point-form, greatly increases the odds of writing an effective essay. The easiest and most efficient way to proceed with writing a "who are you?" essay (or any longer essay for that matter) is to prepare an outline and begin filling in information. Try to envision what you want to put in your essay and then break your essay down into paragraphs. Dedicate one paragraph to each of the points you will cover. The following is an example of a general, all-purpose outline for a "who are you?" essay.

General Outline

I. Introduction

II. Discussion (choose *one* or *more* of the following topics to write about)

    a. Three people who have most influenced you
    b. Three places you have visited or lived in
    c. Three events or situations that have influenced you
    d. Three descriptive traits that best describe you
    e. Three personal strengths and weaknesses
    f. Three hobbies or interests
    g. Other relevant categories

III. Conclusion (optional)

Note that "three" is an arbitrary number, but it is recommended that you cite no more than four items to be covered under each specific category—people, places, events, traits, strengths, hobbies, etc.

The following is an example of a sample outline for a "who are you?" essay. While the subject of beer is a bit outrageous, this is an example of how to build your essay around a theme and still break your discussion into manageable parts, in this case, three people and three events.

Sample Outline

I. Introduction (para 1)

I like beer. Beer explains more about me than anything in the world. Who am I? I am the *beer man* – at least that is what many of my close friends call me. To understand why this gold colored substance tells so much about me, I must mention two things. The first concerns the most important people who have influenced me. The second is about the truly unique events that have shaped me at critical times in my life.

II. Discussion (para 2–7)

a. There are three *people* I have known in my life whose influences have been monumental. Their names are Ms Teacher Go, Businessman Mo, and Aunt Sally, the fortune teller. All three tie into beer....

... Ms Teacher Go (para 2)

... Businessman Mo (para 3)

... Fortune telling with Aunt Sally (para 4)

b. There are three *events* in my life that have had a major impact on my love of beer. These include my coming to America, my role in the armed forces, and my experience as a captive in an African jail.

... Coming to America (para 5)

... Joining the armed forces (para 6)

... In an African jail for 10 days with just water (no beer!) (para 7)

III. Conclusion (para 8)

Three important people and three important events have come together to make me the kind of person who will always be interested in beer. I believe that if any of the above individuals or events had not played the role they did, my life and personal and professional focus would be less than what it is or would otherwise be. What I do know for sure is that this beverage of golden color will continue to play a role in my future. It is a future that will use my past influences and focus them on marketing in the beer industry.

Tip #9: Consider employing a "creative approach".

Creative approaches can help make an essay stand out. In her sample Essay A that follows in this chapter, Audrey (Candidate #1) writes her essay using the Chinese elements of fire, metal, water, wood, and earth. Each of these elements is used as a metaphor to represent aspects of her life. Fire represents the unpredictable events in her life like the burning down of her home in California; metal is a fundamental building material which represents her chosen career in architecture; water separates her ancestral China from her home in America; wood represents her creative abilities; and earth stands for her well-grounded belief systems.

Shannon (Candidate #5) builds her essay around the parts of a wrist watch, her product specialty area at Walt Disney. The headings within the essay include: The dial of creativity, the gears of teamwork, the strap of humanity, the hands of direction, the case of leadership, and the complete watch. Each topic describes her individual characteristics in a complete and multi-faceted manner. Her final sentence serves as a summary: "Creativity, cooperation, humanity, career focus, and leadership are all components in my life which must balance and work together to make sure that I stay 'on time'."

At other times a candidate might want to pick one subject that he or she knows very well and build the whole essay around this one subject. This is especially true with respect to hobbies and interests. A superb pianist might choose to make the piano the focal point of his or her essay. A superb tennis player could break the game of tennis down into three parts, namely training, match play, and mental outlook. Using the game of tennis as a metaphor, these three aspects could be used to describe that person's life. Training could represent the person's background and preparation (in tennis and other endeavors), match play could represent the person's achievements, and mental outlook could stand for those additional things that the person finds important in his or her life.

Tip #10: Consider writing a short introduction for your "who are you?" essay; alternatively you may choose to begin your essay with a summary or lead sentence.

Introductions serve to catch the reader's attention. In short, introductions should be brief, relevant, and memorable. Your introduction could be an excerpt from your actual essay where you choose to highlight an aspect of your background. It might even be a quote that is relevant to your life. In the following sample excerpt, the applicant describes where he is from which provides a glimpse into his family background and helps ground the essay for the reviewer.

Candidates' names, as well as other individual and corporate names appearing throughout the sample essays in this book, may have been changed to protect the confidentiality of the persons or organizations involved. In some cases, essay content may have been altered for presentation purposes.

I was born and raised in Western Canada in the city of Calgary. In terms of preparing me as an individual and businessperson, I see my youth as helping me develop an interest in business and sports. My interest in business is due largely to my father, who earlier in his career, was a salesman and general manager of an oil and gas concern. The oil and gas industry is as fundamental to Calgary as the computer industry is to Silicon Valley and some of the things I learned in my youth include initiative, salesmanship, and mutual cooperation. I was also encouraged to play sports from an early age; I played hockey nearly every weekend from the age of 5 until I switched to skiing at the age of 13. In a few short years, I worked myself all the way up from a beginner to a three-time National Junior Downhill Skiing qualifier. In my last year skiing as a junior, I was invited to join the Canadian National Ski Team to tour and compete in Europe.

If you choose not to write an introduction, a second, more direct approach comes into play. Start your essay using a summary or lead sentence. For example, the candidate cited above could have omitted an introduction and opened his essay using the first sentence of his second paragraph as follows:

I would like to show who I am through a discussion of three special turning points in my personal and career development, through an assessment of my personal strengths and weaknesses, through a selection of the three traits that best describe me, and through a look at what motivates me in my work.

Tip #11: Break your discussion into three or four major parts.

Applicants frequently have problems structuring their essays, no matter what the length and no matter what the essay type. How will you divide up major sections of your essay? How will you group everything?

The best "who are you?" essays are built around themes. You must brainstorm and decide what might be your major theme. The next step is to think in terms of "three's"; break your essay into three parts. Of course, three is an arbitrary number but it is a starting point. Next review all the types of things you can write about in a "who are you?" essay as presented earlier in this chapter under the topic *Tip #8: Make an outline for your "who are you?" essay.*

As already mentioned, a summary or *lead* sentence is a very useful tool for use in writing your essay. A lead sentence is a sentence which summarizes the contents of an entire *essay* or its major *sections*. A lead sentence foreshadows what is to come; it highlights what items you will discuss and, most probably, the order in which they will be discussed. Each item in the lead sentence should be developed into at least one separate paragraph within the body of the essay.

With reference to the candidate above, the following is another example of how a summary or lead sentence is used to summarize a single *section* of an essay.

My personal weaknesses are largely a reflection of the weak points stemming from my background. The weak points of my background include (1) my inability, at an early age, to find and develop my personal strengths and (2) my lack of guidance in terms of educational choices followed during my formative years.

Writing about people, places, events, or situations. Perhaps the easiest way to write a "who are you?" essay is to start with three people who have influenced you. Think of your mother and father. You have some of the traits of your father and some of your mother and, of course, you have your own individual traits. This could be used as a three-part structure. You may choose to view three people as mentors and write about them each contributing a guiding insight. Another easy method is to write about three geographical places. Say that you have lived in England, the U.S., and India for parts of your life. You could spend about a third of your essay covering each area geographically, relating how each has influenced who you are as a person. Another category is events and situations. Certain events and situations can influence us in "geometric" ways—they may last a few seconds but stay with us our whole lives. For example, people who have been engaged in war, been in an accident, or even won the lottery, can testify to this truth. On the other hand, some events or situations are more gradual in their effect. These include going away to college, getting married, getting a promotion, buying a car, making your first investment, etc. Think of the people, events, and situations in your life as representing distinct turning points.

Writing your essay around personal traits. One way for you to approach the "who are you?" type essay is to build your essay around three or four different personal traits. One thing worth mentioning at the outset is that it is not the traits themselves that are most important but rather the support given to the traits. The examples and the specifics are what will determine whether the writing is both distinctive and believable. When using traits to describe yourself, keep in mind that the reader should be convinced from your writing that you do possess such traits. If you say that you are "imaginative, philosophical and industrious" then the reader expects that you will tacitly prove your case.

In writing your essay around traits, you may want to think of your life in reverse chronological order. That is, you are a certain kind of person today, so how did you get this way. You will want to show how a number of different factors—people, places, events or situations, or things—have influenced you and how each plays a role in helping you develop the traits mentioned.

Writing about strengths and weaknesses. Strengths can be a powerful way to tell someone about who you are. Strengths may represent positive traits you possess which are either inborn or which you have acquired or developed as a result of the opportunities and personal initiatives. For example, you may be personable, and this is a positive trait. You may want to write about the events in your background which have helped you become personable, including the many opportunities you have had to meet people and also your family background. How did you and/or other family members become gregarious people?

Weaknesses should ideally be viewed as strengths in disguise. What have you learned from your weaknesses? If you have struggled to overcome them, they may indicate proactivity or tenacity of character. Always express how your weaknesses contain the seeds of greater benefits. For example, for the candidate who was too focused on sports to the detriment of more serious academic achievement, he or she might cite participation in sports as the catalyst to becoming a more well-rounded person.

Tip #12: Choose specific, concrete examples to support what you say.

As a generalization, the difference between a really good essay and a mediocre one is that a really good essay uses specific examples while a mediocre one does not. This could not be more true than in the case of the "who are you?" type essay. To be sure, "average Joe" applicant will not use many examples at all. When you write your drafts, you may want to try to emphasize points by placing "for example" immediately after what you write. That is, if you say you worked for Andersen Consulting and you have analytical skills, put a *for example* after this and cite some evidence. Do not assume that the reader will believe that just because you worked for Andersen Consulting this automatically implies, and therefore guarantees, that you possess good analytical skills. There must be support. The key is to use specific and concrete examples to support whatever you say. If you concentrate on using examples to support what you say in your essay, you are well on your way. See *Tip #88: Try the "for example" technique.*

Tip #13: Consider the use of quotes and anecdotes.

Quotes. To make your essays more interesting, it is probably a good idea to consider including some quotes throughout your essay. What other people say helps make you seem more real. Quotes from famous and familiar people may be used to support a particular philosophy you live by in conducting your personal or professional affairs. In days gone by, candidates could be seen placing random quotes of famous people on the top of each page of their essays in order to impress the reader. Nowadays, reviewers have become more critical and expect an applicant to explain the meaning behind a quote in terms of its special relevance to him or her.

Anecdotes. Anecdotes are little stories used to embellish a point made by a writer. The following anecdote might be useful in describing how an entrepreneur can succeed despite what the others say are realities to the contrary.

My uncle was an entrepreneur who inspired me. He had a little story comparing entrepreneurs to bumblebees. According to my uncle, NASA has done extensive studies on the bumblebee's flight capabilities based on modern scientific theory and, based on their studies at NASA, our friend, Mr Bee, is in imminent danger of crashing. Aeronautically speaking, the bee's wings are too short to support his body weight in flight. Scientists desperately want to communicate to Mr Bee to tell him that he is in imminent danger of crashing. Mr Bee is unaware of all this and scientists do not know 'Bumblebee language'. So in the absence of any direct communication, Mr Bee continues to do what he does best—fly.

Tip #14: Consider the appropriate use of readability tools and keep track of reader friendliness.

Keep track of your readability factor, also known as reader friendliness. In the case of the sample essays written by candidates that follow in this chapter, a number of stylistic and readability tools are employed including: bolds, italics, indents, enumerations, dashes, and some very short sentences. These all help make the essays more readable, but hopefully not too busy-looking. Bolds may be used to emphasize keywords or divide the essay into sections. Italics are best used to draw attention to small but important words such as—*not, don't, no, first*. Headings and headlines are discussed under Tip #47. Lastly, an addendum could be used as a tool to summarize more in-depth information while freeing the main essays from excessive detail. For more on stylistic and readability tools, see Chapter 10, *Packaging Your MBA Essays and Application*.

WRITING THE "CAREER GOALS" ESSAY

The "career goals" essay is the most pervasive and arguably the most important of the business school essay types. The purpose of this type of question is to get you to explain what you want to do in your future work and how your background plays a role. As noted earlier, the "career goals" essay is often combined with the "why an MBA?" and "why XYZ school?" type essay questions. Thus, the purpose of the essay is to find out what you want to do with your career, why you want an MBA, and why you want to attend a particular business school. For example:

"How do you see your career developing? How will an MBA further that development? Why are you applying to Stanford?" (Stanford Business School)

Common mistakes

There are a number of common mistakes that candidates make when answering the "career goal" question. They are:

- Not mentioning what their career goal(s) are or, when doing so, not having reasonably specific career goals.

- Not showing an effective or plausible transition to future goals, particularly with respect to linking their background—work, educational, cultural/international, personal—to support their future goals insofar as career goal is an extension of their background and experience.
- Not using a clear and simple structure to help organize and signpost discussion.

Winning approaches

The following is a summary of how best to write a "career goals" essay.

- Clearly state your short- and long-term career goals early in your essay. You may even want to begin your essay with a statement of your goals, which explicitly defines your career objective in terms of an industry, area, and functional focus.
- Write about your background and experiences in the body of your essay and remember to include all relevant aspects of your background including professional, educational, cultural/international, and personal experiences.
- Draw an outline and use a summary or *lead sentence* to signpost what you will talk about in the main body of your essay. Allocate one paragraph to each of the topics mentioned in the lead sentence.

SEVEN TIPS FOR WRITING THE "CAREER GOALS" ESSAY

Tip #15: Make an outline for your "career goals" essay.

The following is an example of a general, all-purpose outline for a "career goals" essay. The easiest way to proceed with writing your "career goals" essay is to prepare an outline and begin filling in information. The "why an MBA?" and "why XYZ school?" type essay questions are technically separate essays but are frequently combined with the "career goals" type essay to form a single essay.

General Outline

   I. Introduction (brief)

  II. Goals (+ vision)

 III. Background

     a. Professional experience

     b. Educational experience

     c. International experience

     d. Personal experience

 IV. Why an MBA?

  V. Why XYZ school?

 VI. Conclusion (optional)

Again, the two biggest questions you are likely to have in terms of writing this essay type is *what* to write and *how* to divide the essay up. In a combined "career goals" and "why an MBA?" and "why XYZ school?" type essay question, there are essentially four things to write about. The best structure to use in presenting these four items is as follows:

1. Your goals and your business vision.
2. Your background and experience:
   a. Professional experience—work experience (both full-time and part-time).
   b. Educational experience—undergraduate major(s), research projects, which may also include extracurricular collegiate activities.
   c. Cultural/international experience—travel, language, family, country, culture.
   d. Personal experience—hobbies and interests; relevant traits, insights, philosophies, and sometimes mentors, career or personal turning points or setbacks; this may also include community service.
3. Why you want an MBA.
4. Your reasons for wanting to go to a particular business school.

The following is a sample outline written by a candidate interested in pursuing a career in investment banking.

Sample Outline

I. Introduction (para 1)

II. Goals (para 2)

    a. Long-term goal – Investment banker doing IPO (initial public offering) work in Argentina.

    b. Short-term goal – get an MBA, join investment bank in New York, transfer from New York to Argentina.

III. Background and experience (para 3–7)

For the past five years, I have been building a specialty in finance and real estate:

    a. Professional experience (para 3)

        1. began work in "ABC" real estate firm

        2. currently working for "XYZ" bank

    b. Educational background (para 4)

        1. obtained bachelor's degree in finance with minor in real estate

        2. took part in extracurricular activities

    c. Cultural/international experience (para 5)

        1. traveled and worked in Mexico and Spain

        2. languages: speak Spanish and English; have working knowledge of Portuguese and French

In addition to solid work experience, I possess some valuable personal traits and have gained some insights which will be invaluable to my future work in investment banking.

    d. Personal insights and business vision (para 6–7)

        1. first, my sharp people skills

        2. second, my great persistence

        3. third, why technology holds the key to the future of this industry

IV. Why an MBA? (para 8)

    a. Cross-functional skills

    b. Recognized for advancement purposes

V. Why XYZ school? (para 9)

    a. Academic specialties and course offerings

    b. Students, faculty, and facilities

    c. Geographic location and employment opportunities

👆 **Tip #16:** Consider writing a short introduction for your "career goals" essay; alternatively you may choose to begin your essay with a statement of your career goals.

Sample excerpt

What would you pick as the greatest invention of the past 100 years – antibiotics, atomic energy, computers, credit cards, plastics, television, transistors, the jet engine, rockets, mass communication, self-image psychology? What about the greatest invention of all time – the wheel, electricity, mass production? The list of great inventions is long but one that is likely to be near the top of any list is the invention of the *movable type press* which made possible the effective and efficient reproduction of the printed word. This invention gave birth to mass printing and the publishing industry.

The introduction above is catchy and relevant to the candidate's career objective of publishing. Do not spend more than one short paragraph on the introduction because the longer you take before you state your goals, and address relevant aspects of your background, the greater the chance that your essay will get side-tracked. A more direct approach is to just start off your essay with a succinct statement of your career objective. An applicant's goal statements are arguably the most important sentences in the entire application package. Placing your goal statements in the opening sentences of your essay is consistent with their overall importance.

👆 **Tip #17: Create "goal statements".**

The "career goals" essay requires that you make mention of your career objective. The most direct way to express your career objective is through *goal statements*. These statements are the key to showing career focus. You want to make mention of your short- and long-term goals in such a way that the reader can easily figure out what you want to do with your career. How specific should your career goal statements be? The test of specificity is the following: the combination of both your short- and long-term career goals should spell out what you want to do in terms of an industry, area, and functional work focus. The following are two examples of career goal statements.

1. **Poor:** "My goal is to work for a multinational company and obtain an international position."
2. **Better:** "My *long-term* career goal is to be a top marketing executive in the fast-moving consumer goods industry in Asia. My *short- to mid-term* career goal is to pursue work with an international consulting firm and gain a specialty in consumer goods marketing."

The above long-term goal sentence tells us in just *one sentence* that the candidate plans to work in marketing (functional specialization), to work in the fast-moving consumer goods field (industry specialization), and to work in Asia (area specialization). Your two career goal statements are the most important sentences in this essay because they supply your essay with focus. Because of the importance of the career goal statements, you may choose to simply start your essay with your goal statements.

The opening paragraph of your essay will follow:

1. First sentence: "My long-term career goal is to ...."
2. Second sentence: "My short- to mid-term career goal is to ...."

The following are some examples of different functional, industry, and area specialization:

1. Functional specialization, for example, accounting, finance, marketing, manufacturing, personnel, general management, consulting, sales, trading, research, etc.
2. Industry specialization, for example, investment banking, consulting, real estate, marketing, fashion, food and beverage, oil and gas, chemicals, entertainment, pharmaceuticals, communications, hi-tech, Internet, etc.
3. Area specialization, for example, Asia, North America, Europe, Russia, the Middle East, China, South America, Africa, etc.

Some candidates have a company focus within an industry focus. For example, "I have worked five years for GE and I will return to GE after business school." It is by no means necessary to be so specific as to have a company focus—just an industry focus. Likewise a number of candidates may have a country focus within a continental bloc. For example, a number of applicants from Asia may be specific in citing China or India as the place they want to work after business school. Again, it is by no means necessary to have a country focus but it is recommended that you have an area specialization based on continents.

Tip #18: Create "vision statements".

Vision may be thought of as your personal idea(s) or insight(s) about where your chosen industry is heading. Vision is a kind of intangible factor that acts like glue to hold your background and previous experiences to your short- and long-term goals.

Top business schools try to attract people who are not just going to survive in their chosen field but, instead, who will become *leaders* in their respective fields. In order to make a case for your leadership potential, you should indicate why you are likely to become a leader in your future industry. As a future leader, you will be at the cutting edge of your industry. Are you the kind of person who actually thinks and acts "ahead" of industry trends? It is helpful to write a little about the thoughts and insights that you may now have which will signal how you will move your career forward.

Vision may be stated in either a few sentences or a single paragraph. In a combined "career goals" and "why an MBA?" and "why XYZ school?" type essay question, you will probably want to talk about your vision near the beginning of your essay after mentioning short- and long-term goals. An alternative is to wait and include it in the body of your essay during your discussion of your relevant professional background and personal experience. Refer to the general outline for a "career goals" essay (page 44).

The following are examples of vision statements.

- Retail banker: Reveals how technology and brand marketing are the key to future banking but how each is not always a complementary force. Technology helps banks increase product offerings and services to customers. However, such technological products end up becoming commodity offerings as other banks inevitably follow up with similar competing products. Branding, including astute marketing and advertising, is needed to help banks differentiate themselves so customers will not think all banks are fungible or substitutable entities.

- Marketer: States how chip technology—stored information—will affect the credit card industry, and how customization techniques in Europe are the key to understanding trends in other parts of the world.

- Publisher: Mentions why on-demand printing will revolutionize the publishing industry and how multimedia platforms will replace "flat-page" learning materials in the education field.

- Public affairs consultant: Writes about how public affairs is different from public relations and how public affairs is an underutilized strategic business tool. Whereas executives of multinational companies traditionally budget for accounting, legal, and other professional services, they do not typically think about public affairs or how they can proactively lobby governments on macroeconomic and political issues (e.g., tax laws, import quotas, regulations) which could affect their company or industry.

Some tips to help you find vision in your chosen field include:

- Peruse the magazine stand of a large bookstore and look for articles of interest about the people or companies operating in your current or future industry.

- Ask your boss or other knowledgeable persons where they think your chosen industry is headed and reconcile these ideas with your own.

- Use an on-line search system, such as Lexis-Nexis, Google, Yahoo, Hotmail, AOL and search for current newspaper and magazine articles which will supply you with insights and ideas on the market dynamics and direction of your chosen industry.

Goals and vision in sample essays. Consider the following essay excerpts for an individual who is focused on the publishing industry. Based on the way the candidate's goal statements are written, it is easy to figure out what he wants to do in terms of an industry, area, and functional focus. The reader of the essay quickly discovers that the applicant wants to work in the publishing industry (industry focus), in marketing (functional focus), and in Asia (area focus).

> My long-term goal is to become a chief executive of a major publishing house with responsibilities in Europe. My short- to mid-term career goal is to work in marketing and distribution for an established publishing conglomerate, such as Time Life Books (Time Inc.) or Bantam Doubleday Dell (Bertelsmann Group).

In terms of business vision, he presents his ideas about where the publishing industry may be headed.

> The future of publishing will be shaped by those individuals who have the vision to see where the industry is heading – away from a traditional "flat-page" format toward multimedia based platforms which combine entertainment, CD-ROM, and Internet technologies. With three-quarters of the world's population living in Asia by the year 2010, publishing will have to address a growing English language medium in Asia, as well as in almost all other developing countries of the world.

In mentioning personal insights, he reveals that his chosen career path will be cemented by passion and that he has thought about what actions will lead to success.

> My experiences indicate to me that top achievers are not necessarily the smartest or most intelligent people, but that they are consistently well focused. I have noticed that successful people find something they are good at and replicate *that something* over and over.

In the sample Essay B written by Candidate #1, Audrey, she states that her career goal is focused on the corporate interior design and facilities management area. Based on the way she writes her goal statements, it is relatively easy to figure out what she wants to do in terms of an industry, area, and functional focus. The reader of the essay quickly discovers that she wants to work in the corporate facilities field (industry focus), between North America and Asia (area focus), and in an implied general management capacity (functional focus).

> My long-term professional/career objective is to own and operate my own consultancy business focused on assisting multinational corporations to expand and manage their corporate facilities in Asia.
>
> ### Candidate #1: Audrey – Sample Essay B, third paragraph

In terms of business vision, she presents her ideas about a new trend in the corporate facilities area.

> A case in point is StarGate Computers which is one of the first major multinational corporations to adopt and implement a "hot-desking" concept in Asia, specifically

in the People's Republic of China. This concept provides an environment for field workers who use the headquarters or regional office on a first-come, first-serve basis. Files and personal items are transported to their offices via mobile storage units. Utilizing this concept, StarGate Computers has been able to reduce its corporate facilities space requirements by 30–40 percent in China, saving hundreds of thousands of dollars in construction and on-going facilities management costs.

Sample Essay B, third paragraph

She again describes her vision in terms of what she sees happening in the facilities management area in Asia.

> In today's global facilities management industry, corporate success is often determined by factors such as timing and business locale. In a growing marketplace like Asia, a corporation's business success may stem simply from grasping opportunities to strike early in expanding to major worldwide cities and locations. Understanding the process by which to select, implement, and manage global facilities, however, is a relatively untapped area of expertise in Asia. This process incorporates the disciplines of strategic time and project management, knowledge of an individual country's political, social, and business environment, cultural awareness, in addition to effective leadership, interpersonal, and communication skills. Thus far, there is a lack of such qualified individuals with sufficient knowledge and experience to work in such a capacity in the Asia-Pacific region.

Sample Essay B, tenth paragraph

A short case study

Goals and vision work best in tandem. Although a candidate might have a well-defined career objective without sufficient vision, rarely does a candidate have a significant business vision without first having a well-defined career objective. The following are all excerpts taken from essays written by business school students. The first example appearing below is written by a candidate who is eager but lacks a developed idea of how he will become a fund manager.

> Being a graduate majoring in Statistics, I have a solid foundation in quantitative training. In addition, minoring in Computer Science gives me a strong background in information technology. I have always had a keen eye for financial news and still do analysis using computer on stocks and options at home after work. It is necessary for me to acquire a business degree in investment management to broaden my vision in investment and risk management, and the use of information

technology in a career in the financial markets. My immediate goal is to become a financial analyst and my eventual goal is to become a fund manager.

Compare the candidate above with the candidate below who shares the identical goal of becoming a fund manager. The latter has a much more developed idea about why she wants to work in the fund management area and the abilities it will take to succeed.

I view money managing as an ultimate form of art in the financial industry. In order to become a successful money manager, one must be very well acquainted, not only with the whole spectrum within the financial industry including stocks, bonds, interest rates, and foreign exchange rates but also a diverse number of industries. My past experience is limited to the equity market. I feel I need more exposure to the other financial areas in order to become a successful money manager in Korea. Korean financial markets are still in their developmental stages and companies and retail investors in Korea are accustomed to earning 15–20 percent return on their investment due to the high market interest rate. With Korea joining the OECD, all this is going to change in the near future. The interest rates are going to adjust to the levels of the more developed countries and making money is going to become more and more complex with the introduction of futures and derivatives. Currently there exists only eight national and regional investment trust companies, with the three largest ones taking up almost 80 percent of the whole industry. Because of their size, they are slow to change, adapt new ideas, and too conservative in their approach. I expect to see many small sized boutiques booming and I plan to work for one of them.

The characteristics that are necessary to become a successful money manager include a calm demeanor, perseverance, confidence, and of course, strong analytical abilities. All these qualities must be developed through proper education and experience. Only a solid combination of knowledge and experience can guide you through the good as well as the hard times. To gain the knowledge and insight and learn how to link this knowledge with the real world, I have chosen to apply to XYZ business school. Your outstanding reputation in marketing and finance together with the international independent study courses will allow me a chance to apply the knowledge to real world situations. Becoming a bond trader after obtaining my MBA will help me to gain exposure in the bond market which, in Korea, will develop astonishingly over the next ten years.

Vision means having some idea of how and where your future business will come from. The following excerpt is taken from an essay used in applying for the joint Lauder-Wharton MBA program. The candidate clearly highlights how China is important to her future with a family-owned shipping company. Most candidates in talking about China cite generalities such as China is a big country and there will be big growth in the future.

Anyone who is not living in a submarine knows this. You must specifically relate the growth in China with the growth in a specific aspect of the China business you are interested in.

> At Lauder, I intend to concentrate on China. China's relevance to our business is evidenced by the remarkable growth of its liquefied petroleum gas (LPG) sector during this decade. In 1995, for example, LPG imports to China totaled 2.4 million tons, an increase of 92 percent from the previous year. That same year, one-third of this import demand was supplied from a large breakbulk terminal in the Philippines. As volumes into China increase through the next millennium, so will the demand on shipowners to provide value-added services for this trade. Philippines-based vessels are logistically well-suited for this supply route. However, the ability to form close business relationships with Chinese companies will give our company a formidable advantage in the race to expand and develop ventures in this booming market.

The essay below could be said to represent the quintessential "career goals" essay of the average, informed MBA candidate. The point being made here is that simply "wanting to go to business school" is not enough of a reason to be accepted by a top business school. Consider the phrases used: "… transition into a new field and gain some corporate experience … now I want something more … remain open to entrepreneurial possibilities". The critical reviewer will expect a more specific idea about where the candidate is going and a better idea that the candidate is driving his or her career as opposed to merely bumping along. In summary, this essay might be fine for many business schools, but for the top schools, competition will force reviewers to "up the ante" and expect the candidate to have a clearer, more defined direction.

> After graduating from Occidental College in 1994, I established my own restaurant business in Pasadena California. Managing my own restaurant operations over the last seven years has given me well-rounded business experience in that it required me to perform multiple functions and constantly learn new roles in order to become successful. Actively involved in all aspects of operations in my restaurants, I have proven experience as a leader and manager of people and practical hands-on experience in management, accounting, consulting, marketing, business development, and human resources. I believe the skills to effectively and efficiently handle numerous activities simultaneously will translate effectively to any post-MBA career I undertake.

> Upon making the decision to close my company's main restaurant operation at the beginning of summer, I faced a significant setback in my career. I decided it was time to reassess my career goals and analyze my career options. I realized that this was the perfect opportunity to develop myself further by building on my

strong hands-on entrepreneurial experience by undertaking a comprehensive MBA program. Completing a rigorous MBA program would provide me the appropriate foundation to make the transition into a new field and gain some corporate experience.

Considering my background as an entrepreneur and undergraduate liberal arts education, I strongly believe that an MBA is essential to achieve my career goals, through expanding on the skills and practical knowledge I have acquired through operating my own businesses. I feel I have achieved a lot but now I want something more. Business school will help me to round out my practical experience and provide me the opportunity to learn new analytical and quantitative skills. My short-term career goal upon completion of my graduate studies is to return to the Food and Beverage Industry and work for a multinational corporation. I believe I can achieve this goal through utilizing the practical knowledge I have gained from my professional and life experiences and combining it with the fundamental business foundation my MBA will give me. Over the longer term, I remain open to entrepreneurial possibilities, whether they are an opportunity of my own making or the chance to focus on establishing or expanding a business overseas.

I am interested in pursuing a graduate degree at Kellogg based on the quality of the school and its MBA program. Of special interest to me is the International Business & Markets major, which is compatible with understanding business in a global context. This would allow me the opportunity to take part in the Global Initiatives in Management, and receive a strong foundation in international business strategy, accounting, and marketing. I am also interested in taking electives offered by the Entrepreneurship & Innovation major to build on my past entrepreneurial experience. In addition, I am impressed with Kellogg's emphasis on working in teams and the level of communication and partnership between the faculty and students, which clearly distinguishes Kellogg from other graduate programs. The innovative curriculum development process, in which students have direct input in creating new classes, represents a learning environment that I would like to be a part of.

Tip #19: Clarify your career path.

Often the thing that characterizes superior business school applicants is not only their clarity of focus and vision but also their ability to articulate how they will get there. Here is an example of an individual who wants to use his MBA for work in the public sector. The theme is centered around China but, by analogy, the principles used in writing this essay are relevant to candidates with experience in other domestic or international settings. The last paragraph makes it very clear what his career path is. This gives his essay—his career goals—plausibility.

My career goal is an ambitious one: to obtain a senior position in the Ministry of Foreign Economic Relations and Trade (Mofert) of the People's Republic of China. This goal ties my previous ten years of work experience in the pharmaceutical industry in China and Asia with my aspiration to enter top level government work in China. Mofert directly oversees and establishes the policies of foreign joint ventures in the PRC including the Sino-American joint venture of "ABC" company under which I currently hold the title of Manager, China. Mofert also governs all foreign trading activities.

For the past year, my extensive dealings with Mofert have helped me realize the urgent need for effective leadership at the senior level of the ministry. The upper ranks of the ministry are occupied by a much older group of "communists" who are familiar with the domestic situation in China but who are ignorant of modern business practices. In short, China needs individuals to design its economic future.

My greatest asset lies in the fact that I can deal with both sides of China's domestic business equation – private and public – as well as with both sides of the international equation – Eastern and Western culture and business practices. An MBA would give me advanced business skills which, when coupled with my in-depth work experience and significant PRC contacts, would ensure my goal of reaching a top position in Mofert.

After graduation from XYZ school, I plan to join Mofert and work with foreign joint ventures. I will help design policies ensuring the future success of foreign joint ventures. After two years, I would like to transfer to work aimed at attracting foreign capital to invest in modernizing infrastructures such as power plants, telecommunication, and transportation. Also, I would like to work in a trade department position with hopes of being stationed in the U.S. to promote trade between the U.S. and China. After working in several critical departments in Mofert, and having proven myself with significant achievements, I expect to be promoted to a Vice-Minister position.

Tip #20: Break down your background and summarize key elements in the body of your essay.

A person's background may be broken down into four major categories:

1. Professional experience—both full-time and part-time work experience.
2. Educational experience—undergraduate major(s), research projects, which may also include extracurricular collegiate activities.
3. Cultural/international experience—travel, languages, family, country, culture.
4. Personal experience—hobbies and interests; relevant traits, insights, philosophies, and sometimes mentors, career or personal turning points or setbacks; it may also include community service.

The main point is that your background includes more than just your work experience. Many candidates forget to mention their relevant educational, international, and cultural backgrounds. In addition, your background includes your personal beliefs, values, insights, and philosophies, both of a professional and personal nature. A distinction can be drawn between "business vision" and "personal insights". Business vision is used to describe where your company or industry is headed; personal insights are used primarily in a non-business sense to refer to the ideas you have about how to work or live successfully.

The following is an example of how you can summarize your background information and make it easy for the reviewer to read. The preferred approach uses a "top-down" style, placing the summary first.

- **Poor:** "I graduated from college … My first job out of college was with MoeMoe Bank and I worked for three years … Next, I worked for JoeJoe Securities … Finally, I found work with my recent employer, ABC company…."
- **Better:** "For the past five years, I have been involved in developing a banking specialty. This has been accomplished in four important ways. I have secured solid work experience, pursued the relevant education, honed my language skills, and gained a few personal insights about living and doing business in South America."

Tip #21: Choose relevant examples and support them with specific details.

Above all else, examples must be both specific and relevant. Examples must be specific in that they must be detailed enough to support what you say. Examples from your background must also be relevant in order to best support your long-term goal. You cannot include all of your background and experiences—only those aspects which are relevant and which you choose to highlight.

For example, the fact that a person stops on the way to work every morning to get a coffee from the local boutique coffee shop is likely irrelevant, at least for 99 percent of applicants. However, for the applicant whose future goal is to work in the coffee business, this fact may well be relevant. Stopping for coffee every morning might serve the added purpose of keeping abreast of consumer trends in coffee.

Not only must you choose relevant examples to support the things you write, but you must also use specific, concrete examples. As previously mentioned, when writing business school application essays, candidates often write in generalities such as "I have good people skills … communication skills … analytical skills". There must be support. The following examples also serve to give you some idea of how to use standard and personal support points. The basic difference between them is that personal support points give the reader an idea of what the writer personally came away with as a result of such and such experience. Comments of a personal nature stand out in the reader's mind. The following examples are used to give you some idea of how to use standard and personal support points. You will want to review the sample essays that follow in the next chapter to note which examples in these essays stick out in your mind.

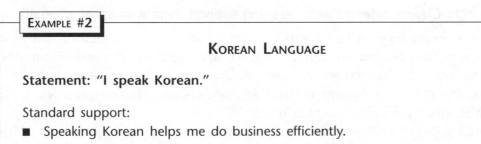

EXAMPLE #1

ANDERSEN CONSULTING

Statement: "I have analytical skills."

Standard support:
- Analytical skills help me work with numbers to both read and interpret financial statements.
- Analytical skills serve as objective measures for the basis of good decision-making.

Detailed support:
"My time spent working at Andersen Consulting helped me develop an analytical mindset. I learned to relate what is said verbally with its financial reality. When a client says his or her problem is high costs, I systematically break down total costs into their individual components. Once I know where the numbers 'point', I look for the stories behind these numbers. Sometimes the problem is not with high costs as the client may have thought but with another factor in the overall system."

EXAMPLE #2

KOREAN LANGUAGE

Statement: "I speak Korean."

Standard support:
- Speaking Korean helps me do business efficiently.
- Speaking Korean helps me understand Korean culture.

Detailed support:
"Speaking Korean, however, is only the tip of the iceberg. Direct communication is important but the ability to understand what Korean people think is more critical. In becoming fluent in Korean, I started to gain a sixth sense about what Korean people were thinking and this became my secret weapon in business negotiations."

THE "CAREER GOALS" ESSAY AS AN ARGUMENT

✍ Tip #22: Test your "career goals" essay by viewing it as an argument in disguise.

The ability to look at essay writing as an *argument* can be useful in order to test its persuasiveness. After all, much of expository writing is "argument in disguise". An argument, as referred to in formal logic, is a claim or statement which is made supported by some evidence. The reason that it is worthwhile to stop and analyze our writing as an argument is that our writing, like any argument, has assumptions. It is primarily by strengthening these assumptions that we in turn strengthen the arguments we make.

First the basics. There are three parts to any argument: conclusion, evidence, and assumption.

- The conclusion is the claim or point that the writer (author) is making.
- The evidence is the facts, examples, information, or data that the author uses in support of his or her conclusion.
- The assumption is the author's unstated belief (unstated evidence) about why his or her claim is right. An assumption is that part of the argument that the author takes for granted or assumed to be correct without stating so. It is sometimes said to be the *glue* that holds the conclusion and evidence together.

EXAMPLE

Argument	**Because Dorothy achieved a high score on her GMAT, she is guaranteed success in business school.**
Conclusion	She (Dorothy) is guaranteed success in business school.
Evidence	High GMAT score.
Assumption	Success in business school requires the same set of skills as does performing well on the GMAT.

Take the case of someone applying to graduate school such as business school, law school, or medical school. Admissions committee members do not make decisions based solely on quantitative measures, most notably candidates' college transcripts and test scores. Instead they try to also evaluate those intangible factors that will not only help the candidate succeed in graduate school but also help the candidate succeed in his or her professional career. After completing graduate school, these factors often determine who will become a leader in their given fields. Any applicant who takes the opportunity to mention intangible factors, such as positive personal traits, insights, and career vision, is helping the admissions committee decide why he or she is the right candidate to be admitted. The point of this is to say that intangible factors in these situations very much form the basis of assumptions.

A classic example is seen in the business school application process when responding to the question, "Why are you applying to business school and what do you want to do with your career?" A candidate applying to business school is essentially saying, "I'll succeed at XYZ school and in my chosen profession as evidenced by my background." The statement becomes an argument.

The "career goals" essay is like an argument which contains a conclusion, some evidence, and one or more assumptions. Your conclusion is embodied by your goals, that is "you will reach your goals". Your evidence is embodied by your background and experience to date. What is your assumption and what will strengthen it? Your assumption is embodied by those traits, personal qualities, and business vision that will ensure your reaching your future goal(s). *Mentioning these kinds of "qualitative" things help you build up more "evidence" and thereby strengthen your assumption and, in turn, your argument.*

Question: What is the conclusion part of your "career goals" essay?

Answer: Your conclusion is that you will reach your short-term and long-term goals. Note that you address your conclusion explicitly if you use goal statements: "My long-term career goal is to ... My short- to mid-term career goal is to...."

Question: What is the evidence part of your argument?

Answer: Your evidence consists of those relevant aspects of your background and experience. Anything that is historical information about yourself can be cited as evidence but it must be relevant. Again, your background typically consists of a combination of your professional, educational, cultural/international, and personal experience.

Question: What is the assumption?

Answer: The assumption is said to be the glue that holds the evidence to the conclusion. Here, it is the belief that you can bridge the gap between your background (evidence) and your future short- and long-term goals (conclusion). Your assumption is simply that your background is sufficient preparation to enable you to reach your goals.

Exhibit 3–1 is an outline of a sample "career goals" essay and serves to show how the "career goals" essay can be understood in terms of a classic argument structure. As previously mentioned, this analysis shows the importance of personal traits and skills which become assumptions in disguise.

Exhibit 3–1   An outline of a sample "career goals" essay

Your business school application essay outline (Career goals + Why an MBA? + Why XYZ school?)	This essay as an argument

I. Introduction
II. Goals
   A. My long-term goal – Investment banker doing IPO (initial public offering) work in Argentina.
   B. My short-term goal – get an MBA, join an investment bank in New York, transfer from New York to Argentina.
	Conclusion:
	"My future business goals are such and such and I will attain them."

III. **Background and experience**
For the past five years, I have been building a specialty in finance and real estate:
   A. Professional experience
      1. began work in "ABC" real estate firm
      2. currently working for "XYZ" bank
   B. Educational background
      1. obtained bachelor's degree in finance with minor in real estate
      2. took part in extracurricular activities
   C. Cultural/international experience
      1. traveled and worked in Mexico and Spain
      2. languages: speak Spanish and English; have working knowledge of Portuguese and French
	Evidence:
	"My relevant background and experience are such and such."

In addition to solid work experience, I possess some valuable personal traits and have gained some insights which will be invaluable to my future work in investment banking.
   D. Personal insights and business vision
      1. first, my sharp people skills
      2. second, my great persistence
      3. third, why technology holds the key to the future of this industry
	Assumption:
	"Sharp people skills and great persistence (in addition to my background) are compelling reasons to believe that I will achieve my goals."

IV. **Why an MBA?**
   A. Cross-functional skills
   B. Recognized for advancement purposes	

V. **Why XYZ school?**
   A. Academic specialties and course offerings
   B. Students, faculty, and facilities
   C. Geographic location and employment opportunities
VI. **Conclusion**	

WRITING THE "WHY AN MBA?" ESSAY

The following is an example of a "why an MBA?" type essay question asked by a leading business school.

"What are your career goals? How will an MBA help you achieve these goals? Why are you applying to Columbia Business School" (Columbia)

Common mistakes

Applicants often make a number of mistakes when answering "why an MBA?" question. The common mistakes are:

- Not showing why an MBA is needed to get from where they are now to their future goals ("missing link" idea).
- Not showing a sincere motivation for wanting to get an MBA. This includes implying that they want an MBA primarily because they "need the piece of paper" rather than for the knowledge or skill to be gained from obtaining the degree.

Winning approaches

The following is a summary of how best to tackle the above question.

- Show a real *need* for an MBA. You will want to evaluate your reasons for getting an MBA and you may want to review one or more of the following:
  a. Functional diversification – "your desire to acquire skills". An MBA can help you acquire different skills through exposure to different courses, such as finance, marketing, operations, human resources, strategic planning.
  b. Career advancement – "your desire to move up in an organization". An MBA can help you advance from an analyst to associate, clerk to manager, manager to executive, etc.
  c. Switch industries – "your desire to switch industries". An MBA can help you move from banking to brand management, accounting to marketing, advertising to accounting, etc.
  d. International placement – "your desire to move into global markets". An MBA can help you switch from being a regional employee to a national employee, or national employee to an international employee.
- Show a sincere *desire* for an MBA. Concentrate on writing about what you want to do with an MBA *not* about what an MBA can do for you.

FIVE TIPS FOR WRITING THE "WHY AN MBA?" ESSAY

Tip #23: Think first and foremost in terms of why you are suited to be a businessperson and what you think the hallmark of a businessperson is.

Tip #24: Mention (or imply) that an MBA is the missing link between where you are now and the future.

Tip #25: Mention academic reasons for wanting to do an MBA including the reason for your proposed major and/or minor in business school.

Tip #26: Mention the need to obtain cross-functional skills (a common example is a person who has expertise in finance and who wants to study marketing or vice-versa).

Tip #27: Evaluate other reasons for wanting an MBA including switching industries, being recognized for advancement purposes, pursuing work in a different geographic region, securing a hedge against job uncertainty, obtaining an important credential, gaining contacts, and making new friends.

Sample responses

The two most common reasons why people seek an MBA degree are a need to acquire cross-functional skills, and to be considered for advancement purposes. These reasons are supported by a desire to move both "across" and "up" an organization or industry. Moving "across" usually means wanting to acquire a variety of different skills, while moving "up" means wanting to be considered for advancement purposes.

Here is the sample response citing the need to acquire cross-functional skills as well as the need for acquiring international managerial skills for the purpose of being considered for promotion.

> Why an MBA? Whereas all my experiences to date have given me a good understanding of basic business practices, and to some extent a specialty in finance and accounting, I must develop a far greater strategic marketing and selling component to use in my future career. Specifically, I will need to be able to select, package, and promote book and related products across Europe. This requires an understanding of all major business disciplines – marketing and brand management, strategic planning, economics, quantitative methods, production, operations, and relationship management. It also requires excellent international managerial skills. Thus, I view MBA training not only as a way to increase my cross-functional skill level but also as a means of ensuring that I am recognized for advancement purposes enroute to becoming a distinguished international executive.

In the sample Essay B written by Audrey (Candidate #1), she mentions her need for acquiring elements of a traditional business background, learning how to evaluate projects from a financial perspective, and being able to speak to high-level businesspersons in a business vernacular.

As I do not have a traditional business background from an educational or professional standpoint, an MBA would provide me with the essential skills and knowledge to be effective as a global corporate facilities management professional in the business world. One critical area of knowledge that I currently lack in an industry that is extremely cost-sensitive is the skills and understanding to evaluate the financial aspects involved in facilities management. In a recent article about career strategies in *Facilities Design & Management Journal*, leading corporate real estate and facilities management executives state that up-and-coming management individuals must have a firm grasp of financial tools and investment management skills. These requirements allow a real estate or facilities executive to be cross-functional, allowing one to be able to speak about finance to a CFO in a language mutually understandable. I need to be able to understand the corporate side of the picture as well as the assets themselves, real estate or corporate facilities. Collectively, I am in search of an MBA program which is strong in the fundamentals of business, including finance and economics, has a renowned international business and management perspective, a celebrated entrepreneurial program, and is located geographically in proximity to high-technology and telecommunications corporations. The Stanford Graduate School of Business is at the crossroads of this search.

Candidate #1: Audrey – Sample Essay B, 11th paragraph

WRITING THE "WHY XYZ SCHOOL?" ESSAY

The following is an example of a "why XYZ school?" essay question asked by a leading business school.

Why is a Stern MBA necessary at this point in your life? (New York University)

Common mistake

One common mistake made by applicants when answering this type of question is:

- Not showing clear and specific reasons for why their goals are necessarily tied to a particular school's business program.

Winning approaches

There are three general areas you may want to cover in addressing why you want to go to a given MBA school and how a school's specific strengths and offerings tie to your plans. Review the following outline when answering this type of essay question.

- ■ **Academic**
  a. Academic specialties, course offerings, teaching method, and class size.
  b. Courses: accounting, economics, entrepreneurship, finance, general management, human resources, international business, management information services (MIS), manufacturing, marketing, new venture management, non-profit, organizational behavior, strategy, etc.
  c. Teaching methods: lecture, case, or combination.
  d. Class size: large class vs. small class size.
  e. Joint-degree programs including MA, law, medicine, and engineering.
  f. Library and research opportunities; independent study courses.
  g. Overseas educational exchange programs.
  h. Special leadership programs, new product labs and work exchanges.
- ■ **People**
  a. Faculty, facilities, and student body.
  b. Renowned professors, diverse student body.
  c. Alumni and networks.
- ■ **Geography**
  a. Location and living environment.
  b. Personal development and diversification: East Coast vs. West Coast; big city vs. small town; weather; linguistic challenges.
  c. Professional development and diversification: internship opportunities and post graduation work opportunities.
  d. Ask: what major companies are located near your prospective business schools which might provide internship/full-time work opportunities?

TEN TIPS FOR WRITING THE "WHY XYZ SCHOOL?" ESSAY

As an overview, the "why XYZ's school?" question is an important essay (or interview) question and you *can* blow it. Most applicants do not get enough detail into this question. First, a lot of information is right in school brochures or on the web. Schools put in a great deal of their effort into producing MBA brochures and admissions officers are understandably perturbed when candidates appear not to have taken the time to read the brochure closely. Second, writing a good response to this question not only shows you have done your homework, but it also shows good salesmanship. It sells the admissions office to their own school. Candidates generally think in terms of convincing a business school on why an MBA is right for them. Actually schools are much more interested in why their particular business school is one of your top choices. It is simply a matter of branding. Deans and admissions directors constantly think about how their schools are perceived alongside other competing business school programs. The following are ten tips for writing a "why XYZ school?" essay.

Tip #28: Mention that a school has a talented, diverse student body, high-caliber faculty, and/or top-notch facilities, and/or strong alumni networks.

Tip #29: Mention academic specialties and special programs offered by the school which attract you to the school.

Tip #30: Mention specific courses which you would like to take and/or mention the names of a couple of professors whose courses you would like to enroll in.

Tip #31: Mention wanting to do some independent research and cite a proposed research topic.

Tip #32: Evaluate other reasons for wanting to attend a particular school including joint degree programs, exchange programs, special leadership programs, teaching methods, class size, and geographic location.

Tip #33: Mention employment opportunities including what you would like to do with your summer internship opportunity (if applicable).

Tip #34: Mention extracurricular organizations you may want to join while attending business school.

Tip #35: Think in terms of how you might contribute to the school as an alumnus.

Tip #36: Employ a search engine—Google, Yahoo, Hotmail, AOL—and search for relevant and current information about a particular business school.

Tip #37: Consult a travel guidebook (e.g., Lonely Planet Publications) to gain more information about the city and the environment around where your chosen business school is located.

Sample responses

In the sample excerpt below, the candidate mentions his reasons for wanting to go to business school at Stanford in paragraphs 11 to 14. Specifically, he cites Stanford as a leading educational institution, acknowledges the strength of the GSB—Stanford Graduate School of Business, and the strength of the faculty and students. He mentions Stanford's particular strengths in marketing, operations, and entrepreneurship and shows how these points are related to his goal of publishing. Moreover, he shows how publishing requires entrepreneurship and venture capital skills, a link that might not otherwise be obvious. In terms of geographical location, a match is drawn between Stanford's location on the West Coast with a Pacific Rim orientation, as well as work and internship opportunities with the "big five" trade publishers, all represented with offices in the Bay Area.

Next, the applicant goes into more specifics by naming professors and actual courses he is interested in. This shows that he has done a little homework and has thought through his decision to apply to Stanford. He expresses a desire to take advantage of the opportunity to study in other departments within the university—an interdisciplinary approach—identifying courses in the Psychology Department and the Law School. In the closing lines of the essay, he proposes a topic of research which he would like to pursue if given the opportunity.

Why Stanford? Stanford is indisputably one of the leading educational institutions in the world. The Graduate School of Business (GSB) is positioned on the cutting edge of today's global management practices. In particular, the Stanford MBA program is known for its strength in *marketing*, *operations*, and *entrepreneurship*. Development in these areas is critical for me in my future career as an executive in the book publishing industry. In addition to its academic specialties, Stanford has a faculty and student body second to none.

I am particularly interested in the venture capital component of the Stanford MBA program. I see many aspects of book publishing as being analogous to venture capital and entrepreneurship. The effective publisher must identify good talent (authors), evaluate among competing projects and choose the most lucrative ones, evaluate risk-reward relationships, and re-evaluate the mix of projects in the company's business portfolio. Jonathan Newcombe, president of Simon & Schuster and book publishing industry spokesperson, has been quoted as saying, "We (book publishers) are the merchant bankers of the intellectual capital markets." (*The Twain Shall Meet*, Forbes).

In addition, the school is located strategically on the West Coast and has a Pacific Rim orientation. The opportunity to study in the Bay Area would make it possible for me to stay abreast of developments in the publishing industry. The Bay Area is known for many innovative publishing concerns and has representative offices for the "big five" trade publishers – Random House, Simon & Schuster, HarperCollins, Bantam Doubleday Dell, and Warner Books. I would welcome the chance to secure a summer internship opportunity with one of these established firms, or perhaps with a new startup firm such as Advanced Marketing Services (headquartered in San Diego), which is currently marketing the "large discount book store" concept and enjoying double-digit growth.

I want to benefit from the best training possible to complement my marketing and production focus. I am impressed by the work of Dr Lamonth in the area of market design and I see the following courses as particularly beneficial: M349 – Managing the Sales Force and Channels of Distribution; S382 – Culture and Management in the Pacific Rim; T362 – Supply Chain Management (Logistics); S355 – Seminar in Selected Entrepreneurial Issues; and G341 – Personal Creativity in Business. I look forward to taking a course in the Psychology Department (e.g., Psychology and Print Media) and one in the Law School (e.g., International Negotiation and Arbitration) in order to better understand the issues of international rights in publishing. Given the opportunity to pursue independent research, I would like to investigate how different distribution systems can cut down on piracy when selling products in developing countries.

Likewise, the sample Essay B written by Audrey contains the following description:

Specifically, I find that as the leader in management education, the Stanford MBA program contains innovative vantage points and opportunities for the development of future international business and management leaders such as myself. These include your first-year core coursework focused on developing an understanding and competence in four areas including the organizational environment of a firm, the external environment (economy and society) of the business, functional areas of accounting, finance, marketing, and operations, and finally, developing skills in the application of quantitative techniques to management problems. In addition, the opportunity to learn from a diverse and unique class of students with a broad range of professional and personal achievements would provide a unique perspective to the coursework. The emphasis on global issues as an integral part of your MBA program is particularly attractive to my career pursuits.

I am interested in pursuing the Global Management Program Certificate as it directly relates to my career goals in Asia. In addition, in order to provide me with the education and applications to complement my Asia focus and finance, real estate, and management focus, I would find the following courses particularly beneficial: G306 – Real Estate Investment; F323 – International Financial Management; F321 – Investment Management and Entrepreneurial Finance; and R372 – High Performance Leadership. Since my ultimate career goal is to own and operate my own consultancy business, your renowned entrepreneurship education would be vital to my success. Finally, I would be thrilled to be back in the beautiful Bay Area, my hometown, with my fresh experience and vision from a global perspective and share with my fellow classmates as we work together toward obtaining our respective MBA degrees in anticipation of making a positive difference in the global business environment.

Candidate #1: Audrey – Sample Essay B, paragraphs 12–13

OVERVIEW

The following narratives highlight the major themes contained in the "career goals" and/or "who are you?" essays written by each of the candidates. Note how, consistent with Tip #5, each of these essays is built around a single theme. Although there is no limit to the number of themes possible, the following seven essays do represent recurring themes among MBA applicants.

Candidate #1

Audrey's theme is "the creative person". Her career goal involves working in real estate/ facilities management. Her "who are you?" essay is built around five Chinese elements which she uses as a metaphor to describe different aspects of her life. Creative approaches can be useful devices to use when writing "who are you?" type essays. The inherent advantage in using creative approaches is that they are catchy and interesting; the disadvantage in using creative approaches is that they may appear contrived. This is not the case with Audrey's essay and it is likely one of the most outstanding "who are you?" essays you will likely see in the realm of business school application essays.

Candidate #2

John's theme is "the leader". His career goal is built on two aspects of his leadership: His writing style is clear and concise and he employs a sufficient number of short examples as support. Here is an excerpt from his introduction: "My six years of work experience has taken place in two of the premier organizations in the world: The United States Marine Corps and The Coca Cola Company. The Marines taught me to lead and Coke taught me to market. Both organizations provide practical, hands-on experience in the fundamentals of management in the international arena. I want to pursue an international general management career after obtaining the professional qualifications provided by an MBA from Columbia Business School. My long-term goal is to become an International Group President for Coca-Cola. My short to mid-term goal is to obtain a masters in business administration from CBS and return to The Coca-Cola Company to run a small international unit."

Candidate #3

Vivian's theme is "the culturalist". Her career goal is to be a leading ethics/corporate citizenship consultant. Her "who are you?" essay is focused on her Hungarian ethnic background. She essentially says that who she is can be best understood by examining her Hungarian roots. The advantage of this approach is that it exudes warmth and flavor; the inherent disadvantage is that the writer's individuality may be overshadowed by a description of the culture which he or she is a part of. Vivian avoids any such problem by maintaining an individual voice throughout and by making sure she mentions what she believes are her unique attributes.

Candidate #4

Fritz's theme is "the entrepreneur". He builds both his essays around the ever more popular topic of entrepreneurship. Such essays will usually emphasize self-initiative and energy as required to launch new products, businesses, or commercial ideas. Fritz writes his "who are you?" essay by stating that he is representative of a new breed of German entrepreneur and goes on to define what this means and how his background supports his definition. His "career goals" essay omits an introduction and begins with a clear statement of his three distinct career goals, one of which includes eventually taking his two Eastern European-based companies public.

Candidate #5

Shannon's theme is "the team player". Her long-term career objective is to continue to build her career in consumer goods marketing. In writing a "who are you?" type essay for admission to (Tuck) Dartmouth College, Shannon also uses a creative approach, cleverly relating her personal and professional background to the parts of a wristwatch, which is her product specialty area at Walt Disney.

Candidate #6

Kenji's theme is "the traditionalist". His essays are both built on a banking theme. His great grandfather, grandfather, and father have all worked to build the family bank and he is following in their footsteps. Who he is and where he is going are best understood in terms of his family and their banking traditions. His future goals stem naturally from his background. The inherent advantage of this approach is the logical and coherent way it ties a person's career goals to his or her background. The disadvantage of this approach is that it can be predictable and lackluster. However, Kenji writes in an interesting, story-telling way. Note in particular how his two essays look and feel as if they are one unit even though he is answering different essay questions, e.g., "who are you?" and "career goals". A high degree of symmetry between two such essays is a sign that the personality of the candidate matches the career direction of the candidate.

Candidate #7

Gary's theme is "the individualist". This short essay is written in response to the "who are you?" type question: "Please describe yourself to your MBA classmates." (Stern Business School, New York) Each of Gary's first three paragraphs is dedicated to describing how he sees himself viewed from a British, Jamaican, and Taiwanese perspective. He further uses music as a way to link all three paragraphs together. His essay uses a creative writing style that employs many short sentences in a matter-of-fact manner. It is sometimes called the stream-of-consciousness writing approach because it gives the reader the impression that the writer is putting down on paper whatever comes to mind. Such a style gives the impression of spontaneity, openness and straightforwardness. Due to the energetic writing style demanded, essays of this kind tend to be short in length.

SAMPLE ESSAYS

Candidate #1

Candidate's biography: Audrey is female, Chinese-American, educated in the U.S.

Outline for Essay A – "Who are You?" Type Essay

I.   Introduction (brief) (para 1)
II. Discussion

    a. Fire – unpredictable events (para 2–5)
    b. Metal – field of architecture (para 6–7)
    c. Water – Chinese culture and international background (para 8–9)
    d. Wood – artistic and creative abilities (para 10)
    e. Water and Metal and Wood – international career in architecture (para 11–12)
    f. Earth – belief systems (para 13–15)
    g. Leadership roles (para 16)

III. Conclusion (para 17)

Outline for Essay B – "Career Goals" Type Essay

I.   Introduction (brief) (para 1)
II. Goals (+ vision) (para 2–4)
III. Background

    a. Working in Hong Kong (para 5)
    b. Male-dominated workplace (para 6)
    c. Language skills (para 7)
    d. Business skills (para 8)
    e. Future opportunities in Hong Kong (para 9)
    f. Career outlook (para 10)

IV. Why an MBA? (para 11)
V. Why Stanford Business School? (para 12–14)

Essay A: Each of us has been influenced by the people, events, and situations in our lives. How have these influences shaped who you are today? (Stanford)

Introduction

Creative structure

Throughout history, mankind has tried to explain the events and situations encountered in life through philosophical and mystical means. The Chinese have a unique way to explain their lives and their world through an understanding of the five elements which comprise all matter: *fire, metal, water, wood,* and *earth.* In the same way that these elements can characterize all matter, they can metaphorically characterize each of our lives, our health, and destiny, not to mention how we interact in society, how we affect others and our immediate surroundings and vice-versa, and ultimately, how we affect the world. These elements, collectively, produce both a creative and a destructive cycle, eventually bringing balance and harmony in our lives. Through a review of the symbolism of each of these elements, I would like to explain the influences of how the people, events, and situations in my life have shaped who I am today.

Fire is representative of unpredictable events in my life. The Oakland Hills fire of October 20, 1991 that raged through the Oakland and Berkeley Hills, reduced thousands of homes to ashes and destroyed the once beautiful tree-nestled hillside community in the East Bay. Unfortunately, our family home of 20 years was among one of those thousands. I still vividly remember that Indian summer day. My mother, teenage brother, and I were the only ones home that Sunday morning as my father was called away to the hospital to perform an emergency surgery and my sister was away at law school. Suddenly, the blue skies turned into dark gray clouds and the news flashed that a wildly spreading fire was raging out of control over the hill at Hiller Highlands. We were given 15 minutes to evacuate our home.

My mind in a blur, I directed my little brother's actions and together with my brother, we comforted our mother as she collapsed in her bedroom in panic and fear. In our haste to escape, as the fire raged down the mountainside near our home, we were not able to salvage much. I did manage to save most of my sister's wardrobe that she bought with her hard-earned money in preparation for her professional career as a lawyer. As for the rest of the family, we were able to save my father's diplomas and medical certificates and my recently completed portfolio of architectural projects and a small box of mementos. The most devastating among our many losses were our family photos and heirlooms. To this day and forever forward, we can only cherish those images in our minds as those precious photos and possessions are gone forever.

I will never forget the sight of the charred and smoldering land where our family home once stood when, two days after the fire, my mother and I were finally allowed to view the damage in person. My mother is a locally famous personality in the Asian community through her success as a restaurateur in the Bay Area. Chinese TV Channel 26 apparently was in the area filming some of the damage from the fire and, recognizing my mother, caught us on film as we broke down at the brick footsteps of the mountain of ashes which had once been our home. That footage was aired repeatedly on the news throughout the evening. In these ensuing years, my family frequently laments the tragic loss of our home and its contents. However, through it all, I have learned that nothing is more important to me than the safety and togetherness of my family. We had survived the drastic event together and it no longer mattered to me that I had lost forever all my yearbooks, family heirlooms and photographs, mementos from our past, and even my third grade papier-mâché elephant that had made my father very proud.

> **Motif**

The unpredictable metaphor of "fire" once again put me through another trying time in my life. Shortly after the fire, while I was completing my last semester at the Academy of Art College, my mother was diagnosed with colon cancer. After going through abdominal surgery, she required intense chemotherapy. Since I had the most flexible daytime schedule, I took on the responsibility of taking my mother to her daily chemotherapy sessions and caring for her during the day as she went through bouts of uncontrollable shivering and loss of appetite, hair, and weight. My mother persevered through it all from the time of the unexpected diagnosis to the arduous completion of chemotherapy sessions. During that period, she exhibited qualities of strength, optimism, and resilience. I was so proud of her. She is now into her fifth year of remission, a period by which the doctors told her that if there were no recurrences of cancer, she would be considered completely cured. I learned a valuable lesson about optimism, determination, and endurance in those months with my mother and have applied the same characteristics toward my own life struggles in times of weakness. I also took to heart the Chinese saying: "It is on disaster that good fortune perches." In those months of my mother's recuperation, I maintained my own determination to complete my second degree and did so by achieving a 4.0 GPA in that last semester. At the same time, acting as family architect, I completed the design of our new family home in Piedmont, which replaced the one destroyed by the fire.

> **Bolding is a device to help the reader**

Metal symbolizes my chosen profession in the field of architecture. As a major construction material in buildings, it is metal which permits a building to tower many stories above the ground once the foundation is set. How my career steered toward this profession reverts back to my days as a child. As with many Chinese families, our Sunday family tradition was to have dim sum lunch with my grandmother. The adults spent the afternoon playing rounds of the Chinese table game mah jong. During their breaks in the game, my parents often found me at the table constructing challenging buildings out of the mah jong tiles. I would explore the rectilinear shapes of these tiles, treating them like bricks in the shaping of forms with windows, archways, and other fenestration. I remember sometimes imagining I was inside these structures wandering about and discovering that some structures felt open and exhilarating while others felt cold and uninviting. This was the beginning of my fascination with architecture and the influences it has on human perception.

My childhood interest led me to choose a college major in architecture, a discipline which merges both artistic and scientific applications. For my college education, I chose to attend U.C. Berkeley for its architectural program's strength in theory and design. Berkeley's program is unique compared with other schools in the country for its emphasis on theory rather than practical application. The belief is that practical application can be learned on the job whereas design theory cannot. Architectural design theory contributes a sense of responsibility to the shape, form, and function of a structure toward a sense of the balance and harmony of the environment around the structure. A favorable attribute of the architecture and design professions is the tangible results generated from our work. Our work often serves as a functional, civic, and/or aesthetic value for society to use and enjoy. Architecture has been influential in my life as an art form that integrates multiple disciplines in both its academic approach as well as professional application. Through my undergraduate studies and working career, I have infused the multiple disciplines of the profession into daily use in the form of critical analysis, strategic thinking, and creative problem solving. Whether I am designing personal sentiment cards, working on a college design charette, or solving a professional facilities problem, I always create applications in this manner, which subsequently generate richer and more satisfying results. There is a certain reward in creating a built environment which provides me with a feeling of contributing to the progress of society. I am proud to be an architect.

Use of examples ✓

The element **water** is representative of my Chinese cultural and international background. The Pacific Ocean is the body of water that connects East, my ancestral home of China, to West, my physical home of the U.S. This waterway has had a profound influence on my life in many ways, including my multi-lingual abilities. The travels experienced in my earlier years most profoundly influenced me in my language abilities. I was born in the U.S. and had spent the first four years of my life there until my family moved to Hong Kong. As a four-year-old going to kindergarten in Hong Kong, I was compelled to speak, read, and write Chinese, although I only knew how to speak English at the time. By the time I had begun to learn and understand some Chinese, my family moved to Seoul, Korea where my father served in the U.S. Army as a medical officer. There, at the International School, I was taught in English but also was exposed to the Korean language. A year later, we moved again, this time back to the States to Monterey, California.

In Monterey, my first grade teacher, Miss Takata, noticed my language struggles created reading skills inferior to that of my classmates. She set about to change this by suggesting to my parents a tutoring program whereby I attended school one hour earlier each morning and in addition, completed extra homework assignments. By the second grade, attending school in Richmond, after my father left the Army and started a private medical practice, I reached the head of my class in reading and writing. The next year, my parents decided to buy a plot of land in the Oakland Hills' Montclair District to build our family home. Once again in a new school environment, I was accepted in the Oakland Unified School District's Gifted And Talented Education (GATE) program for academically-gifted students. This program gave such students opportunities for advanced education in math and English, including the opportunity as a high school senior to study calculus at U.C. Berkeley as an honorary participant in the Accelerated High School Student Program (AHSSP). I owe this part of my educational development to Miss Takata, without whose dedicated efforts during my formative learning years I might not have been able to become so accomplished a student.

Motif

Wood is symbolic of my artistic and creative abilities. As the source material for all paper products, wood symbolizes a relevant point in my childhood. At age eight, I was the youngest person at that time to have exhibited a piece of artwork at the Oakland Museum. In my third grade class, I had created and hand-painted entirely from mental images, a papier-mâché Thai elephant which was so realistic in its effect that my teacher, Mrs O'Neill, presented it to the school principal. The school principal suggested and arranged for it to be exhibited at the Oakland Museum to encourage program support for art studies at the elementary school level. After the exhibition was over, my father proudly featured my elephant on his desk in his private den. Throughout my life, it proved as a constant reminder to me that I had creative skills which set me apart from most other people and encouraged the artistic development of my young mind. The elephant papier-mâché project saw the beginning of my artistic and creative aspiration, which has been a common thread in my life, whether this talent is applied toward my work, my hobbies, or my perceptions and appreciation for aesthetic values in life.

Water, as an element of my Chinese background, has combined with metal, my architectural background, and wood, my artistic and creative abilities, as a means to broaden my career horizons toward an international career in architecture. In August of 1993, I was granted a three-month overseas job assignment to consult for the Hong Kong-based architecture firm, the Inchcape Group, in the project management of their 125,000-sq. ft. Chase Manhattan and Chemical Bank merger project. I was selected for this unique assignment on the basis of my skill-set and cultural qualifications. These included my Western education, professionalism, work ethics, cultural background, and bilingual abilities. Although I had to grapple with languages and a struggling academic performance in the early years of my life, the multi-lingual exposure resulting from my family travels and life abroad ironically has provided me with this unique opportunity to live and work in Hong Kong for the past three years. According to the Inchcape Group's Managing

Director, Robert Marlin, I have a "dynamic combination of skills seldom found in the design industry". At the arduous completion of this three-month assignment, involving numerous 12-hour work days, rigorous deadline schedules, and challenging client interfacing, I was offered a permanent position with the firm. This position, which has blessed me with incredible work experience and cultural enrichment these last three years, would have never been realized if it were not for my language skills and ability to bridge Eastern and Western business practices.

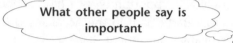

What other people say is important

As a result of the international exposure in my childhood years and professional life, I have also developed an ability to interact positively with people in any circumstance. This includes the present challenges and experiences I face as a female architect working in an industry and a region of the world, Asia, which is male-dominated. When I initially attended client meetings in my boss' presence, clients naturally assumed that I was his administrative assistant attending the meeting for the purpose of taking notes. In my oral communication, it became apparent that if I was to command any respect, I would need to speak effectively, intelligently, and most importantly, confidently. Today, I attend client meetings as a sole representative of my firm, and often run all-male project coordination meetings, utilizing my bilingual capabilities, in both English and Chinese.

In its elemental form, **earth** symbolizes my well-grounded belief systems. As an earthquake tests the stability of the ground, so have my belief systems been tested by the professional endeavors I have undertaken. Last year, Mr Neil Lau, who is unfortunately typical of the current locally-hired in-house facilities managers in large corporations in Hong Kong, gave me the international symbol for bribery by rubbing the palms of his hands together in a circular motion. Despite the fact that we had completed a series of successful projects and expressed an interest in securing future work with this French banking institution, Credit Indochine, we ultimately were not invited to do so. Mr Lau chose to operate his department in an unethical manner which ultimately brought down the department and tainted the sound reputation of his employer.

Ethics

I strongly recommended to my managing director not to capitulate to the bribery while risking not being awarded the project. He concurred with my conviction and although we ultimately did not get awarded the project, I take pride in the professional manner in which I managed the delicate situation and made the proper ethical recommendation to my managing director.

Another aspect of my belief systems is my receptiveness for others' ideals. This has come about through my architectural training and work experience whereby I have learned to value and respect matters which are subjective in nature. As a result, I find it difficult to pass judgment upon others' practices and ideals, and I respect the views and perceptions of others. The aforementioned Mr Lau was accustomed to a manner of handling business through a method he had been exposed to, unethical as it was. Although I respected his viewpoint, I could not let his unethical business practice go unnoticed. Unfortunately, these business practices are becoming more commonplace in Hong Kong as the People's Republic of China takes on an increased role in the business community. I have not again personally been confronted with a similar situation since the Credit Indochine occurrence. However, I find myself in touch with peers and other members of my industry who are confronted with such decisions with increasing frequency. My advice to them is to do their best to discourage the development of such behavior and to uphold the principles by which our industry has traditionally thrived.

In making a positive difference in my life's pursuits, I often take on various leadership roles in my personal and professional life or in social and extracurricular activities. In each organization that I join or volunteer my time, I take an active leadership position either as an elected officer or a volunteer participating in organizing and scheduling events, brainstorming ideas, or offering my creative skills in pertinent applications. In social events, I generally take a lead in organizing activities or recruiting assistance. I enjoy feeling that I made a contribution to a cause and even better, helping to educate others. For example, I was a nominated delegate to participate in a panel discussion regarding present trends and future developments of the workplace in a professional forum in the spring of this year. The sponsoring corporation, Mammoth, flew in expert advisors on the subject matter from the States to lead the panel. Unfortunately, many of the other delegates did not participate in the discussion. Feeling a bit embarrassed for the Mammoth representatives, I quickly led a discussion with regards to the changing workplace as a result of technological advancements in today's corporate environment. I was able to offer my knowledge from both my experience in the States as well as in Asia. After the panel discussion was completed, Mammoth's leading representative, Nicholas Ottenburg, personally thanked me for my participation and input.

Leadership qualities

In conclusion, I have found the five elements, when applied to aspects of my life, to be complementary and at times contradictory in nature. Life's situations have both positive and negative outcomes, and through both types of events, I have gained positive lessons and personal attributes which have strengthened my perspective on life. Independently, and collectively, the five elements are representative of aspects of my life which have been significant in shaping who I am today. My career in architecture, for example, symbolized by the element *metal*, has been fueled by *wood*, my artistic abilities, transported over *water*, with respect to my overseas architectural work experience, and grounded by *earth*, my solid belief systems. The relationship between water and fire is equally significant. In the same way that water can put out a fire, so can the strength of my Chinese roots and family unit ("water") survive turmoils such as the fire which burned down our family home. This same fire that destroyed all of my personal belongings, including my once cherished papier-mâché elephant, could not, however, destroy the artistic skills which created it. My artistic and creative abilities are deeply imbedded in my character and lay at the foundation of my personal and professional aspirations. As the Chinese philosopher Lao Tzu said, "What is firmly rooted cannot be pulled out."

Motif

Essay B: How do you see your career developing? How will an MBA further that development? Why are you applying to Stanford?

Introduction

Many multinational corporations are faltering in their approach to expand their corporate facilities, whether purchased or leased, due to inexperience in working on and understanding the complexities of design and construction projects in Asia. I have first-hand experience and have participated in discussions with corporate real estate directors and facilities managers regarding this occurrence. Most corporations hire interdisciplinary design consultancies such as my current employer, the Inchcape Group, to assist them in their global facilities planning. Business entities have come to realize that maintaining a well-managed and highly efficient facility is critical to success. However, there exists a lack of understanding of Asian business practices and the pace with which different countries operate. There is a growing niche in the global corporate facilities management industry for qualified individuals to bring vital business applications to this region of the world thirsty for Western business and management approaches with an Asian sensitivity.

The culmination of my work experience thus far has been in specializing in the field of corporate interior design and facilities management. Whereas I am an architect by trade, the corporate interior design and facilities management field involves the practice of coordinating the physical layout and efficient use of space in collaboration with the needs of the corporation, its management, and its employees. It integrates principles of business administration, architecture, and the behavioral and engineering sciences. The international work experience gained during the last three years has given me the opportunity of creating a career emphasis in the successful completion and strategization of corporate interior projects stemming from growth patterns of multinational corporations in the Asia-Pacific region. In this time, I have executed projects in major Asian cities including Hong Kong, Taipei, Tokyo, Singapore, Jakarta, Beijing, Shanghai, Guangzhou, Seoul, New Delhi, and Manila. I have reached a point in my career in which an MBA is necessary to provide me with the tools and skills to promote corporate facilities management growth for multinational corporations in this region of the world.

Goals

My long-term professional/career objective is to own and operate my own consultancy business focused on assisting multinational corporations to expand and manage their real estate/corporate facilities in Asia. The services I would provide include: developing global real estate plans, strategizing growth plans, occupancy cost management, financial analysis, and management of corporate facilities as a financial asset. My intermediate career goal is to be in a position of management and planning, working in the Corporate Facilities Management Division of a high-technology or telecommunications corporation which has plans to expand to Asia. I have chosen this focus group because my past major clients have included StarGate, Microsoft, Sequent Computers, Cisco Systems, AT&T, and MCI. Such corporations are often in the forefront of pioneering new ideas in effective facilities management. A case in point is StarGate which is one of the first major multinational corporations to adopt and implement a "hot-desking" concept in Asia, specifically in the People's Republic of China. This concept provides an environment for field workers who use the headquarters or regional office on a first-come, first-serve basis. Files and personal items are transported to their offices via mobile storage units. Utilizing this concept, StarGate has been able to reduce their corporate facilities space requirements by 30–40 percent in China, saving hundreds of thousands of dollars in construction and on-going facilities management costs.

Vision

Another reason I am looking to work with high-technology and telecommunications corporations is the vast expansion these corporations are experiencing due to globalization. This vast expansion requires intensive planning and strategization sessions for such corporations to effectively grow, due to the fact that different business arms are growing concurrently, yet at different rates. Successful completion of such expansions are often affected by a host of different social and economic factors such as property development rates, quality of labor force, availability of building materials, and infrastructure, to name a few. Working for a few years in this capacity will provide me with a greater understanding and sensitivity to the vital elements of the corporate and business environment that stimulates global expansion.

My three years in Hong Kong have provided me with unforeseen opportunities to grow at tremendous rates as a design and management professional with an Asian specialty. Personally, I have also grown as an individual living and working in an environment differing in many ways from that of the world I had grown up in and had been accustomed to in the U.S. From a career standpoint, I have found it essential to learn skills quickly and apply myself in all aspects of my industry, from marketing and client relations development, to project, organizational behavior, and financial management. Two main issues which make my work in Asia different from that in the U.S. include cultural awareness and working in a male-dominated workplace.

Examples ✓

In Vietnam, for example, where I recently managed a hotel renovation in Ho Chi Minh

City, I experienced the involvement of the Socialist government intervening upon the importation of specified goods required for the project. Through this experience, I learned about viewing business practices from another's perspective and came to a solution whereby local products were used in conjunction with the imported products to both the client's and government's satisfaction. Legal issues also take a different precedence in Vietnam. A signed and approved contract for our consultancy services proved invalid when the hotel owner decided to cancel the contract upon the successful completion of our work. No reasons were provided nor did the owner find any need to substantiate his right of cancellation. I was sent to Ho Chi Minh City to re-negotiate our contract in a closed meeting session with the members of the all-male board of directors. I was able to successfully re-negotiate our contract on the basis of the sound business relationship we had established during the course of the project, explaining delicately our perspective and involvement in the project professionally and financially.

Cultural sensitivity ✓

Regarding language barriers, as a form of cultural awareness, the subtleties exchanged through the use of the Chinese language have been tantamount to my abilities in working effectively with our Chinese clientele. An example of such a challenge came recently when I prepared to present a design and project management proposal entirely in Cantonese in order to clinch a new project in Guangzhou, China. The client was one of China's leading pharmaceutical companies, Guangzhou Pharmaceutical Industry Company Ltd. I went to this presentation accompanied by our Beijing office associate. When we arrived, it became apparent that Mandarin was to be the spoken language, not Cantonese. As my Mandarin was quite inferior to my Cantonese, it became necessary for my colleague to give the presentation in Mandarin. As my colleague had not prepared the presentation, I gave the presentation in Cantonese and my colleague translated it into Mandarin for our potential clients' understanding. This experience required the ability to maximize opportunities and resources, exude confidence, and most of all, thinking as a team. The joint presentation effort led us to the successful award of the project. New experiences come in all shapes and sizes in my work in Asia. It has been tremendously helpful to develop a focused mindset, maintain a high energy level and alertness, be motivated, and results-oriented.

As a female architect and manager in a male-dominated industry in Asia, I have had unique opportunities to prove my effectiveness in a manner to command the respect and support I readily deserve. In communication, I am forthright; in project management, I am decisive and timely; and in industry knowledge, I am informed. I am most excited about my chosen career path, thus far, for the multi-faceted disciplines required to be effective and successful. I have not been short of opportunities and challenges which have allowed me to grow as a professional and future management leader.

Presently, as I reflect upon a period of my career that has been filled with solid Asian work experience and personal growth, I am thankful for having been granted the opportunity to live and work in Hong Kong. The timing could not have been better as all of Asia is teeming with growth and economic opportunities for development and I was able to partake in and influence this development through my work and travels throughout the region. Hong Kong is a society that has created for itself, through its evolution as a major business and financial capital of the world, an environment stretched with an overflowing population, subsequent pollution and environmental damage to the land and surrounding waterways, and a fast-paced way of life where the attribute of patience is not welcome. As well, it is undergoing tensions and change as it prepares itself for a transformation from a British colony to a Special Administrative Region of the People's Republic of China on July 1, 1997. It is at the helm of a new era that I am prepared to pursue my next venture of attaining an MBA from Stanford University which will enable me to bring vital business applications to this sector of the world thirsty for Western business and management approaches with an Asian sensitivity.

Vision

In today's global facilities management industry, corporate success is often determined by factors such as timing and business locale. In a growing marketplace like Asia, a corporation's business success may stem simply from grasping opportunities to strike early in expanding to major worldwide cities and locations. Understanding the process by which to select, implement, and manage global facilities, however, is a relatively untapped area of expertise in Asia. This process incorporates the disciplines of strategic time and project management, knowledge of an individual country's political, social, business and cultural environment, in addition to effective leadership, interpersonal, and communication skills. Thus far, there is a lack of such qualified individuals with sufficient knowledge and experience to work in such a capacity in the Asia-Pacific region. My career development, coupled with the professional skills that I possess, is preparing me for a long-term career in global corporate facilities management. However, critical skills and knowledge are necessary to facilitate this goal. An MBA is the important building block in this process.

As I do not have a traditional business background from an educational or professional standpoint, an MBA would provide me with essential skills and knowledge to be effective as a global corporate facilities management professional in the business world. One critical area of knowledge that I currently lack in an industry that is extremely cost-sensitive is the skills and understanding to evaluate the financial aspects involved in facilities management. In a recent article about career strategies in *Facilities Design & Management Journal*, leading corporate real estate and facilities management executives state that up-and-coming management individuals must have a firm grasp of financial tools and investment management skills. These requirements allow a real estate or facilities executive to be cross-functional, allowing one to be able to speak about finance to a CFO in a language mutually understandable. I need to be able to understand the corporate side of the picture as well as the assets themselves, real estate or corporate facilities. Collectively, I am in

Citing articles

search of an MBA program which is strong in the fundamentals of business, including finance and economics, has a renowned international business and management perspective, a celebrated entrepreneurial program, and is located geographically in proximity to high-technology and telecommunications corporations. The Stanford Graduate School of Business is at the crossroads of this search.

Mentioning courses adds credibility

Specifically, I find that as the leader in management education, the Stanford MBA program contains innovative vantage points and opportunities for the development of future international business and management leaders such as myself. These include your first-year core coursework focused on developing an understanding and competence in the four areas including organizational environment of a firm, the external environment (economy and society) of the business, functional areas of accounting, finance, marketing, and operations, and finally, developing skills in the application of quantitative techniques to management problems. In addition, the opportunity to learn from a diverse and unique class of students with a broad range of professional and personal achievements would provide a unique perspective to the coursework. The emphasis on global issues as an integral part of your MBA program is particularly attractive to my career pursuits. I am interested in pursuing the Global Management Program Certificate as it directly relates to my career goals in Asia. In addition, in order to provide me with the education and applications to complement my Asia focus and finance, real estate, and management focus, I would find the following courses particularly beneficial: G306 – Real Estate Investment; F323 – International Financial Management; F321 – Investment Management and Entrepreneurial Finance; and R372 – High Performance Leadership. Since my ultimate career goal is to own and operate my own consultancy business, your renowned entrepreneurship education would be vital to my success. Finally, I would be thrilled to be back in the beautiful Bay Area, my hometown, with my fresh experience and vision from a global perspective to share with my fellow classmates as we work together toward obtaining our respective MBA degrees in anticipation of making a positive difference in the global business environment.

The Stanford MBA program is in search of individuals who are focused, achievement-oriented, motivated, energized, and command the respect of others, have the ability to maximize opportunities and resources, have academic aptitude, and have strong communication and interpersonal skills. My career and life experiences have collectively provided me with opportunities to develop the certain qualities that prepare one to meet the challenges that make managers become leaders. As a professional and community service-driven individual, I have demonstrated my leadership abilities and management potential. From my first full-time position out of college, as a select member of the Neiman Marcus Executive Management Training Program to my present position as Project

Director and Senior Designer at the Inchcape Group in Hong Kong, I have exemplified a strong foundation in management skills. My broad-ranging Asia experiences include learning to articulate my ideas through language abilities, single-handedly negotiating contracts in developing countries like Vietnam, and crisis management on project sites. Through all my experiences, I have always maintained a focused drive that demonstrates a combination of ideals like motivation, focus, and interpersonal skills, to name a few.

In conclusion, my individual skill-set and background, coupled with the extensive knowledge and experience that the Stanford MBA program provides, would equip me with an uncommon foundation with which to achieve my long-term goal of owning and operating my own consultancy business in the specialization of global corporate facilities management. The MBA program at the Stanford Graduate School of Business will not only teach me the skills necessary to work in and contribute to the corporate sector of global facilities management for a high-technology or telecommunications corporation, but also will provide me with personal development skills necessary in shaping my career direction. As sound architecture is based on solid training, precision, and graphic communication, so is sound business based on strong theory, practical application, and vision. Collectively, I see a Stanford MBA as helping me to complete a "blueprint" for my ultimate business success in the world of global corporate facilities management.

Candidate #2

Candidate's biography: John is male, American, educated in the U.S.

Outline – "Career Goals" Essay

I. Goals (para 1)
II. Background

    a. Marine Corps (para 2–4)
    b. Coca-Cola (para 5–6)

III. Why an MBA? (para 7)
VI. Why Columbia? (para 8)

Essay: What are your short- and long-term career goals? How will the Columbia Business School MBA program help you achieve these goals? (Columbia)

My six years of work experience has taken place in two of the premier organizations in the world: The United States Marine Corps and The Coca-Cola Company. The Marines taught me to lead and Coke taught me to market. Both organizations provide practical, hands-on experience in the fundamentals of management in the international arena. I want to pursue an international general management career after obtaining the professional qualifications provided by an MBA from Columbia Business School. My long-term goal is to become an International Group President for Coca-Cola. My short to mid-term goal is to obtain a masters in business administration from CBS and return to The Coca-Cola Company to run a small international unit.

Clear writing ✓

Thorough preparation, self-confidence, and credibility are all traits of a leader and my four-year block in the Marine Corps is testimony to this. Leadership in the Marines is unique in that it comes with great responsibility and commitment to personal safety. As Infantry Company Commander Captain, I managed and led 250 Marines including 5 officers. Some of my responsibilities included setting mission objectives, establishing training goals, writing performance evaluations, conducting career counseling, disciplining Marines, and managing the Company's fuel and ammunition assets. I also conducted numerous live fire evolutions that involved over 300 Marines. One Division operation required conducting a live fire company attack at night and also performing in a simulated chemical environment. Before I left the Marine Corps, I was ranked #1 out of 12 Captains in the Battalion by the Commanding Officer and awarded the prestigious Navy/Marine Corps Commendation Medal for my service.

The flow of illegal drugs through the border between New Mexico and Mexico has long been a serious problem. In April 1997, when I was a 1st Lieutenant in the United States Marine Corps, I was the mission commander for a Joint Task Force operation along the border. In this real world mission my unit worked alongside the U.S. Border Patrol. To highlight the seriousness of this mission, the unit that replaced mine, had an altercation with a Mexican teenager that resulted in his death. For this operation I independently planned, organized, budgeted, and executed the mission that was successful in preventing $1,000,000 worth of illegal drugs from entering the U.S. An equally important success of the mission was the fact that no Marines were injured, no equipment was lost or damaged and all 45 Marines involved conducted themselves in a highly professional manner. The reason for our success was due to the amount of planning, intense training and preparation that we undertook before we ever arrived on the border. I have learned from this experience that success stems from well thought out and organized planning.

It was also in the Marines that I developed a real international focus. I spent one year in Okinawa, Japan, during which we trained alongside military units throughout Asia. This military experience has been invaluable in the formation of my leadership and international philosophy. Believing that I had accomplished my military goals, I turned my attention to a career in business.

Working for Coca-Cola in the Atlanta Headquarters has allowed me to understand the company's progressive international distribution network. Working in the International Bottling Division, I support the needs of bottlers worldwide and work with the Bottler Annual Plan to outline and monitor specific performance targets. I spearheaded a Parallel Product Tracking System that resulted in a 45 percent drop in illegally transshipped products to overseas markets.

Although Coca-Cola is an enormously large company, it has recently taken steps to undergo a significant change in business practice and philosophy including aggressive plans to double shareholder value within five years. First, the company has redefined its market: Traditionally it has been a Carbonated Soft Drink Company with 85 percent of the world's market. Now it is a Ready-to-Drink Beverage Company with only 25 percent share of the market. This has posed challenges to the marketing team! Second, the company is no longer solely a "carbonated beverage company" receiving orders from Atlanta, but has become a total beverage company requiring small unit leadership, product innovation and local marketing expertise. In the midst of a significant structural change, I have gained substantial exposure in innovative marketing concepts and mediums that include the Internet and cashless vending.

To accomplish my career objectives it is vital that I obtain the necessary formal training from a top business school. I see myself going back to work for Coca-Cola in a business planning and development role for an international division. In this role I will be responsible for business development in emerging markets to include innovative marketing concepts, financial structures and investments, distribution methods and operating efficiencies. Following this role I would become the country manager of a medium sized county. It is in this role that my concentration in general management and consumer marketing from Columbia Business School would be of most value.

Even though my experiences to date have provided me with a good understanding of basic international business practices, I am aware of my need for more formal training in finance, consumer marketing, and business planning in order to be a cross functional general manager. The Columbia Business School arguably has the best resources, people and technical skills in the U.S., if not the world. The New York location provides an excellent opportunity to learn in an invigorating environment. I plan to focus on General Management while selecting electives from the international business and marketing departments. I am particularly interested in the International Marketing and High Performance Leadership Courses. I feel that my varied background will be a contribution to the class, which employs the teaching method of lectures, case studies, guest speakers and breakout time.

Candidate #3

Candidate's biography: Vivian is female, Hungarian-American, educated in the U.S.

Outline for Essay A – "Who are You?" Essay

I. Introduction (brief) (para 1)
II. Discussion

    a. My parents and my Hungarian-American upbringing (para 2–4)
    b. Hungary and Hungarian inventions (para 5–6)
    c. College days and personal initiative (para 7–8)
    d. Hired by GE for work in Hungary (para 10–11)
    e. Doing the right things; commercialism/community well-being (para 12–13)

III. Conclusion (para 14)

Outline for Essay B – "Career Goals" Essay

I. Introduction (brief) (para 1)
II. Background

    a. Graduate of General Electric's FMP Program (para 2–3)
    b. Working for GE in Eastern and Western Europe and Asia (para 4–7)

III. Goals (+ vision) (para 8–10)

    a. Previous experience in ethics consulting (para 11)

IV. Why an MBA? (para 12)
V. Why Stanford Business School? (para 13–15)

Essay A: Each of us has been influenced by the people, events, and situations in our lives. How have these influences shaped who you are today? (Stanford)

Of all the countries of Europe, Hungary is truly unique. Situated in Central Europe, between Austria and Romania, Hungary is considered neither Slavic nor Balkan. Its language is a linguistic anomaly, sharing only a slight similarity with Finnish. Owing to its unfortunate geographical location on the crossroads of East to West, Hungary has been the subject of numerous conquests and invasions – from Mongols, Romans, Turks, and Habsburg to the Russians. However, throughout their 1,100-year-old history, Hungarians have managed to not only retain their unique culture, but also amalgamate the best attributes of their captors. Even the resulting oppression and deprivation suffered during occupation have had a positive spin. Being Hungarian means being distinctive yet adaptable, and by necessity, ingenious and intensely motivated. As the traditional saying goes, Hungarians can "make steel from wood." Its proximity to the grandeur of Western Europe has produced a "poor relative" syndrome, sparking both envy and ambition in its people. Being Hungarian means proving you can do it too.

All about Hungary

There is an engine running inside of me, always purring and propelling me forward toward my dreams.

My parents fled Romania for America in 1965 with US$75 in their possession. As ethnic Hungarians living in Oradea, a region belonging to Hungary before WWII, they had been subject to constant discrimination at school and in their profession. When I was born four years later, they were still struggling to make a living in their adopted country. For years, my father studied at night for his optician's degree while holding a full-time job. My mother learned English by watching *Sesame Street* with me. Growing up as a first-generation American, straddling two worlds, the old and new, has left a deep impression on me.

My Hungarian upbringing has imbued me with a heightened empathy toward other cultures. I speak three foreign languages – Hungarian, Spanish, and French. My parents, as immigrants, continually emphasized the great importance of education, hard work, and determination. They passed down to me their belief in the "American Dream". My American background has given me the spirit, self-confidence, and the opportunity to go out and create that dream. Being half-Catholic and half-Jewish, from my mother's and father's side respectively, has allowed me to understand different religions and accept different religious beliefs. One of my friends even joked that I am both "half chosen" and "half forgiven". This combination of different cultures, religions, and values has imbued me with empathy, insight, and well-roundedness.

Both influences, Hungarian and American, have taught me to not expect anything to be handed to me. In fact, I become suspicious when things go too easy. I am diligent, ambitious, and determined, always juggling many jobs, projects, and responsibilities at once. I make things happen. Yes, I do expect to achieve great things in life. There is an engine running inside of me, always purring and propelling me forward toward my dreams. On account of my parents' immigrant background, I am very pragmatic. I know if I want something, I will have to initiate action myself. I find or make opportunities and approach each job and each task with great creativity and resourcefulness. My family may not have had a lot of money, but they gave me an enormous amount of love, attention, and encouragement. Because of this, I believe that I can do anything I set my mind to.

Only by knowing and understanding where you are from, do you know who you are. I too have invented and created in my own small way.

Landlocked, with minimal mineral wealth and natural resources, Hungary has a population of less than ten million. Although representing only a tiny fraction of the world's population, Hungarians have played major roles in enormously significant 20th century inventions including the television (Kalman Tihany), the computer (Janos Neuman), the world's first mass production car (Jozsef Galamb), and the atom bomb (Edward Teller). Modern-day Hungarians such as George Soros, George Lucas, Estee Lauder, and Andy Grove, *Time Magazine*'s Man of the Year for 1997, are vanguards of industry, commerce, and entertainment.

Most people do not know that the above inventions were fostered by Hungarians or that these luminary figures are of Hungarian descent. But for me, my Hungarian ancestry has been instrumental in shaping my personality. In fact, I feel I cannot explain what influences have shaped who I am, without first explaining what it means to be Hungarian. Only by knowing and understanding where you are from, do you know who you are.

I too have invented and created in my own small way.

While in high school in Florida, I graduated with high honors, as president of the Spanish Club and co-editor of the school newspaper. Diligence, self-motivation, and inventiveness characterized all my endeavors. While most of my friends were going to football games or to the movies, I was home studying or concocting fund-raising schemes for the clubs I was member of. One of the most successful of my entire senior year was my idea to raise money for the annual Spanish Club cruise. We sold small bottles of suntan lotion attached to cards, which we arranged to be sent to homeroom classes right before spring break. Not in all the years of my high school in Florida, I was later told, had there been a fund-raiser involving suntan lotion.

Personal initiative and energy have always been a key facet of my personality. This key Hungarian characteristic stands out. I am extremely motivated. In college at Boston

University, I had an internship or job each semester. If an internship did not pay, I would double and take a paying job as well. I did so in part because I had to work for financial reasons and in part because I figured the real world experience would help me land a good job after college. Ever pragmatic, I reasoned that internship experience would be more valuable than working at a coffee shop or a clothing store – although I did those as well – or joining a sports team or sorority. By the time I graduated, I had worked in seven different fields and over nine different jobs. These included: Allied Irish Bank, Mrs Miller's Muffins, Smith Barney, Harris & Upham, Pierre Deux (French lifestyle store), *Interview Magazine*, Houghton Mifflin Publishers, *Madame Figaro* magazine, *Boston Magazine*, and Coffee Connection. I even had the distinction of being the youngest person to have an article published in *Boston Magazine*. The news director had been impressed with my resume and numerous articles I had written in high school. He hired me during my freshman year even though it was company policy to only accept juniors.

This shows energy

They never dreamt that at 21, I would return to the country they (my parents) left behind, ironically, at the very same age.

As an American-born Hungarian, my family was surprised when I went to Hungary after college to work. They never dreamt that at 21, I would return to the country they left behind, ironically, at the very same age. Within two weeks of graduation, I was hired into General Electric (GE)'s two-and-a-half year Financial Management Program (FMP) and began work at General Electric Lighting Tungsram in Hungary. The political environment in Eastern Europe in 1991 and the fall of Communism opened up the chance to pursue my goal.

During my five years in Hungary, I discovered how four Hungarian characteristics – distinctiveness, adaptability, ingenuity, and personal motivation – continued to play a major factor in my own personality and accomplishments. My strong commitment to my Hungarian roots prompted me to create Hungary's first expatriate volunteer association.

In 1991, I created the Hungarian International Association (HIA) while working for GE Lighting Europe in Hungary. My motivation to create HIA was rooted in my strong belief in ethics and my indebtedness to the Hungarian community. Through HIA, I united and motivated foreign-born professionals of Hungarian ancestry, like myself, to support and give back to the local community. For my work, General Electric awarded me the prestigious Phillippe Award for outstanding leadership in community service, GE's highest worldwide service honor, in August 1994. As president for four years, I brought my vision of an expatriate service organization to life. I achieved success by leading and organizing HIA like a business and by applying all four essential Hungarian characteristics – distinctiveness, adaptability, ingenuity, and personal motivation.

How do we as individuals do the right things and how do we promote commercialism while fulfilling community well-being?

I am a person who has vigorously pursued a greater understanding of what my Hungarian cultural background means to me. I believe that culture is important because the better a person understands one particular culture the better he or she can understand other cultures. For me, this importance foreshadows my plan to spend a good deal of my life working internationally. At this stage of my life, I am fortunate to have studied and worked with many interesting overlaps. I graduated with a Bachelor of Science degree in Journalism and have proven my communication abilities on and off the job. I have excelled in English – a language that initially mystified my parents and I have learned the nuances of the Hungarian language, which initially mystified me. I have also achieved a complementary relationship between words and numbers, which is useful and very powerful. At times, one needs numbers to communicate ideas, and other times one needs words, as in giving speeches. My strength lies in my ability to listen, synthesize ideas – whether quantitative or qualitative – and articulate concepts – verbal or written – in a way that is concise and eloquent.

I have worked full-time for six years for GE, a general management leader, but have also worked part-time (while in college) for small privately-run companies. I have worked across a myriad of industries: I have worked on different continents, namely Europe, North America, and Asia, and in different countries following different economic, political, and religious systems. I have, for the time being, achieved a decent sense of material well-being. The question I now ask myself is not only how do I proceed but how do we as individuals do the right things and how do we promote commercialism while fulfilling community well-being? My lifetime aspiration is to fulfill my goal of becoming a leading business ethics/corporate citizenship consultant. The world is closer than ever before and now it is necessary to actually do the right things. When individuals, corporations, and countries do the right kinds of things, quality, morale, and goodwill come about. When individuals, corporations, countries mistreat each other, the effects are viewed quickly. When we mistreat the environment, the environment speaks back at us. Every person, corporation, and country finds itself living in front of a mirror. Technology in the form of news information and high-tech weaponry, makes doing the right kinds of things more critical. It is no longer just for our peace of mind.

Like the Hungarian inventors before me, I feel a need to create and express myself through my work. *Munka* is a Hungarian phrase that means "work makes you noble". Being Hungarian and seeing the real-life examples of success among so many famous Hungarians have given me confidence in my own abilities and showed me what is possible with ingenuity and motivation. I feel a strong debt to my parents, to the U.S. for the opportunities it has provided to all of us, and to Hungary for being situated on an unfortunate but eclectic crossroads.

Essay B: How do you see your career developing? How will an MBA further that development? Why are you applying to Stanford?

Strong opener

Extreme self-motivation, diligence, and a talent for leadership characterize the diversity and scope of my personal and professional accomplishments. My global work experience in Hungary, Hong Kong, and the U.S. and my educational background in communication and business have given me a broad perspective on the commercial world. These accomplishments have instilled in me a unique and formidable blend of skills and competencies.

Graduate of General Electric's prestigious Financial Management Program

I graduated from General Electric (GE)'s two-and-a-half-year Financial Management Program (FMP) in December of 1993, and in doing so, joined the alumnae of GE's top finance managers and CFOs. I view this as my most substantial accomplishment because graduating from GE's FMP demonstrated my self-discipline, intellectual stamina, and strength in applied quantitative skills. FMP honed and sharpened my skills and gave me a firm foundation in finance and business.

One of corporate America's most prestigious and most competitive financial training programs, FMP is an intensive and grueling combination of a full-time on-the-job finance experience and formal educational training. Concurrent to taking five graduate level finance courses such as Financial Reporting, Financial Accounting, and Auditing, trainees or "FMPs" rotate through five six-month assignments in all functional finance departments, from General Accounting, Investment Finance, Sales and Marketing to Manufacturing Finance.

Key positions with General Electric in Eastern Europe, Western Europe, and Asia

For the past six years, I have held a series of intensive and challenging managerial positions in Eastern and Western Europe and Asia with General Electric. Achieving the responsible and visible level of these assignments demanded extremely hard work, excellent analytical and quantitative skills, and top management approval and support. I regard the attainment of these positions as significant work accomplishments. It took enormous diligence and dedication not only to be chosen for each position, but also to move quickly through the ranks at the relatively young age of 26.

From my leading role as manager of the Western European Internal Audit Department for GE Lighting in Europe (GELE) to my present position as finance manager of the CNBC Channel for NBC Asia in Hong Kong, I delivered results and success. At NBC I created my position from scratch and provided financial counsel to management as the *first* financial manager of the channel. At GELE, I created all audit plans and led all business reviews throughout the Western European affiliates. I demonstrated not only my financial and business acumen through these varied roles, but also great adaptability, stamina, and a large threshold for hard work and rigor.

I took advantage of all avenues and opportunities to learn and grow professionally at General Electric Lighting Europe. Even during my first year of work, I requested and received additional assignments. One of my first assignments was to implement GELE's *first* investment tracking system for over US$44 million worth of capital investments. After successful completion, I went on to help spearhead the company's first ever detailed analysis of product pricing and profitability by lighting product line. I received a management award for my recommendations which generated US$5 million in incremental margin in 1991.

Above all, however, I value my work because I achieved success in vastly different and enormously complex environments. Environments that spanned different continents, cultures, and industries – from Eastern Europe to Asia and from manufacturing to broadcasting. I lived in foreign countries far from home for over six years and worked in new and often struggling corporate divisions.

When looking into the future, my real aspiration is to become the preeminent leader in business ethics/corporate citizenship consulting, specializing in work for large multinational companies. While most businesses know that ethics compliance and a larger social conscience are important, if not pivotal, business leaders have a hard time: (1) quantifying ethical practices and (2) implementing strategies and programs. Quantifying ethics is a key step in selling ethics to individual managers and corporations. Currently, most talk of ethics leaves businesspersons shaking their heads in general agreement but ethics is viewed as compliance in nature. I feel that my greatest long-term contributions working in this field will be measured by: (1) my ability to find ways to define and quantify in "dollars and cents" terms the benefits of ethics and corporate citizenship and (2) my ability to sell corporations on the proactive benefits of these programs as a means to market the company, products, and employees. This translates to opportunity through proactivity, not compliance by requirement. I would cherish the day when ethics becomes a separate line entry on the corporate income statements and balance sheets of the world's major companies.

> **Contrasting terms serve to clarify**

Whereas *business ethics* is about individuals within a corporation, *corporate citizenship* is about the larger corporate entity and its relationship with the community. Corporate citizenship involves linking corporate-giving strategies with business strategies to develop a corporate social vision, enhance corporate reputation, and make a positive contribution to the communities in which businesses operate. The average corporate manager is likely to be unfamiliar with corporate-giving strategies. A few large multinationals such as General Electric and Lockheed Martin have implemented worldwide ethics and compliance training and organized company-wide charitable fund-raising programs. The need for well-defined programs is critical for U.S. companies operating in the international sector. In China, for example, a few multinational companies have thought about ways to manage corporate citizenship programs. One U.S. company is reported to have bought an antique Ming dynasty furniture set at an auction in continental U.S. and then donated the set to the Chinese government as part of a business presentation in Beijing. Obviously this donation is completely legal and may go a long way in bolstering the company's reputation as a social do-gooder in China. In juxtaposition, other foreign companies have suffered negative reputations and have been described by the Chinese as, "we only have eyes for money".

Cultural tidbits ✓

I feel I am the person ideally suited to reaching my goal. I have been fortunate to have built my career to date within a general management dynasty – General Electric. My seven years' work experience with General Electric has allowed me to understand the workings of one of the world's most successful companies. My experience is key because, after completing my MBA, I want to continue working with GE or another multinational, to help implement ethics policies and training programs. An alternative option would include working with an international consulting firm such as McKinsey with exposure to large corporate clients or working within a specialized department of a professional organization such as KPMG's new 'Business Ethics Consulting' section.

My previous work experience in ethics consulting is relevant and began while I was working for General Electric in Hungary. I worked for Eva Somorjai, Chief Ombudsperson for General Electric in Hungary, for over a year. Eva's work as Director of the 'Helpline' – GE's company-wide hotline for reporting and resolving integrity and ethics-related issues – in Hungary has become a 'Best Practice' throughout GE's Western and Eastern Europe businesses. I assisted Eva in implementing the Hungarian 'Helpline' in 1994 and helped in over 25 Integrity cases, ranging from 'whistle blowing' termination to collusion. I also personally led compliance audits in Spain and France in my role as Western European Internal Audit Manager for GE Lighting Europe. In these roles, I found that my strong sense of fair play, my investigative abilities and my excellent interpersonal skills dovetailed with the requirements for this position. My background in finance and journalism provided the right mix of skills and aptitudes – from accountancy and investigation to communication – as well as the right mindset – principled and fair – to resolve issues quickly and successfully.

Leadership in this new field will be through research, study, and advanced education

My long-term goals in ethics and corporate citizenship represent a shift in my present career in finance. My six years' international finance experience and my work in ethics consulting have exposed me to my intended field of study and provided me with an invaluable foundation, but the route to leadership in this new field will be through research, study, and advanced education. A top MBA program would provide me with the education, resources, and time to further my business ideas. An MBA would expose me to distinguished professors, experiences of my peers, and both independent and related summer study. I would be able to pursue my goals full time with all my energy and commitment.

For a person like myself, pursuing a career in a new field such as business ethics, Stanford Business School's course flexibility and emphasis on the development of ideas will be essential to achieving my career goals. Very few graduate programs today offer the immense selection of wide-ranging elective courses and the opportunity to organize independent study with distinguished professors. Along with the business school's entrepreneurial focus, all these factors will be critical to hone and organize my ideas into a roadmap. Courses such as Ethical Dilemmas in Management and Corporate Governance, Power, and Responsibility will combine ethics on an individual level with corporate governorship on a corporate level.

One of my goals will be to develop case studies in ethics and corporate citizenship

As a Stanford Business School student, one of my goals will be to develop case studies in ethics and corporate citizenship consulting. I want to couple my practical and anecdotal international work experience in business ethics at a major general management dynasty – General Electric – with research currently undertaken at Stanford Business School. I want to offer my experience in the most recent General Electric corporate ethics initiatives and programs. According to Larry Ponemon, National Director of Business Ethics Consulting at KPMG, GE now has one of the best ethics compliance programs in existence.

I have been following a series of seminars given by the American Chamber of Commerce in Hong Kong relating to the topics of ethics and corporate citizenship. I want to work with other students at Stanford to present a series of seminars on ethics for first-year students. By referring to ethics and compliance cases I worked on at GE Lighting, I can contribute real-life examples arising from different geographical and cultural settings as well as different industries and functions. For example, I have worked in the U.S., Hungary, the U.K., France, Spain, and Hong Kong and in different industries, such as broadcasting and manufacturing, as well as different sectors, such as finance and marketing and sales.

Candidate #4

Candidate's biography: Fritz is male, German, educated in Belgium

Outline for Essay A – "Who are You?" Essay

I.   Introduction (brief) (para 1–2)
II. Discussion

    a.   New breed of German entrepreneur (para 3)
        1.   Internationally educated (para 4)
        2.   Linguistically adept (para 5–6)
        3.   Sales-oriented and technically competent (para 7–8)
        4.   Culturally rounded (para 9–11)
        5.   Focused on more than just money (para 12–13)

III. Conclusion (para 14)

Outline for Essay B – "Career Goals" Essay

I.   Goals (para 1)
II. Background

    a.   Starting my own two companies (para 2)

III. Vision

    a.   Next step: From manufacturing to marketing (para 3)
    b.   "Anonymous" buying versus relationship buying (para 4–6)
    c.   A Russian market by default (para 7–9)

IV. Why an MBA? (para 10–12)
V.   Why Stanford Business School? (para 13–17)

Essay A: Each of us has been influenced by the people, events, and situations in our lives. How have these influences shaped who you are today? (Stanford)

I see myself as a new breed of German entrepreneur. I envision similarities between myself and Jens Michael Reuter, CEO of Softbank Corp. Mr Reuter is the Bill Gates of Germany. He is German, started his empire in East Germany, and later expanded to Western Europe. His life is intertwined with three countries – Germany, England, and the U.S. My life is intertwined with four different cultures – German, Russian, Swedish, and Belgian. I am German by birth; educated in Germany and Belgium; started my first two companies in East Germany; and have plans to expand to Russia, in addition to Western Europe. While Mr Reuter is concentrating on Internet multimedia development and computer software distribution, I intend to move from manufacturing to focus, in the longer run, on telemarketing.

> Quite an accomplishment

In 1995, at the age of 26, I started my two companies – Spatuck Limited and Rusk (Germany–Russia) Co. Ltd. Spatuck Limited is engaged in the marketing of diversified consumer products. Rusk (Germany–Russia) Co. Ltd. is engaged in the manufacturing of hair wigs and related products. These two companies are an extension of my father's field of business. Rusk (Germany–Russia) Co. Ltd. is the major supplier of products and sells products through Spatuck Limited. Through these two companies, I manage about 200 people with annual sales of US$3.5 million. As to be discussed in Essay B, my goal includes taking my companies public in five years' time while concurrently helping my Swedish father-in-law enter the Russian market.

> Clear set-up

I feel I am a new breed of German entrepreneur, defined as one who is: (1) internationally educated, (2) linguistically adept, (3) sales-oriented and technically competent, (4) culturally rounded, and (5) focused on more than just money.

Internationally educated

What could be more diverse I thought? I am a German citizen, educated in Belgium, hired by a French company to work in Russia. It was like going from one new world to another new world. I was hired by Banque Paribas to work in the Moscow office after I graduated from Versalius College in Belgium. My academic and professional experiences include expertise in the Russian language and culture, finance, and manufacturing. After finishing high school in Munich, I was admitted to the Versalius College in Belgium. Later I graduated from Versalius College, majoring in Russian language studies. I went to Versalius College because of its undergraduate reputation in languages and business. During the time that I was in university and college, I spent some time in Sweden and Poland in order to deepen my knowledge of other European languages.

Linguistically adept

If I could endeavor to speak to a large crowd for ten minutes in a third language after only five months of study, there would be no greater language challenge I will likely face in the future. When I was studying at Versalius College in Belgium, I competed in the university-sponsored Russian Speech Contest with all students in Belgium who were

studying Russian. At that time I only had five months of Russian study and I had to compete with people who had one to two years of Russian study. Although I finished in the middle of the contestants, I began to have an interest in Russian culture.

I am very proud of my ability to speak multiple languages. Although my native tongue is German, through my early years studying English in Germany, I have developed good speaking and writing skills in English. My study of Russian in college and later during the year that I worked in Russia enabled me to speak and write Russian without much problem. And because I studied in Belgium, I have become proficient in French. I have spent one summer in Stockholm University in Sweden to learn Swedish. And as my wife is a native of Sweden, I also have a good working knowledge of Swedish.

Sales-oriented and technically competent

When I was in grade 12 in Germany I ranked among the top 11 in the Euclid Math Contest, a national math contest. During that summer I was sent to the University of Munich (Ludwig-Maximilians-Universitaet Muenchen) to receive a two-week advanced math training. There I met another 59 students who were amongst the brightest math students in Germany. It was a very good experience to work with all these bright people. My eyes were 360 degrees more open since then. The new breed of young German businesspersons are sales-oriented, not just technical craftsmen. Germans are stereotypically known for their technical ability, and in particular for their manufacturing skill. Being German, I have also excelled in technical endeavors.

While I was working for Banque Paribas in Moscow, I was exposed to the world of finance as a complement to my Russian language studies. A year after I came back to Munich to work for my family company, Haas Hair Beauty Co. Ltd., I learned about the manufacturing process which is very different from finance and accounting. However, it is my sales ability that I will rely on most in the future. Mr Olson, my business partner in Rusk (Germany–Russia) Co. Ltd. says, "All my customers seem to like me." Mr Olson has more experience than I do in the wig business, but I generate more sales in terms of dollars than he does. Now I generate about 60 percent of the business for Rusk (Germany–Russia) Co. Ltd. My secret is to be open with my customers on pricing. I know we are not the only wig manufacturer. My customers probably have business relationships with other factories. I need to make my customers feel that they can trust me. So I am very open in analyzing with my customers my cost breakdown, and I always make sure my analysis sounds like I am making but a moderate profit.

Support for the candidate's good sales ability

Culturally rounded

The French say, "The customer will be full just by looking at it." Although German food is famous for its meatiness and Swedish food is famous for its wholesomeness, French food is famous for its elegance. The appearance of French dishes such as Orange Duck, Warm

Truffle Salad, and Panfried Gooseliver with Raspberry Vinegar are always so elegant. During my two years of study at Versalius College in Belgium, I met many French people. I admire the French culture. I found the French to be hardworking, conscientious, and talented. I think France is very advanced compared to the other European countries in more areas than just cuisine.

Enumeration helps readability

Through my training in French culture, I possess an attitude of perfection, discipline, and diligence. I used these qualities to turn around an earlier family business project with Mattel Germany. My perfection, discipline, and diligent attitude allow me to correct three problems: (1) delivery delay, (2) improper product quality, and (3) waste due to inefficient operation procedures. We were one of the two vendors of the production of the wig part of "Barbie 1994". We had a lot of problems with the order. First, we could not deliver on time. It was our first time dealing with a toy firm, making large quantities of doll hairpieces in a short time. We had a lot of complaints from Mattel about our delivery delay. We were told we would be cut out of the order if we could not bring up our speed. Second, we could not keep pace with the quality requirement as we tried to work fast. Third, we had too much waste. We lost money at the beginning on every piece we made. During that time I had a lot of meetings with our factory engineers discussing the ways to improve the production process. We ended up improving our efficiency so much that we beat our competition; a firm that had worked with Mattel for ten years. As a result, Mattel gave about two-thirds of the total order quantity to our factory. We ended up making approximately three million hairpieces for Mattel that year.

My experience in Germany helps me to extend my business relationships with the Russians. Through my business connections, I met Mr Olson of Rusk Co. Ltd. in Belgium. In 1995 Mr Olson and I set up a joint-venture company, Rusk (Germany–Russia) Co. Ltd. We built a factory outside of Berlin. Mr Olson has joint-ventured with the Russians because the Russians are famous for technical expertise in the wig field and our representative in Russia, Mr Smirnov, is a very well-known man in the wig-making industry. As a very typical German, Mr Olson is very united with his people. He treats all workers as his family members and he expects workers to stand up for the factory if there are any problems. Mr Olson is 55 years old. He is very detail-oriented and very tough. He always says to me that East Germans say "ja, ja, ur machen das schom" (it will do). Whenever he asks our East German workers to do something, he never really expects they will do 100 percent of what he asked for. For example, he asked once our workers to make some working tables for the factory. Mr Olson gave them the specification and measurements but the tables ended up a half-inch longer here and a half-inch shorter there. My factory manager and I were thinking we might use them anyway since we had already made them. But Mr Olson said no. He said we had to remake them from beginning until the tables were perfect.

Focused on more than just money

My father told me that when he was five years old, he was so poor that he had to earn money by guarding cows on a farm in order to have a meal. If he did not work that very day he would starve. I was influenced by my father a lot. Education and family are two of the most important values that I inherited. My mother and father emigrated from East Germany to West Germany in 1962 as a result of a rare scientific and technical exchange between the two countries. Although my father's family was very established in East Germany before the war, after the war during the time my grandfather died, my father's family lost everything and became very poor. Neither my father nor my mother could afford to have higher education after graduating from high school in East Germany. As a result, both of my parents especially my father, always wanted us to have as much education as possible. In terms of family, my father never really had a family. My grandfather died when my father was born and my grandmother died when my father was only four months old. So my father always stresses the importance of family to my two sisters and myself. As the oldest and the only son in a German family, I inherit a lot of expectations from my father.

My Swedish father-in-law's company "Rohan", is among the top 20 largest conglomerates in Sweden. His business interests are very diverse in many different industries – chemical, textile, insurance, finance, computer networking, telecommunication, etc. When I first met my father-in-law in his office in Stockholm, I was very impressed by his plain but powerful looking office. There was nothing on his desk except a few pictures – one of a chemical plant and the others of him standing with some important people such as the prime minister of Turkey. My father-in-law is a Christian. He always says that if God gives you abilities, you should not waste them and use them as much as you can. At the age of 63, I do not think he feels he should slow down, rather he is expanding his company at speed. He told me once he likes to see that he is creating jobs for other people. He likes to help others. As a tradition, every Christmas Eve he will go to one of the most remote villages in Sweden to distribute presents to those old people. He has been doing this for 25 years. He too is interested in more than just money.

I see myself in the new age of European entrepreneurship. Even though I was born a German, I have never really thought of myself as purely German. A former prime minister of Germany once described Germany as "Capitalism with a socialist hat and a feudal belt". I think of myself as a West German with an East European heart. My life experience so far has equipped me with crossover characteristics of German, Russian, French, and Swedish. I have a disciplined mind like that of a German person, yet I have a flexible demeanor like a French person. My French education taught me to see things with an open mind and be direct. I am somewhat strong-minded like a Russian. Continuous perfection becomes part of my attitude toward whatever I do. My exposure to Scandinavian culture affects me so much that family and stability are always two very important aspects of my life. My background helps me to act properly when I deal with different cultures in business. I feel like I am a bridge connecting the gap between Western and Eastern Europe. I am carrying on the traditions of an old generation to meet the demands of a new global generation.

Essay B: *How do you see your career developing? How will an MBA further that development? Why are you applying to Stanford?*

My professional goals are ambitious ones. Within five to ten years, I plan to: (1) take my two German-based companies public on the Frankfurt Stock Exchange, (2) launch consumer products into major Eastern European countries including Russia, and (3) assist my Swedish father-in-law in his effort to launch magnetic tape products into the German market.

Two years ago in 1995, at the age of 26, I started two companies – Spatuck Limited and Rusk (Germany–Russia) Co. Ltd. Spatuck Limited is engaged more in marketing and Rusk (Germany–Russia) Co. Ltd. is engaged in manufacturing. Spatuck Limited makes a lot of OEM products for various mail order catalog companies. Most of the products that we make are being sold to customers through TV infomercials. Rusk (Germany–Russia) Co. Ltd. manufactures hair wig-related products. Rusk (Germany–Russia) Co. Ltd. sells products through Spatuck Limited. Although not directly related to my intended career field – telemarketing, Rusk (Germany–Russia) Co. Ltd. provides me with ample cash to expand my other businesses. The total sales revenue of these two companies is about US$3.5 million. I have a factory outside of Berlin with about 200 people. Although my companies are still at the first stage of the telemarketing business, I will eventually directly market our products through infomercials and become a major player in this new East European industry.

Headlines increase readability

Next step: From homogeneity in manufacturing to heterogeneity in marketing

As a generalization, Germans are good at manufacturing. In the European context, Germany and England are manufacturing leaders today. In the world context, we must add the U.S., Japan, and Korea to the list of manufacturing giants. The trend I see occurring is a global world that produces products that are of relatively high quality across the board. Take for example notebook computers. Today most brands are of good quality. Ten years ago this was not the case. In the future, with the emergence of more and more countries in the global marketplace, product quality will be viewed as a "constant" so to speak. Marketing will be the final untapped variable in the business equation. As in mature marketplaces like in the U.S., this trend has given rise to the marketing phenomenon known as telemarketing or infomercials. Telemarketing is on-line, real time selling. My goal is to fully anticipate this trend of telemarketing and be at the forefront in the East European and Russian marketplaces.

Business vision

"Anonymous buying" versus relationship buying

I foresee "anonymous buying" as a term to describe the way consumers will buy in the future. "Anonymous buying" is really the opposite of relationship buying. Relationship buying is very much rooted in the way East European or communist countries do business. Traditionally, Eastern European businesspersons viewed business as "webs" of close relationships.

Arguably the most successful businessman in Germany, Mr Kuhn, relies heavily on close relationships. He hardly does business with people whom he does not know. His major customers and suppliers are basically unchanging. My father started his company some 25 years ago. Almost every decision my father makes is based on relationships. The hair and beauty industry, for example, is a relatively small industry and very relationship-oriented. My father once traveled all throughout Europe to meet his customers to keep secure his relationships.

It might be true that relationship management plays a big part in certain industries such as petroleum. Your suppliers and customers basically remain your suppliers and customers. You really need to know the right person in order to be in. Once you are in, you are pretty safe. But this is increasingly not true for consumer products. In fact, there is really no critical need for knowing whom you are buying from or selling to. The Internet supports this idea of invisible customers.

A Russian market by default

An analysis of the East European and Russian markets leads to a curious observation. Large conglomerates of business in major West European countries like England and Germany have no choice but to enter the Russian market. North America is already very advanced and the markets are quite saturated with strong competition. Asia is a fragmented marketplace both culturally and linguistically. Latin America has its own problems including political and economic uncertainty. Africa is too poor to consume yet. That leaves Russia. From a European perspective, Russia is big and close by. Russia has more than 300 million people. Also, from a non-Asian international perspective (e.g., European), Russia may be the logical business choice based on size, as well as proximity.

My wife's family is from Sweden. My father-in-law owns one of the top 20 largest conglomerates in Sweden call "Rohan". His company is involved in many different businesses such as textile, chemical, petroleum, insurance, and telecommunication. The company has factories all over the world including Greece, Morocco, China, and Indonesia. He and his company also own a few venture capital companies in the U.S. In Germany, for example, Rohan owns part of the BASF Magnetic, a former subsidiary of the BASF group. In Sweden, his company has a joint-venture partnership agreement with New York Life. My father-in-law's company also has a desperate need to enter the Russian market in order to keep up with the growing pace. Just recently Rohan opened a US$20-million factory in Turkey to manufacture plastic materials.

My goal is to fully anticipate these realities and partner with companies to enter the Russian market. My significant exposure to different cultural backgrounds including German, Russian, French, and Swedish will enable me to be a gatekeeper of future East European business. I received my education in four different places namely, Germany, Belgium, Sweden, and Poland. My educational experience at the University of Versalius in Belgium involved the Russian language. My professional experiences with Banque Paribas in Moscow involved finance; my family company, Haas Hair Beauty Co. Ltd., and later my own companies, Spatuck Limited and Rusk (Germany–Russia) Co. Ltd., involved manufacturing. I am looking to make my greatest impact selling products across international markets. This will complete the cycle I set for myself – "count, make, and sell" – accounting, manufacturing, and selling.

Why an MBA?

I need a superior MBA education to: (1) give me a macro framework for analyzing business markets, (2) help me in crucial micro decision-making for my growing business, and (3) expose me to smart, young businesspersons who aspire to develop a continuous learning process to cope with a fast-paced growing society.

Nowadays the advancement in information and communication technology makes the world closer. We are living in a more competitive environment. I really need an MBA education in order to have a framework of analyzing complex business situations systematically. I believe if you are surrounded by smart people all the time, you can be smarter too. I believe it does open your mind to a broader platform and you can utilize the unused parts of your talent.

During the time studying in the MBA program, I will assign a general manager to handle my current business operations. During the summer holiday, I would like to find some summer jobs in some big conglomerates such as News Corp or GE Capital to learn about the different aspects of satellite advertising. After I finish my MBA program I plan to go back to Germany to expand my business.

Why Stanford?

As a new breed of German entrepreneur, I would like an MBA education to help grow my current and future businesses. I have chosen the Stanford program as a result of the following: (1) student body and small class size, (2) faculty and academic reputation, and (3) location and employment contacts and opportunities. Stanford's diverse student body and the small class size would enable me to learn as much as I can from the school as well as from other students in a cooperative environment. The outstanding faculty would give me the advance insight and ideas of many business aspects. Stanford University is located in the heart of Silicon Valley. There are many high-tech startups and venture capital firms which can give me a lot of opportunities to talk to them and exchange ideas of manufacturing as manufacturing is part of my background.

The renowned faculty members in Stanford University such as Nobel laureates Professor William F. Sharpe attract me. I would like to learn about Capital Asset Pricing Model from Professor William F. Sharpe, Auction System from Professor Robert Wilson and Professor Paul Milgrom, and New Growth Theory of Economics from Professor Paul Romer. Courses such as Strategy and Action in the Information Processing Industry would give me the chance to talk to prominent business leaders such as Mr Andrew Grove, the President and CEO of Intel Corporation.

Stanford Business School's course flexibility and emphasis on the development of ideas will be essential to achieving my career goals. I am particularly interested in entrepreneurship and am also applying to the Global Management program. I would like to take as many elective courses as I can. Courses such as M356 – Global and International Marketing; E302 – International Development Management; S354 – Entrepreneurship and Venture Capital; S356 – High-technology Entrepreneurship; E323 – International Financial Management; and R393 – Cultural Diversity and Organizations all looked very interesting and challenging to me.

I would also like to participate in a few extracurricular organizations while at Stanford University. I would like to be active in the Stanford Venture Forum, the New Enterprise Forum, and the Entrepreneurship Conference. I also would like to take the opportunities to join as many student organizations as I can such as Multimedia Club, Manufacturing Club, Telecommunications Club, Venture Capital Club, Entrepreneur Club, Outdoor Adventure Club, Golf Club and Wine Circle.

I have a unique perspective from dealing every day with German and European culture. I believe I could be forthright in presenting my opinions in class and would welcome the opportunity to assist in developing case studies with an in-depth cultural component. Perhaps in the years to come, I could serve as an alumni representative to help individuals in finding appropriate employment opportunities in Europe.

CANDIDATE #5

Candidate's biography: Shannon is female, American, educated in the U.S.

Essay: With the admissions policy statement in mind, describe those personal or professional characteristics that distinguish your candidacy for admission to Amos Tuck. (Dartmouth)

> Try describing who you are in terms of a wrist watch!

Is your watch accurate?

Like the components of the Disney watches which I develop every day, my individual characteristics must function together to truly represent who I am.

The dial of creativity

The dial or face of a watch can often show its personality. Printing a character on the face can bring the watch to life and set it apart from other watches. Often when I am working on a project, especially for Disney, I create many options for our product assortments. Although I am not, nor ever will be, a professional artist, I often generate rough concepts for product or dig through hundreds of artworks to find just the right one to support our brand. In doing this, I focus on the target customer, the retail market, and the technical limitations of the product whether it be watches, clocks, mugs, pewter, or stationery.

Likewise, I find creativity is often needed when solving challenging problems. During my undergraduate studies, I spent my junior year abroad at Stirling University in Scotland where I volunteered to help teach mentally-impaired adults at a local day-care center. One lovely elderly lady I was teaching found it extremely difficult to understand the abstract concepts of money and coins. After two sessions on this topic, we were both quite frustrated. I decided to show her monetary value on a more practical level, so I brought some basic supermarket products from home and we played shop. Although it was a bit juvenile, she began to grasp the use and value of the different British coins in making her daily "purchases" and was soon adding them up to "buy" the items she desired.

The gears of teamwork

The gears inside of a watch movement work together to achieve their shared goal of accurate time. I believe that cooperation, similar to that in a watch movement, is vital to the success of any organization.

After seven years of debate competition I have learned the value of teamwork. The enormous amount of research necessary to be competitive in policy and parliamentary debate could never be accomplished by a single individual. Over the years, I have researched a tremendous number of topics on everything from acid rain to third world nuclear proliferation to world hunger. Throughout my debate career, I made a point of sharing new and important findings with my other team members so that we could all be more competitive. I continuously helped to coach younger debaters by giving them both my research and time. Through cooperation with my team, I was able to qualify for finals in multiple debate tournaments, win the highly competitive AAA Georgia State Debate Championship in high school, and break the Guinness Book World Record for the longest debate as a freshman in college.

The strap of humanity

When an individual wears a watch, the strap holds the watch in place on the individual's wrist. On many watches, there is a soft, pseudo suede material that provides comfort to the skin beneath the strap, no matter what type of material may be on the outside. As my organization faces different external pressures, I believe it is imperative to maintain certain core values which are always "strapped" in place beneath our group (i.e. social, ethical, and community responsibilities) that will not waiver under any circumstances.

At Disney, we often develop watches that could potentially have fantastic monetary results in the retail market. However, if the product is not completely safe for children due to small parts, sharp edges, or other potential safety issues, my decision to forego the style is unquestionable, irrelevant of the potential sales generated from the product. The safety of children comes first.

Whether as a leader or member of an organization, I believe it is my duty to be a role model for ethical and responsible behavior. As a manager, I hold myself and my team at Disney accountable to a high ethical standard. Certain business practices make working in a purchasing organization quite difficult at times due to "entertainment" invitations and "gifts" from suppliers. By politely turning down these offers and returning personal gifts, I try to show my staff that the acceptance of this type of "compensation" is not acceptable in our organization.

Commitment to the needs of others is also quite an important aspect of my personality. Working with a group called Hospice of Scotland County in North Carolina, for example, was emotionally the most difficult endeavor I have ever undertaken. Hospice is an organization that takes care of terminally-ill individuals who have stopped receiving treatment for their illnesses. I was a volunteer caregiver in this group and had several patients that I would visit weekly. Developing a relationship with them, while knowing they will soon die, can be a heart-wrenching experience. However, the knowledge of how much you can help a family or an individual far outweighs the emotional strain.

The hands of direction

The hands of a watch must be set, and re-set as needed, to consistently point to the accurate time. My professional goals are the same. Without direction in my career, I would find it difficult to continuously decide the life choices I need to make or to dedicate myself to performing at my full potential. From my initial decision to double major in International Business and International Politics at St. Andrews College in North Carolina to my decision to leave a good job at Silicon Watch Company to join Walt Disney, I have always had a vision. Although re-adjusted and fine-tuned, my goal to work in international business dealing with consumer products has remained constant. It was commitment to these career ambitions that actually led me to Geneva four-and-a-half years ago.

While finishing my Bachelor of Arts degree in North Carolina, I spoke with several consumer product companies who indicated that only senior level employees could work in their international areas. With encouragement from my dean, I decided to move to Geneva to gain international work experience in the area of fast-moving consumer goods. Geneva was the perfect choice as Geneva and Zurich collectively manufacture over 50 percent of the world's watches along with a vast majority of other related products. Thankfully, I had already spent one year studying in Scotland, so leaving the U.S. to live in a country I had never visited was not a difficult concept. Therefore, after graduation from college, I moved to Geneva, resume in hand, to find a job in consumer products. Thankfully, my plan worked. Three weeks after arriving in Geneva, I was hired by Silicon Watch Company for its marketing department. Although I was the youngest employee in the company when I started, I was assistant manager of the watch division by the time I left to join Disney in Geneva two years later.

I have always held the basic tenet that most goals worth achieving require a great deal of hard work. My career goals are no exception. In preparing myself academically to work in the international arena, I spent many hours developing my knowledge base, researching and writing papers as well as interacting with professors and classmates. As a result, I not only graduated Magna Cum Laude, but I was better equipped to handle many business and political issues which have presented themselves to me here in Europe such as analyzing my division sales and costs as well as better understanding the cultural barriers when manufacturing and distributing in Europe.

While developing my experience in consumer goods here in Geneva, I have worked hard to learn many of the production processes we use in order to fully understand how items are made and the limitations for their development. I have visited dozens of factories in smaller locales and asked so many technical questions that I am positive some of the plant managers were ready to strangle me by the end of the tour. Furthermore, in creating growth for my divisions at Silicon and Walt Disney, I spent many hours sourcing new suppliers, evaluating our business needs, and developing my teams. Only through hard work combined with cooperation and creativity were we able to create a level of customer satisfaction that has kept our business on a continual increase.

The case of leadership

The case, or housing, of a watch is actually one of its most important aspects. The case holds all of the other components together so that they can work in unison. The face, hands, and movement are contained inside the case while the strap is attached externally. As both a leader and a manager, my role mirrors that of a watch case. I bring together the different individuals in my organizations, whether professionally or personally, so that we can work to meet our goals.

Initially, I refined some of my leadership skills as elected President of the St. Andrews College Model United Nations Delegation in North Carolina. In order to attend the National Conference at the real United Nations in New York, we had to raise several thousand dollars and comprehensively prepare all issues to represent our country properly. I divided the responsibilities amongst my officers and created individual task force teams to accomplish our goals. The reason I decided to take this approach, as opposed to having everyone work on all aspects needed to attend the conference, was to empower my officers and to give everyone specific responsibilities. By asking each member of the team to take partial "ownership" of his/her task force, the work necessary to meet our goals was more evenly balanced and several creative ideas for problem solving were actually generated.

As a manager or leader in any organization, I have always considered my role to be the stimulus for creating teamwork and to make sure that everyone is properly motivated to do their individual tasks so that we can achieve our goals together. At Disney, I try to provide continual support for my team in helping them to solve problems with product, suppliers, or customers and to give them guidance as needed. I do not believe that being a good leader means coming up with every idea or giving directions consistently from the top downward. I believe in listening to my team members and empowering them to make decisions, assuming it is within their capability and responsibility. In my group at Disney, we share in both the problems and the achievements of our area. Only by supporting those under my supervision can I help the members of my team to grow and learn, making them more valuable to our organization and to themselves.

The complete watch

The dial, movement, strap, hands, and case of a Mickey Mouse watch form a complete timepiece. Individually, the components have little value. However, when combined, they create substantial worth. Such is the same for my individual characteristics. My leadership abilities and career focus mean very little without the necessary creativity and cooperation. Moreover, my core values and compassion are ingrained within all aspects of my personality. Creativity, cooperation, humanity, career focus, and leadership are all components in my life which must balance and work together to make sure that I stay "on time".

Candidate #6

Candidate's biography: Kenji is male, Japanese, educated in the U.K.

Outline for Kellogg – "Who are You?" Essay

I. Introduction (brief) (para 1)

II. Discussion

    a. Receive
        1. Family background (para 4)
        2. Travel experience (para 5)

    b. Invest
        1. Oxford (para 6)
        2. Legal education (para 7)
        3. Maples Law Firm (para 8)

    c. Return
        1. My proposed contributions to Kellogg (para 9)

III. Conclusion (para 10)

Outline for Kellogg – "Career Goals" Essay

I. Career objectives and professional outlook

    a. Industrial Bank of Osaka (para 1)
    b. Goals (para 2)
    c. The role of banking (para 3)
    d. Vision (para 4)

II. Development to date

    a. Maples Law Firm (para 5–6)
    b. European versus Asian legal perspectives (para 7)
    c. Legal studies versus business studies (para 8)

III. Why Kellogg? (para 9–10)

Essay: **Each of our applicants is unique. Describe how your background, values, and non-work-related activities will enhance the experience of other Kellogg students. (Northwestern)**

All living organisms on our planet, and by analogy, organizations, survive and make contributions by carrying out fixed behavioral patterns. Although these patterns vary rather significantly depending on the organism or organization concerned, our very survival depends upon repeating patterns that govern our lives. As I have been born and raised in a banking family, I would like to structure my answer to the question in a way that reflects the basic pattern that all banks follow. A bank carries out the following tasks: firstly, it *receives* deposits from its customers; secondly, it *invests* the money received by making loans; and finally, it *returns* money to its depositors with interest. By focusing on what I have personally received and invested thus far in my life as well as what returns I hope to make, I would like to show how my background, values, and non-work-related activities will enhance the experiences of other Kellogg students.

> **Interesting way to link banking with biology!**

Receive

"In the same way that a bank receives money from its depositors, each of us receives, at birth and during childhood, certain assets that we take for granted."

In the early 20th century, my late great-grandfather left his small rural village in Japan to travel to the city of Osaka to search for the basic necessities of life. This situation led him to become involved in the steel and shipping industries, where he built up his wealth during the Great War (World War I). To diversify his business, he founded the Industrial Bank of Osaka in 1907. The Bank has grown along with the Japanese economy, experiencing good times and bad, profiting from Japan's enterprising and dynamic business environment and in turn contributing to its growth. It is in this setting that my life began.

I am the eldest member of my generation of the Kamimura family. As such, I was groomed from youth to play an active part in the family business. Thus, I was encouraged to spend much of my life outside school in the Bank during my childhood days. I was reluctant to give up my free time, although I now realize that it brought me extraordinary learning opportunities about "dollars and cents" in action. Furthermore, it made me aware at a young age about the role that I would be required to play as well as the responsibilities that I would have to accept. This experience has nurtured my interest in the finance industry and gave me a sound understanding of the business from a young age.

I was very fortunate to have closely witnessed the events connecting Japan's economic upturn in the 1980s with those events marking Japan's economic downturn in the 1990s. As my father was the standing chairman of the Basic Corporate Law Drafting Committee

(Diet) in 1992, I was able to be present at numerous informal meetings with Japanese corporate and government leaders. From hearing discussions with figures such as Foreign Minister Keizo Obuchi and Policy Research Council Chairman Taku Yamaski, I learned that the relationship between government and the business community is a symbiotic one. While businessmen look for effective governmental policies which encourage wealth creation, government, in turn, depends on investment from the business community to boost the economy.

Aside from devoting time to furthering my financial knowledge, I have traveled to many places of interest. While traveling, I enjoy walking down local streets and observing how people live, how business takes place, and how different cultures affect the business climate. In Tibet, for example, people are devoutly religious and, although technologically backward, are quite advanced in terms of social cooperation. I also have been privileged to have had the opportunity to meet with various political and industrial leaders who are friends of my parents. Meeting people who have achieved significant leadership positions has given me a sense of respect for their achievements and seasoned me, in that, I am not intimidated when meeting high-ranking individuals merely because of their positions. In short, I have learned to judge people by their characters and accomplishments, not by their titles and status.

Invest

"In the same way that a bank holds a fiduciary duty to prudently invest the assets that it receives from depositors, an individual must strive first to identify and then to invest wisely the unique assets he or she has been given."

After attending Hibiya High School in Tokyo, I chose to go on to study law at Oxford University, England. For me, the opportunity to be surrounded by some of the brightest students from all parts of the world was a great learning experience. Apart from academic pursuits, I actively participated in many extracurricular activities. I was a member of the Steering Committee for the Oxford University Cancer Campaign, Treasurer of the Asia-Pacific Society, and arranged the Overseas Japanese Ball. These activities enhanced my leadership, creativity, organizational, and teamwork skills. Above all, they developed my capability to work effectively with people from different cultural backgrounds.

Despite my strong interest in finance, my reason for studying law and gaining legal qualifications lies in the fact that all business decisions have to be made within a legal framework. I believe having a sound foundation in this area and also having the legal discipline will benefit me immensely in my later banking career. In addition, I feel that law has furthered my ability to analyze complex problems as well as to structure persuasive arguments. An activity which I enjoyed while at university is the Mooting Competition. It is a competition amongst law students from different colleges, and at times different universities, to argue a legal scenario in a court-like environment. As a side often consists of as many as four people with a significant amount of research required, I realized the importance of teamwork, which I found to be the pivotal ingredient for success.

While my legal experience has benefited me in various respects, I have noticed that a good lawyer is not necessarily a good manager. This is because lawyers are either working on their own or with a very limited number of people, and they work in-depth in a narrow, specialized area. As I am conscious of the need to develop my managerial potential, I worked hard to become the youngest member to sit on the firm-wide Focus Group of Maples Law Firm. This committee meets regularly and examines possible organization and process changes that could be made to improve the effectiveness of the firm. I have gained satisfaction from participating in this committee, particularly from seeing some of my ideas being implemented.

Return

"In the same way that a bank is expected to yield a return for its depositors, it is up to each of us to give back to our families, friends, and society an unexpected but tangible return."

Having been raised in a privileged family setting, I have had the opportunity and feel the need to contribute to the betterment of society. Education is something that I have always valued as it has made a great difference in my life both qualitatively and quantitatively. Thus, it is an area where I hope to make a long-term contribution. In the context of my proposed Master of Management education at Kellogg, I want to: (1) share with fellow Kellogg students my ideas and experiences relating to Asian business dealings, (2) join an organization aimed at advancing education standards in the local Chicago community, and (3) assist the Kellogg School in placing students in international employment positions in the finance sector.

In conclusion, all living organisms, and by analogy, organizations, exhibit fixed behavioral patterns, the most intelligent of which are carried out for a purpose. A bank hopes to profit by repeating the cycle of receive, invest, and return. To me, the cycle of *receive* and *invest* will not only result in profit being added to the family banking business, but also intangible *returns* which the next generation of family members, friends, students, and business associates will *receive* and *invest*, and hopefully, yield greater *returns* to society.

Conclusion mirrors
introduction ✓

Essay: Briefly assess your career progress to date. Elaborate on your future career plans and your motivation for pursing a graduate degree at Kellogg. (Northwestern)

Career objectives and professional outlook

The Industrial Bank of Osaka was founded by my great-grandfather and has been run by my family since 1907. From modest beginnings, the Bank is now a highly recognized independent local Japanese bank in Japan with total assets of nearly US$30 billion. Apart from having nearly 100 branches in the country, it has established its presence not only in many Asian countries, but also in England, Canada, the U.S., and the Caribbean. At present, the Bank ranks 147th in the world, based on asset size.

Just as my father is committed to building the Bank as a member of the third generation of the Kamimura family, it is my aspiration as a fourth-generation Kamimura to build further on our banking traditions and to lead the Bank in new directions. After completing my Master of Management, I hope to gain two years' working experience in an American financial institution, particularly to learn more about their approach to modern technology. My longer-term aim is to work in the Industrial Bank of Osaka as a managing director for foreign operations and ultimately, if I demonstrate the requisite talent, to become the CEO.

Banking is one of the most fundamental businesses in any economy. In the context of a developing Asia, the term "developing economy" presupposes that an efficient banking system exists to fuel growth and development. In one respect, financial institutions are the central element in the growth equation. Without the ability to access capital, individuals and their businesses would cease to function.

In my view, the future of banking involves a marriage of technology with branding which can be both complementary and divisive forces. Technology is the driving force behind banks' increasing product offerings and services to customers. For example, "smart cards" are set to revolutionize our payment systems. Smart cards will soon be the medium of money, replacing notes and coins. However, such technological products and services could end up becoming commodity offerings as other banks inevitably follow up with similar offerings. Branding is needed if banks expect people to associate financial services with a particular bank. It is clearly not in the interest of banks to be seen as a group of fungible or substitutable monetary institutions which consumers cannot tell apart. Thus, while technology is needed to provide better service to customers and therefore attract more clients, it also has the means to erode close customer relationships. Astute marketing and advertising on the part of the banks will be required to build brand image.

Development to date

While my long-term objective is to pursue a career in finance, I entered the legal profession to gain an understanding of the framework that governs all business activities. The training that I received from Maples, a leading international financial law firm based in New York has provided me with broad experience in today's fast-moving business world. Thus far, I have participated in transactional management and documentation of transactions of a wide-ranging nature. Apart from transactional work, I have advised on regulatory as well as procedural frameworks for financing structures, and have been involved in a number of contentious matters, such as international fraud cases and minority shareholder disputes.

I believe that my legal experience has greatly benefited me. When a good lawyer comes to draft an agreement, he or she seeks to protect the client against all potential risks that could arise during the life of the contract. Thus, I am now used to stretching my imagination to contemplate not only the foreseeable risks, but also the unforeseeable ones, and to address them at the outset. During the last two years, I am delighted to have had the opportunity to work in both London and Tokyo. I believe this has given me the chance to learn about European and Asian styles of business dealings as well as to understand internal workings of corporations of different geographical origin.

For example, whereas Europeans see a contract as a "clear set of rules", Asians tend to look past the details and to view the contract as merely a document to "start a business relationship". From their point of view, details are meant to be worked out on a daily or on-going basis. Thus, there exists a significant margin for potential conflict, since Europeans will demand strict adherence to contractual terms from the outset and Asians will want to alter terms as business progresses. As a young lawyer, I have tried to admonish Asian clients to think more in-depth about the actual terms of a contract prior to entering an agreement in order to avoid future conflicts. The internal workings of European and Asian corporations also vary because of cultural and organizational differences. The European system is much more organized and structured than the Asian system. This means that, in the Asian context, the person you are dealing with has more influence over a business transaction, and you must be more aware of how personality will affect a business outcome. On the other hand, the European system is less subject to the vagaries of the individuals concerned.

My academic and practical legal training thus far has helped me to solve problems by thinking primarily in an inductive manner. Legal work requires one to combine the details of relevant laws with authoritative decisions in order to form a conclusion for clients on their proposed course of action. Although this type of thinking process will be relevant to doing future business, I hope to be able to perfect my ability to think deductively as well. I believe an MM degree will assist me in this respect, as case studies develop one's ability not only to use the details of a specific case to draw an overall conclusion, but to think deductively by bringing related business themes to bear on the situation at hand.

Why Kellogg?

Having acquired full qualifications to practice law in both the English and Japan jurisdictions, I feel I have come to an important turn in my life, namely to divert my focus away from the legal field toward the finance industry. Thus, I am attracted to the Kellogg Graduate School of Management, which is widely acknowledged to be at the pinnacle of academic institutions for business management and marketing. I believe the Kellogg MM program will provide me with essential skills and knowledge to be effective as an international financier with a marketing outlook. This can be seen in the broad core subjects that are compulsory for all first-year students. As I feel that a sound understanding in finance, marketing and information systems will be very useful for my career, I would find the following courses most beneficial: *Complex Financial Structures and Global Risk Management*; *International Technology Management*; *Competitive Intelligence, Strategies, and Structures*; *International Marketing Channels*, and *Managing Strategic Alliances*. In addition, I am delighted to learn that students have the opportunity to do a research paper during the second-year term of the MM program at Kellogg. If I am admitted, I hope to have the opportunity to work with the school's renowned professors on the essential micro-economic reforms that Japan will have to undergo early in the next millennium.

Since I have lived all my life in an environment with either strong British or Japanese traditions, I would like to experience another way of life. I am most eager to acquire a flavor for life in Midwestern U.S.; I have been told that Chicago has more aspects of America than any other American city. My reasons for wanting to attend Kellogg are four-fold: first, many of the brightest students are at Kellogg; second, interdisciplinary learning is emphasized; and third, the Kellogg School attracts top business leaders, such as Bill Gates, Howard Martin, Robert Crandell, and Marlene Johnson, to share their views in their areas of expertise. Fourthly, for my summer internship during the first year, I hope to work at the World Bank to gain some exposure to global banking and to learn how the IMF deals with debt in emerging countries.

Candidate #7

Candidate's biography: Gary is male, British of Jamaican heritage, educated in England

Essay: Describe yourself to your classmates. (New York University)

This is the creative writer's approach

I am a British citizen of Jamaican ancestry living in Hong Kong. Walking down Market Street in Manchester, England, I wonder how I am viewed by the onlookers. To the British person I would probably be viewed as second-generation West Indian, and they'd be right. Short-cropped, neat hair. Head upright, with a straight-backed gait. An Englishman may take it as a strut. There is a lilt to my English accent that marks me a Jamaican. Folks assume I am loaded with streetsmarts. At the pub I drink Guinness and thump to the sounds of Oasis, Manchester natives, British rock at its best.

On High Street in Kingston, Jamaica, how do Jamaicans see me? My cousins tell me I "WALK like an Englishman". Folks mark me as British from a hundred metres away. And my Jamaican Patois, so cool back at home, sounds contrived around the boys on the beach. "It is the Queen's English," they tell me. They think I must have money. Anyone who comes from England must have money! They think I am soft, not really street-tough. I try to stroll barefoot along a stony beach in Montego Bay. Oh, how I wince. My younger cousin laughs and shakes his head. At the dancehall we drink Kingfisher beer and groove to the heavy reggae bassline and mellow beat of Frankie Paul.

On Hsin Hai road in Taipei, Taiwan, I accidentally bump into an elderly gentleman and apologize to him in Chinese. He smiles and asks me where I am from. I tell him I am from England. "You're joking! You have black people in England?" he asks. He (he has watched a lot of NBA) and knows I am not dark enough to be African! And how in the world can I speak Chinese? My head is bopping. At the Hard Rock Cafe, I sip a bottle of Tsing Dao beer and bop to Chinese rock-pop diva Faye Wong. I have a tough time keeping up with her lyrics (she sings in Mandarin), but I have an equally tough time with rapper Snoop Doggy Dog, and he speaks English.

On three different continents I am viewed quite differently. And on three different continents I can adapt to each environment. My experiences across the globe have enabled me to appreciate the differences amongst people and to utilize the similarities we have to flow between different cultures. I have adopted some of the traits of my various "hometown" locals: the hardworking nature of the Chinese, the perseverance of the West Indians, and the dry wit and humor of the British. I am a music lover – a jazz freak, because it transcends language to unite all cultures. You do not have to be from South Asia to move to a higher plane listening to a 15-minute version of John Coltrane's *India*, recorded live at the Village Vanguard in 1961.

My sights are now on a U.S. education. Where will I fit in? Will I join Stern's Black Business Students Association, the Asian Business Students Association, or the International Business Club? Maybe I will join all three. Maybe more. The point is, I could feel comfortable with each group. I look forward to sharing my quirky diversity with my fellow classmates. And I look forward to learning from theirs. At Stern, with its healthy cultural and ethnic mix, I expect to fit right in.

CHAPTER 4

Essay Writing Part II:
The *Other* MBA Essay Types

"The applications that I think are the most disappointing are those that talk about only one dimension. All four or five essays will talk about an element of their job, or their personal life, or a particular aspect of their professional accomplishments. This inability or unwillingness to capture the variety of life contrasts greatly with the multi-thematic flavor we see in the applications of successful candidates."

Jon Megibow, former Director of Admissions,
Darden Business School, University of Virginia

WRITING THE "BACKGROUND AND DIVERSITY" ESSAY*

Like most of the essay types included in this section, "background and diversity" essays are used by business schools to get an idea of who you are. In other words, these essays are often used as shorter substitutes for traditional "who are you?" essays.

> **EXAMPLE**
>
> Because GSIA students work closely together, we would like to understand what there is about your background and your experiences that would make a contribution to the diversity of the entering class and the educational experience of the other students. (Carnegie Mellon)

Common mistakes

The following are common mistakes made by applicants when writing a "background and diversity" essay.

- Not using the full-range of your background and experience as is often the case when you talk only about professional experience.
- Not mentioning the significance of how your background contributes to the diversity of the incoming class.
- Not using a clear structure to discuss your background.

Winning approaches

Bear the following tips in mind when writing a "background and diversity" essay. They are:

Tip #38: Break your background down into four parts including professional, educational, cultural background, and personal experience.

You may break down your background into: (a) professional experience—work experience which may include both full-time and part-time employment, (b) educational experience—undergraduate major(s), research projects, which may also include extracurricular collegiate activities, (c) cultural backgrounds and international experience—travel, language, family, country, and culture, and (d) personal experience—hobbies and interests, relevant traits, insights, philosophies, career or personal turning points or setbacks; this may also include community service.

---

* Business schools make yearly revisions to their application materials, where one or more essay questions are likely to be revised. You can access a school's website to download application packages containing current essay questions.

Tip #39: Find your "diversity trigger".

Analyze your background and ask yourself: "What one thing represents my greatest diversity? What one thing can I count on to stand out?" Generally "diversity triggers" center on one of three areas: culture, geography, or employment. Perhaps your ethnic background is really different. Perhaps you are from an unusual place (or your parents or forefathers are from an unusual place). If for example you have lived on three different continents, then you must tell why this is important. This may signal a better understanding of doing business in these geographical areas or perhaps you have a superior understanding of the culture and language of these areas.

Perhaps neither your culture nor your geography defines you, but the nature of your employment does. Perhaps your true diversity is a personal hardship, unusual childhood experience, or exceptional achievement. The sample essays in this chapter and in Chapter 5 provide numerous examples of diversity.

Tip #40: Use a workable structure and signpost your discussion.

As mentioned, a summary or lead sentence can be a useful tool. For example, "My potential contributions to the entering class in terms of my diversity of background and character can be seen in my work, education, culture, and personal outlook." In this example, the reader will expect at least one paragraph to cover each of work, education, culture, and personal outlook.

SAMPLE "BACKGROUND AND DIVERSITY" ESSAYS

Candidate's biography: John is male, Caucasian-American, educated in the U.S.

Columbia Business School is a heterogeneous environment. Please discuss a life experience of yours that shows how you will contribute to the class. (Columbia)

Comparing two bottles of Coca-Cola one would likely, and hopefully, find a very homogeneous product. However, the process behind Coca-Cola's homogeneous product quality is very much heterogeneous, bringing together people of diverse cultural and technical ingredients. Similarly, my unique leadership and international experiences will contribute like a "Secret Formula" to enhance the community of Columbia Business School.

The Secret Formula

For over 100 years the beverage industry has attempted to identify and mimic the Coca-Cola secret formula. My own secret formula consists of quite varied and distinctive real world *leadership* experiences. I have led by example, as wrestling team captain in high school, running the extra mile and staying late after practice. I have led by command as Company

Commander in the United States Marine Corps, directing the attack and disciplining the unruly Marine. I have led by supervision in Coca-Cola, managing market development projects and writing performance evaluations for my team. I have led by persuasion, working daily with the bottling partner in Macau and Mongolia, providing the profit story and selling successful worldwide practices. Each of these varied leadership experiences has helped to hone my own unique leadership style that will contribute to the class.

"I would like to buy the world a Coke"

No other company in the world can match the international distribution capability of Coca-Cola. Company Management has learned over the years, and continues to learn, the best and most efficient means to provide a cold Coke to the farthest stretches of the world. I have learned from my varied *international* experiences – as a tourist viewing the Soviet Union behind the iron curtain (1985); as a peacekeeper in the Marine Corps sitting off the coast of Jakarta, Indonesia (1998); and as a business manager living and working in Hong Kong (Jan 1999 to present) – to adapt to the best local practices. In the same way that I use my experiences everyday to help form decisions, these international experiences will also contribute to the incoming class.

Marketing is the key in making Coke the most recognized brand in the world. The T.V. commercials, the radio jingles, the neon lights, all work together with the great taste to spark spontaneous purchase. Combining my varied leadership experiences and vast international exposure, I too have a heterogeneous product that will spark conversation, while providing valued insights and real world examples to my classmates.

Candidate's biography: Priyanka is female, Indian, educated in India

Please provide us with a summary of your personal and family background. Include information about your parents and siblings, where you grew up, and perhaps special memory of your youth. (UCLA)

Gandhi once said, "Any generalization about India is likely to be wrong." India is indeed a big country with immense diversity. In India a person will hear a new language, see different clothing, and get different food to eat after every five kilometers of travel. India is a home to so many different cultures and religions; a person can find people of each and every religion, including Hindus, Buddhists, Jains, Parsees, Muslims, or Christians. In spite of our differences and diversity, we are still one and united. Indians are peace loving and take pride in their "unity in diversity."

In terms of my personal and family background, I see a combination of both traditionalism and progressiveness. My father served in the Indian Army for 25 years and is currently working as Hospital Administrator with The Heart and Vascular Institute and Research Center. He was a valiant soldier and earned a lot of respect during his career. He was decorated in the 1971 Indo-Pak war, at a time when he was a mere 19 years of age. He was also deputed (posted) in Sri Lanka during the IPKF Operations. The Army provided us with an excellent quality of life and its influence gave me and my brother a disciplined upbringing. Because of my father's job we got to see almost all of India. I have inherited the joy of traveling from my dad. I have seen the Thar deserts in the west of India and the beautiful sand dunes of Jaiselmer. I have toured the whole of southern India and seen the beautiful beaches and backwaters of Kerala, the famous temples in Tamil Nadu, and the awesome Menakshi temple, whose shadow does not fall on the ground at anytime of the day. I have also been to the beautiful tea gardens and mountains in Eastern India. My father was posted in Darjeeling for two years and from there we got a chance to visit the Natula Pass, which towers at the height of 14,000 feet. As a result of my father serving in the Indian Army for 25 years, it gave us an opportunity to learn in depth about my rich Indian heritage and different cultures.

My father never let us get used to the comforts provided by the Army and made sure we earned everything we acquired. As a result, I can manage anywhere and everything on my own. He always encouraged me to do different things and supported me in whatever I chose to do. What inspires me most about him is his sincerity and honesty. Like my dad, I am a very straightforward person, and he has taught me to stand up for what I believe in. For example, in India, people have a very bad habit of throwing litter on the ground instead of using a bin. This is a sensitive issue for me and whenever I see people throw litter around I often approach them and ask them to acknowledge the bin.

My mother is an extremely talented person and a perfectionist. She loves to learn new things and does not leave anything incomplete. She is an excellent cook, painter, and, believe it or not, an astrologer! She does wonderful embroidery, knitting, and tailoring. I have inherited her creativity and her passion for painting. She had started learning to paint from a very early age and eventually shared her knowledge of painting with me. She learnt it from 'guru' Satyanad, who was a very renowned painter and tutor of his times. My mother paints on almost anything and everything – canvass, tiles, ceramic pots, and glass and on earthen pots as well. All the paintings in our house and my grandmother's house have been made by her. My mother has a very pleasant and calm nature. I have never seen her unnecessarily worried and bothered. Her presence is very comforting in difficult times. She is my best friend and we share a good relationship with each other and we have always done things together such as shopping, going to a movie, and cooking dinner. I know I can call her up anytime with any problem and she will always have a solution. This 'sisterhood' that my mother and I have developed is responsible for my sensitive nature and my willingness to help my friends and sit with them for hours to help solve their problems. My younger brother, too, is a very helpful, kind, supportive, and intelligent. Though at times he tends to be a more easy going person and I hope he becomes more aggressive with his opportunities. In spite of this difference and the fact that we fight a lot, we share a good relationship with each other.

In terms of a special memory, when I was in third standard (eight years of age) my father was posted in Wellington, a small hill station in South India. The accommodations on Gorkha Hill housed the officer's families and there were many children around. It was a beautiful and a peaceful place and we could see the beautiful valley with a stream running through it and on the hill facing our houses was the college and the main market area of the small town. Adjoining to Gorkha Hill was another hill that had patches of terrace farming interspersed with jungles, and there was a big cross with the statue of Christ on the top of that hill, which had intrigued us children very much. One day we could not hold our curiosity and we decided to go climbing on the hill to find out what was there on the top of the hill. We took permission from our parents and packed our picnic bags. Excited to explore the unknown, we were also a little scared. First, we crossed the terrace farms annoying the farmers as we trampled their crops. Then came the jungles, which were thick and spooky, and as soon it started raining, we all stuck together. But our curiosity to see what was at the top overpowered our fear. We kept on climbing and soon the jungle gave way to tall grass and beautiful flowers. With the sun shining again, we were all exhilarated and overwhelmed at the beauty of the nature. There was the big cross standing at least ten feet high. And from on high we could see the whole city below. This small experience has stayed embedded in my memory, as it has become symbolic of the small struggles still faced on daily basis and the importance that the role of determination, courage and hope plays on the path to victory.

■ ■ ■

Candidate's biography: Karen is female, Chinese-Canadian, educated in Canada

Columbia Business School is a diverse environment. How will your background and experiences contribute to this?

My Western education and Chinese heritage will certainly enhance the diverse community of Columbia Business School. Having lived and studied in Hong Kong, England, and Canada, I feel that I am in a position to share with my potential colleagues the different experiences that I have encountered in these places. During my five years at boarding schools, I have learned to be independent and considerate of those who are around me. Moreover, my multi-lingual skills (Cantonese, English, Mandarin, and rudimentary knowledge of French) enable me to communicate effectively with people from different places and adapt to new environments quickly and easily.

Joining AIESEC is one experience that I will never forget. AIESEC is the French abbreviation for the International Association of Students in Economics and Commerce. It was a valuable opportunity to make friends and exchange ideas with students from all over the world. I held many different positions during my period of involvement at the University of Toronto (1991–93). I joined as an office manager, where I maintained regular office hours every week. My duties included recruiting new members and answering questions about AIESEC on the phone and from walk-ins. Later, I joined the marketing team. We would set up appointments with recruiting managers of various corporations in

Toronto and try to help arrange traineeships for those students who lived abroad but wanted to work in Toronto. We also organized many fund-raising activities to support the programs that AIESEC had to offer. For example, we called up many companies and corporations to solicit sponsorships to support the University's Career Day and various seminars. As the culmination of my involvement in AIESEC, I was chosen as one of six delegates from AIESEC Toronto to attend the 1992 National Congress in Fredericton, New Brunswick on the east coast of Canada.

I consider myself fortunate to have traveled extensively over the years. My international network of friends has proved to be valuable time and again and during the first two years of my career. Exchanging ideas and information on a constant basis allows us to stay at the forefront of the business world. Since graduation, I have worked in a listed public corporation with over 150 employees and a small Hong Kong company of eight persons. Both companies taught me how close-knit teamwork among employees is essential for a company's expansion. I also had the chance to meet people of all levels during business trips to many Asian cities. Currently, I am working on a US$2 billion theme park project with the Mainland Chinese and Japanese. Being part of the team, I am exposed to the new generation of Chinese businessmen and the dynamics of Japan's advanced technology. I could not have dreamt of this opportunity several years ago. If I am admitted to the Columbia Business School, it will be my pleasure to share my unique background and international experiences with my colleagues.

WRITING THE "STRENGTHS AND WEAKNESSES" ESSAY

"Strengths and weaknesses" type essay questions are used by business schools to get an idea of who you are. In other words, these essays are often used as shorter substitutes for the traditional "who are you?" essay.

EXAMPLE

If we asked three of your closest associates to describe you, what would they say? Which adjectives would they use and why? What would they say are your strengths and weaknesses? (London Business School)

Common mistakes

The following are some of the common mistakes made by applicants when tackling this kind of essay.

- Not being honest. Stating fake weaknesses.
- Not using specific examples and details to make the reader believe the stated strengths and weaknesses.

- Not showing how their strengths have helped them become a better person; not showing how their weaknesses can be overcome.
- Not using a clear structure to develop a discussion of your strengths or weaknesses.

Winning approaches

The three tips below will help you approach a "strengths and weaknesses" essay.

✍ Tip #41: Be honest. Don't try to outguess the admissions committee.

If one of your strengths is that you are an "information sponge", say so. If your weakness is procrastination, say so. Keep it nice and simple. Be candid. If you really have problems trying to evaluate yourself, then ask a close friend what he or she thinks. Friends are usually right on the mark. Too often, candidates try to "figure out" what weaknesses are "acceptable" based on what they think the admissions committee wants to hear.

Be careful not to mention "fake weaknesses" such as "I'm too hardworking" or "I'm too generous." The reviewer will likely not believe you. After all, what should you do— become less hardworking or less generous?

✍ Tip #42: Summarize any discussion of personal weaknesses by showing how each is a strength in disguise or at least what you have learned as a result of struggling with your weaknesses.

There is a saying that "every cloud has a silver lining." This means that every diversity carries with it the seed of greater benefit. In a similar way, every weakness may be viewed as a strength in disguise.

For example, you say that you are a slow decision-maker. However, your slowness might nevertheless result in a fair degree of thoroughness when making significant decisions. Perhaps you are a slow adopter of new technologies but this has allowed you to remain a traditionalist and not be easily swayed by gimmicks. If your weakness is "detail" you nonetheless may be good at the "big picture". If your weakness is the "big picture" you may nonetheless be good at hiring people who see the bigger picture and who enable you to attend to important details.

✍ Tip #43: Break up your discussion of strengths and weaknesses by first discussing strengths and then discussing weaknesses.

The easiest structure proceeds as follows: "My strengths are A, B and C and my weaknesses are D and E. In terms of strengths, I would like to talk about A (mention this trait and give it one paragraph). Next there is B (mention one trait, one paragraph). Lastly there is C (mention one trait, one more paragraph). In terms of weaknesses, I would like to talk about D (mention one trait, one paragraph). Next there is E (mention one trait, one paragraph)."

Sometimes another structure will work better for you. For example, "My strengths and weaknesses can be seen through my work on two different projects with ABC Company. First, my work on project A shows my ... (mention one positive and one negative trait). My work on project B shows my ... (mention one positive and one negative trait)."

Tip #44: You may employ a "creative approach" to describe your strengths and weaknesses.

The creative approach has already been discussed under Tip #9. Whereas the following essay written by Sameer illustrates a direct, straightforward approach (per Tip #43), the succeeding essays written by Cedric, Alfred and Elena exemplify creative approaches. Cedric models his strengths and weaknesses around skiing, Alfred relates his personal strengths and weaknesses in terms of the geography of Innsbruck, and Elena cleverly depicts her strengths and weaknesses in terms of Russian Matryoshka dolls.

SAMPLE "STRENGTHS AND WEAKNESSES" ESSAYS

Candidate's biography: Sameer is male, Indian, educated in India

Please explain what your experience at work tells you about your likely strengths and weaknesses as a manager? (London Business School)

I made a decision nine years ago, when I completed my B.Eng. in 1987 to go into the field of construction chemicals, in a sales/marketing position, which was perceived as highly unconventional in civil engineering. The field of construction chemicals was in its infant stage, but I could see that organizations dealing in construction chemicals were growing beyond the US$20 million/year marker.

Since then my work has taken me to various countries and three continents. During that experience, I have worked with different nationalities (35) and at different levels of construction industry, that is, from on-site workers to functional managers, like site supervisors/QAQC managers, to decision-makers like project directors/project managers.

As my employment history will testify, I am a self-motivated and proactive person, who has achieved goals consistently throughout my career due to perseverance. This is demonstrated by the fact that I have never obtained a position in my present field of the construction industry by responding to advertisement. I have always gone job searching in India and the Far East at my own expense and secured employment from the organizations concerned. My passion and will to succeed which have helped me all along in my career have enabled me to take innumerable challenges and risks. They are my biggest strengths and what I am today, is a product of those two qualities.

Working in Dubai over the last four years, I came across a number of unforeseen work situations and problems. These were due to the need to build the city's new airport (due to political situations) faster. I had to provide solutions, using my products to solve various problems. Providing a solution to a problem is one of my assets and I have the vision to see ahead and beyond the problem. This experience will be of significant importance in my MBA classes to me and to my fellow students.

Dubai being a cosmopolitan city, a melting pot of diverse people, culture, and language, provides an insight into the effects on people caused by social, technological, and political changes around the world. My intense personality and ability to thrive in diverse environments have enabled me to understand the psychological makeup of the markets (people) of many countries and their implications in the future. This skill has helped me and will help me in cross-cultural negotiations which will be a key element to do business in world business of the 21st century.

I am very ambitious and a natural leader through my ability to express myself and organize people and things. I like to make decisions quickly which sometimes has created problems with my administrative staff. I set a very high standard for myself, which I also expect from my staff. This creates problems because the need to find solutions quickly unnerves some people. However, I do not do this intentionally.

My weaknesses are largely connected to my strengths and one of my most glaring weaknesses is my impatience. I am a person who does not like to waste time nor do I like to wait. I find because of my impulsiveness, sometimes I come across as abrasive and overbearing. Over-enthusiasm sometimes puts pressure on my colleagues. However, because of my impulsiveness and enthusiasm, I do not lack decisiveness. Another weakness which I have observed over the last few years is a lack of good business report writing skills, and a knowledge to use the latest information technology tools. While my communication skills and vocabulary have continued to increase through reading and speaking, I recognize the ability to put ideas in a systematic written form as vital; I definitely see the above skills of paramount importance in business.

■ ■ ■

Candidate's biography: Cedric is male, French, educated in France

Give a candid description of yourself, stressing the personal characteristics you feel to be your strengths and weaknesses and the main factors which have influenced your personal development, giving examples when necessary. (INSEAD)

I am a natural team-player with strong negotiation and communication abilities and solid analytical skills. However, I tend to procrastinate when I am not under pressure. During my second year of engineering school (ENST), I was the president of the ski club. My passion for this sport very much parallels my strengths and weaknesses.

While president of the ski club, I co-organized with peers from two other "Grandes Ecoles" the "3's Cup". Working with a strong teamwork spirit was the only way to successfully set-up the event, a 3-day ski trip and competition in the French Alps for 300 students. In addition, I was able to share my passion for skiing with fellow students and recruit more competitors to double our ski team size. During my numerous experiences around the world, being a team-player and my ability to share my interests and perspective enabled me to better communicate with people from different nationalities and diverse backgrounds.

Skiing in powder parallels my strong negotiation and communication abilities. In powder, you must gain speed, make smooth turns and control your rhythm while enjoying yourself. While talking with potential customers or negotiating contracts, I analyze issues precisely, answer them with finesse and creativity, and still enjoy these relationships and learn through them. At 9TELECOM, I successfully led negotiations with France Telecom, because I could listen well to and understand others' points of views, articulate my opinion properly, and argue persuasively.

I use my strong analytical skills in ski races to judge the level of risk I will need to take. I match my strengths and weaknesses with those of fellow competitors, as well as those of the natural elements around me. My math-intensive education and my logical mind enable me to tackle complex problems and handle multiple tasks at once. These analytical abilities proved beneficial during my internship at Divicom. I developed pre-processing algorithms to improve the encoding of digital video, which were later patented.

Skiing can also parallel my strongest weakness. Since I perform at my full potential under pressure, I tend to procrastinate and get bored when I am not under pressure. In much the same way, when skiing through big moguls, you have to go straight through them keeping the pressure, or else a fall is certain. A tool I use to fight this tendency is task managing software, listing all the tasks I have to perform with associated deadlines and urgency levels. Moreover, I believe the intense MBA experience at INSEAD will help me further refine my time and task management skills.

■ ■ ■

Candidate's biography: Alfred is male, Austrian, educated in the Netherlands

Provide a candid assessment of your strengths and weaknesses. (Harvard)

In giving an assessment of myself, I would like to introduce the city of Innsbruck, where I grew up and spent 20 years of my life. The 800-year-old town, with 130,000 inhabitants, is the fifth largest city and situated in the western part of Austria. Innsbruck has gained prominence from its beautiful landscape and the Alpine mountain ridge that surrounds the city.

Though a small town, Innsbruck has hosted the Olympic Winter Games twice and is today a Mecca for hiking and skiing tourists from all over world, giving the city an international flair. Assisting my parents in their restaurant, I was exposed to guests from different nationalities, enabling me to early acquire global perspectives. Through my summer jobs working for Swarovski selling crystals to French, Italian and Chinese tourists, my university studies in Holland, Belgium and the Far East and my current position as a management consultant, I have not only constantly refined my competence in working with people from different backgrounds and origins, but have also achieved fluency in some of the world's preeminent languages (English, French, German and Mandarin).

Innsbruck citizens are characterized by their genuine character and straightforwardness. People say that the mountainous terrain and rough weather conditions have shaped people to be direct and open. Having adopted these traits, I consider it one of my strengths to be candid and not to be afraid to speak out, especially in uncomfortable situations. This has sometimes brought me criticism, but in the end people value my honesty. Today my senior staff members appreciate my sincerity and integrity and often ask for my opinion, especially with regard to clarifying tensions within the project team or issues with the clients.

Innsbruck lies in a valley (580 meters above sea level) and is enclosed by mountains. Due to its unfavorable and isolated location, historically, people always had to endure much physical hardship to cross the mountain pass to get to the other communities. This gave them a perseverant and enduring character, which is still present today. I am not afraid to overcome difficulties and challenges in the pursuit of my goal. For example, despite having asthma, I mastered the rescue swimmer's rigorous training module and became a certified rescue swimmer eligible to practice in pools and also the open sea.

Growing up in a small and remote town with little of the fast-paced cosmopolitan atmosphere of large cities, I see myself as less aggressive in behavior and more individualistic than many people from big cities. This can be considered a weakness; however, I feel that without this character I would not have achieved what I have today. I believe in a supportive and collegiate team culture and I look forward to contributing my strengths to the HBS student community as well as learning from my fellow classmates.

■ ■ ■

Candidate's biography: Elena is female, Russian, educated in China

Give a candid description of yourself, stressing the personal characteristics you feel to be your strengths and weaknesses and the main factors, which have influenced your personal development, giving examples when necessary. (INSEAD)

"Matryoshka" is a special word in Russian. This traditional Russian souvenir, consisting of a series of painted wooden dolls which fit one inside the other, is a symbol of Russia and Russian folk art.

Playing with Matryoshka, one cannot see what each inner doll looks like until the outer one is first removed. Because one big doll holds many small dolls inside, it is quite irresistible to want to open each up to see what's inside. "M-Dolls" force me to be inquisitive. Looking back at my pre-school and school years, I remember myself tormenting parents and teachers with questions. My strong desire to learn more about a subject forced me to prepare reports containing material one couldn't find in a textbook at school. I even read encyclopedias and dictionaries without any special purpose, just for enjoyment. I spent a lot of time traveling during my university vacation time. I have been almost everywhere in China, have traveled across India, enjoyed Australia, traveled from North to South Vietnam, and crossed the Cambodian border and seen the famous Angkor Wat. In my professional life a good doctor must be inquisitive, as medicine is both an art and a science. Even the intuition that I discovered during childhood in Russia is now stronger as a result of my years of living in China and the Far East.

Originally considered as a toy, Matryoshka is as much a puzzle, and can represent an analytical way of thinking, progressing from big to small, and from small to big. My analytical skills serve as objective measures and the basis of good decision-making in both work and life. The progression of going from bigger to smaller leads to cures in medicine. It starts with the "big" patient and then progresses to smaller and smaller clues as to what the cure is. My country and family background and creativity equally help me to find solutions to confusing situations in my everyday life.

Each of the dolls is made individually, and they differ not only in terms of size but in styles and colors. They are made by hand, so the decoration is original. Typically, each doll is smiling, colorful and friendly. The creative process of making the dolls involves no measurements, relies on intuition and requires skill and patience. Referring to my strengths, I would add that I am a friendly and approachable person and one with whom people feel comfortable. In a doctor's practice, one of the crucial elements of success is to find rapport with a patient. A doctor must be open-hearted and friendly to be able to listen to a person in need. This trait helps me in my professional and personal life. While studying and traveling, I interact with people from different countries to find out the details of their lives. There always exist distinct differences with respect to inter-relations, gift giving, face, humor, and food. It is these details which are very important for getting along with people. The fact that Matryoshkas are made of soft woods (lime and birch), reminds me of how people are all impressionable (one can leave a dint on the dolls) but the dolls are also firm enough in makeup (wood is pretty solid), so one must be able to adapt to another person's personality, peculiarities and disposition, without demanding that they be different.

The ability to enjoy M-Dolls and to look closely at their composition and coloring and appreciate their distinctiveness also seems to indicate a type of weakness. For even though it brings satisfaction, examining them so closely may not be a practical thing to do. As in medicine, one can forever analyze and contemplate and study possibilities but limited time and imperfect information require acting. My potential weak points as a business person arise from my training as a doctor: I can be overly attentive to details and a perfectionist. I am a very responsible person and like to force co-workers to check off all the details. While being overly focused on details is necessary in medical practice, in business this may narrow the "panoramic view" of the problem.

WRITING THE "GREATEST ACCOMPLISHMENTS OR LEADERSHIP" ESSAY

A "greatest accomplishments or leadership" essay seeks to find out what you have done. Any "team building" type essay question (i.e., "please discuss an example of how you worked effectively as a team member") is really a sub-component of the greatest accomplishments or leadership essay.

EXAMPLE

Describe your most substantial accomplishments and why you view them as such. (University of Toronto)

Common mistakes

Some of the common mistakes made by applicants when writing such essays are:

- Not mentioning any of their non-work-related accomplishments. In other words, mentioning *only* work-related accomplishments.
- Not stating what they have learned from their experience or what their accomplishments tell about who they are as a person.
- Not using a clear structure; not providing a preview of their accomplishments before going into a full-blown description.

Winning approaches

The following are some advice on how to write "greatest accomplishments" essays.

Tip #45: Consider the "mix" and order of your accomplishments.

When asked for two accomplishments, consider choosing a personal accomplishment to complement a professional accomplishment. When asked for three accomplishments, consider choosing two non-professional accomplishments (e.g., academic, extracurricular, community service) to complement your professional accomplishment. Obviously if two of your three accomplishments are work related then position them as your first and third accomplishments and sandwich a non-business accomplishment in between. Typically your strongest accomplishment should be placed first.

☞ **Tip #46: Test your accomplishment by making sure it has the "wow factor!". Imagine yourself as the reader. Ask, "Is this difficult? ... is this impressive?"**

Suppose you write in your essay that you did a benchmarking study while working as a consultant. Describing or summarizing what you did may not be enough. You know it was a difficult project. So play the devil's advocate for a moment. Ask yourself, "Is that difficult?" Oh yes, you say to yourself, and give a long list of reasons. Okay, now, record what you are answering. Some of these details should be included in your essay. Make it action-oriented. This will help you prove the difficulty of your accomplishment. Do not buy into the assumption that just because something is perceived to be difficult, it therefore proves it is difficult.

☞ **Tip #47: Consider using "headlines" to summarize and highlight your accomplishment(s).**

Headlines or caption headings exist to summarize or pre-phrase information and/or to capture the reader's attention. An example of the use of headlines is easily seen in the upcoming "greatest accomplishments" essay written by Shannon: (i) "Broke Guinness Book of World Records for 109 Hours of Continuous Debate to Raise Money for Oxfam"; (ii) "As a Fresh Graduate of 22 Years of Age, I Uprooted Myself from North Carolina to Obtain My First International Position in the Watch/Clock Industry in Hong Kong"; (iii) "Working with Hospice of Scotland County Was Emotionally the Most Difficult Endeavor I Have Ever Undertaken." Headlines are usually placed in quotations or bold or italicized.

An alternative to headlines is the summary or lead sentence, which is placed at or near the top of your writing piece. Sometimes a headline and a lead sentence are interchangeable. For example: As a Fresh Graduate of 22 Years of Age, I Uprooted Myself from North Carolina to Obtain My First International Position in the Watch/Clock Industry in Hong Kong. Because this is a complete sentence, it can serve either purpose, and as an opening sentence it would give the writing clear direction.

☞ **Tip #48: Do not define "leadership" too narrowly.**

Leadership has many dimensions. Depending upon your particular work experience, leadership could be best shown by example, command, inspiration, competency, persuasion, empowerment, crisis, emergency, etc. Whereas one candidate chooses leadership by command and uses his or her involvement in the military as an example, another candidate chooses leadership in crises and cites his or her involvement in curtailing a public relations debacle. The point is that there is no uniform definition of leadership and admissions officers will allow you to interpret it as you see fit.

SAMPLE "GREATEST ACCOMPLISHMENTS OR LEADERSHIP" ESSAYS

Candidate's biography: Vivian is female, Hungarian-American, educated in the U.S.

Describe your three most substantial accomplishments and explain why you view them as such? (Harvard)

Extreme self-motivation, diligence, and a talent for leadership characterize the diversity and scope of my personal and professional accomplishments. My global work experience in Hungary, Hong Kong, and the U.S. and my educational background in communication and business has given me a broad perspective on the commercial world. These accomplishments have instilled in me a unique and formidable blend of skills and competencies.

Scholarship: Successfully completed General Electric's prestigious corporate Financial Management Program (FMP)

I graduated from General Electric (GE)'s two-and-a-half-year Financial Management Program (FMP) in December of 1993, and in doing so, joined the alumnae of GE's top finance managers and CFOs. I view this as my most substantial accomplishment because graduating from GE's FMP demonstrated my self-discipline, intellectual stamina, and strength in applied quantitative skills. FMP honed and sharpened my skills and gave me a firm foundation in finance and business.

One of corporate America's most prestigious and most competitive financial training programs, FMP is an intensive and often grueling combination of a full-time on-the-job finance experience and formal educational training. Concurrent to taking five graduate level finance courses such as Financial Reporting, Financial Accounting, and Auditing, trainees or 'FMPs' rotate through five six-month assignments in all functional finance departments, from General Accounting, Investment Finance, Sales and Marketing to Manufacturing Finance.

Global work experience: Attained key positions with General Electric in Eastern Europe, Western Europe, and Asia

For the past six years, I have held a series of intensive and challenging managerial positions in Eastern and Western Europe and Asia with General Electric. Achieving the responsible and visible level of these assignments demanded extremely hard work, excellent analytical and quantitative skills, and top management approval and support. I regard the attainment of these positions as my second most significant accomplishment to date. It took enormous diligence and dedication not only to be chosen for each position, but also to move quickly through the ranks at the relatively young age of 26.

From my leading role as manager of the Western European Internal Audit Department for GE Lighting in Europe (GELE) to my present position as finance manager of the CNBC Channel for NBC Asia in Hong Kong, I delivered results and success. At NBC I created my position from scratch and provided financial counsel to management as the *first* financial manager of the channel. At GELE, I created all audit plans and led all business reviews throughout the Western European affiliates. I demonstrated not only my financial and business acumen through these varied roles, but also great adaptability, stamina, and a large threshold for hard work and rigor.

I took advantage of all avenues and opportunities to learn and grow professionally at GELE. Even during my first year of work, I requested and received additional assignments. One of my first assignments was to implement GELE's *first* investment tracking system for over US$44 million worth of capital investments. After its successful completion, I went on to help spearhead the company's *first ever* detailed analysis of product pricing and profitability by lighting product line. I received a management award for my recommendations which generated US$5 million in incremental margin in 1991.

Above all, however, I value my work because I achieved success in vastly different and enormously complex environments. Environments that spanned different continents, cultures, and industries – from Eastern Europe to Asia and from manufacturing to broadcasting. I lived in foreign countries far from home for over six years and worked in new and often struggling companies.

Communication: Proven communications abilities as journalism major from Boston University and professional writing experience

I regard the acquiring of my strong communication skills as my third most substantial accomplishment. I graduated with a Bachelor of Science degree in Journalism and have proven my communication abilities not only by being the youngest intern at *Boston Magazine*, but also by having published an article in the magazine. As a first-generation American, I have also excelled in a language – English – that my parents never taught or spoke with me. They emigrated from Hungary in 1965 without being able to speak English. I have also achieved a complementary relationship between words and numbers, which is unique and very powerful. At times, one needs numbers to communicate ideas, and other times one needs words, as in giving speeches. My strength lies in my ability to listen, synthesize ideas, and articulate concepts – whether quantitative, qualitative, verbal, or written – in a way that is concise and eloquent.

■ ■ ■

Candidate's biography: Brett is male, American, educated in the U.S.

Choose a recent experience in which you acted as a leader, describe your leadership role, and then explain how you were effective and what you learned. (Harvard)

As Chairman, I led a 14-person, hand-picked high school reunion committee and, over a period of six months, the committee managed to organize two events with a plus 200-person attendance. This endeavor also involved producing an hour-long video and an interactive class directory with photos. We raised $20,000 for the school, noting that neither was the Reunion an ongoing event nor was any support given from the school. During the process, we had an 85 percent attendance rate at all of our bi-weekly meetings and 96 percent of attendees were on time with delays of no more than 10 minutes. Given the "15 minutes late habit" for most social events, I consider this outcome exemplary.

My role as leader involved selecting the right people for each role, clearly identifying the responsibilities required and setting up a clear and accountable agreement, known as the Constitution. The structure precluded future miscommunications and confusion of roles. Furthermore, I never assumed I had solutions to any problems but instead relied on steering a group of intelligent people to the right direction by providing macro objectives then allowing the team to creatively deal with each situation. I often instigated laughter as a means of inspiration.

The structure I proposed also clearly identified those who were not committed and the system removed them naturally, which allowed the committee to remain enthusiastic through out the process. Of course good food was an added bonus since all of our meetings were held over dinner at selected or recommended restaurants.

Subsequent to the success of my reunion event, I was invited to join the six-person fund raising development sub-committee of the school's Landmark Fund Raising Campaign targeting $300 million in five years.

■ ■ ■

Candidate's biography: Peter is male, Chinese-American, educated in Australia

Please cite one or two of your most important accomplishments and state why do you view them as such. (Wharton)

My proudest achievement, mentioned in my previous essay, is the promotion that I received, from sales engineer to my current position of marketing executive at ASEA, BROWN & BOVERI in Hong Kong. Started at the bottom of the management tree, I now report directly to the regional director.

Part of the reason that I was given this great opportunity was because of my vision. Before my promotion, I was constantly complaining to management that we lacked company recognition and we needed aggressive marketing tactics. I was asked to do something about it. Since assuming this position, I have combined the marketing efforts of various departments which previously operated independently. It was definitely a case of the whole being greater than the sum of the individual parts. I have also implemented an aggressive advertising and media campaign to increase public awareness and create a positive image. In the past I only had the opportunity to work in one industry – glass. Following my promotion I now also deal with printing equipment, telecommunications, medical equipment, and power production.

Hong Kong is also the place where I achieved my greatest non-work-related accomplishment, involving language. I have developed an 80-percent proficiency in Cantonese and 70-percent proficiency in Mandarin after living in Hong Kong for four-and-a-half years. In addition, I am now able to write over a thousand Chinese characters. As I grew up in essentially an English-speaking household, I originally could not speak any Chinese at all. When I first came to Hong Kong I only understood some very basic Mandarin. Now I have reached a level where I am able to conduct business in Chinese, both Cantonese and Mandarin. Four-and-a-half years ago I could not even write my Chinese name.

It is only through my self-motivation that I have been able to achieve this. The difference between two Chinese dialects can be likened to the difference between two European languages, say German and English. It may be possible to catch a few words here and there, but overall there is no comprehension. The majority of overseas people who have lived in Hong Kong for many years (sometimes almost their whole lives) have only reached a "taxi-level" of Cantonese where they can tell drivers street names, turn right, stop, etc. Apart from people whose families speak Cantonese at home, I have only met two or three people who have reached my level of fluency. All of my overseas friends have tried at one stage or another to learn Chinese, but most have given up. I stuck to my guns.

Another achievement came at an earlier age. I took up the trumpet at the age of 11 and when I reached high school I became a member of the "City of Perth Brass Band". I participated in numerous competitions, both as a band member and as a soloist, coming in first or second many times. The highlight of my music "career" was taking second place in the Western Australian under-19 brass instrument section and also during the same competition, first in the under-19 duet. At that time I was 14 years old. Without my commitment to time-consuming daily practice such an achievement would not have been possible. I was very proud of this achievement as it was the direct result of my many hours of hard work.

■ ■ ■

Candidate's biography: Shannon is female, American, educated in the U.S.

Describe your three most substantial accomplishments and explain why you view them as such? (Harvard)

Broke Guinness Book World Record for 109 hours of continuous debate to raise money for Oxfam

After a four-year high school debate career including a Georgia State Debate Championship title and a trip to the National Debate Tournament for public speaking, I was still not prepared for the challenge which awaited me in my freshman year of college.

Our Debate Society at St. Andrews College decided to make an attempt to break the Guinness Book World Record for the longest four-person debate.

The existing world record was 104 hours, but used more than four people. However, we were determined to use the same four people for the entire debate. With world hunger as our topic, we set out to increase awareness on this issue, raise money for Oxfam (an international relief organization), and break the world record.

The team spent months gathering sponsorships, designing T-shirts, researching every aspect of world hunger and training our bodies to function with minimal sleep. We started our debate on the Thursday before Thanksgiving with the entire campus supporting our efforts. Individual dorms even took turns "camping out" with us overnight and by the third day, the student center looked like one big pyjamas party. During the five days, several close calls with physical exhaustion almost made us stop. But, on the fifth day, delirious from sleep deprivation and surrounded by reporters and cheering students, we broke the Guinness Book World Record. When we finally quit, we had surpassed the previous record by over five hours, using only four people, and raised well over US$1,000 for Oxfam. It took me three weeks to recover, but the satisfaction of our achievement will be with me always.

As a fresh graduate of 22 years of age, I uprooted myself from North Carolina to obtain my first international position in the watch/clock industry in Geneva

The second accomplishment of which I am proud is the risk I took in moving overseas to gain international work experience in consumer products. While finishing my BA in International Business and International Politics in North Carolina, I spoke with several consumer product companies who indicated that only senior level employees could work in their international areas. With encouragement from my dean, I decided to move to Geneva to gain international work experience in the area of fast-moving consumer goods.

Geneva was the perfect choice as Geneva and Zurich collectively manufacture over 50 percent of the world's watches along with a vast majority of other related products. Thankfully, I had already spent one year studying in Scotland, so leaving the U.S. to live in a country I had never visited was not a difficult concept. Therefore, after graduation from college, I moved to Geneva, resume in hand, to find a job in consumer products and to gain international management experience. Three weeks after arriving in Geneva, I was hired by a watch and clock manufacturer to work in their marketing department. Although I was the youngest employee when I started work at Silicon Watch Company, I was assistant manager of the watch division by the time I left to join Disney two years later.

Working with Hospice of Scotland County was emotionally the most difficult endeavor I have ever undertaken

Although I have participated in numerous charity organizations, working with a group called Hospice of Scotland County in North Carolina was emotionally the most difficult endeavor I have ever undertaken. Hospice is an organization that takes care of terminally-ill individuals who have stopped receiving treatment for their illness. I was a volunteer caregiver in this group and had several patients that I would visit weekly.

I consider working in Hospice to be a significant accomplishment due to the emotional issues I had to overcome in order to spend time with these patients. Developing a relationship with them, while knowing they will soon die, can be a heart-wrenching experience. However, the knowledge of how much you can help a family or an individual far outweighs the emotional strain. Easing the pain of others, even if it is only on a small scale, is an accomplishment that only needs to be recognized by the individuals involved.

■ ■ ■

Candidate's biography: Brian is male, African-American, educated in the U.S.

Describe a personal achievement that has had a significant impact on your life. In addition to recounting the achievement, please analyze how the event has changed your understanding of yourself and how you perceive the world around you. (Wharton)

Last year, I was involved in a very personal, challenging, and significant achievement that demonstrated the importance that family, love, and fellowship play in my life. It also highlighted personal qualities that have influenced my current career success, and will impact my future success as well. This involved locating my sister and her sons, and reuniting them with our family. Twenty-one years ago my sister converted and married into the Islamic faith. She and her husband were both African-Americans who chose to convert in the U.S. from their Christian upbringing to this religion. During their marriage they were blessed with five sons whom they planned to raise in their new faith. My sister's and my brother-in-law's zealous beliefs created tension and distance between them and our parents as well as other family members. Gradually both my sister and nephews became more and more isolated from all of us. This distance was made more complete when nine years ago my sister moved to Cairo, Egypt with her five sons in order to raise them in an Islamic environment. Her husband had moved them to Egypt but continued to live, work, and support them from the U.S. This left her husband as our most direct link to my sister but, by his choice, normal channels of communication with him had broken down.

Unexpectedly, my father received a distressing letter from my sister describing poverty-level living conditions and what appeared to be an abandonment of the family by her husband. The letter did not contain enough information to send any correspondence or help and we were unable to verify the contents of the letter with her husband. This made it necessary to personally visit Egypt in order to locate my sister and her sons. Based on my experiences and contacts developed while living overseas, it evolved that I would lead this effort.

In reflecting on the challenges and obstacles overcome in trying to locate and reconcile my sister with our family, I recognize several new discoveries about myself that were made on this journey. First, traveling to Egypt to find my sister uncovered my ability to quickly adapt, assimilate, and construct the tools or relationships needed to function effectively in a new environment. Egypt represented a region of the world for which I had little knowledge. Not only did I not speak the local language, but I also had never pursued any study of the region or its culture. The lack of advance warning for this trip limited my time to prepare for what I would experience. Egypt was my first experience in an Islamic country run under a dual bureaucratic and Koranic law. This would require me to work within the construct of Islam, which is unique in that it is at once an inseparable cultural, religious, and legal entity. Moreover, as a personal situation, I did not have the option of walking away from it. With limited time and financial resources, quick and efficient operation in this new environment was essential. My success in this matter resulted in finding my sister and nephews within three days of my arrival in Egypt.

This search might have taken weeks if it had not been for my ability to rapidly analyze the problem and find a path of communication in a foreign environment that would allow me to engage local people and obtain information. Using a local guide who spoke English, I was able to ask others in Arabic about the directions and address that I had of my sister from her letter to my father. The English translation of the Arabic address led us on a labyrinth-like search on the outskirts of the city. Eventually, my sister and nephews were found in a poor and isolated area. Despite the years apart with no contact, my sister lovingly greeted me and openly told me her story of isolation and abandonment by her husband who had left her without the financial wherewithal to support herself or to leave the country.

The trip to Egypt crystallized how much I had learned about tolerance and adaptability to other cultures. It also identified how communication is the key to bridging the gap between people and cultures. As I assisted my sister and nephews with their immediate needs, the application of the three-part principle of listening, observing, and adopting a non-judgmental attitude enabled me to deal with the new intricacies and mysteries of Islam and Egypt. Travel in other third world countries has shown me that success depends on a high tolerance for ambiguity. Method, priority, and urgency have different emphases than in Western culture, with more time and patience required for anything I wanted to accomplish. Being someone who likes things very well planned, this experience demonstrated that no matter what the task, there is a limit to the ability to prepare or plan for an event. One must be able to adjust quickly to situations in flux. This journey enhanced my ability to do this as I recognized and seized opportunities and good fortune along the way.

Equally important in all of this was knowing when, and not being afraid, to ask for help. These qualities were manifested in my sourcing of a local guide who served as my primary means to successfully find my sister. Realization of my own limitations also meant that I did not go on this trip alone. Another sister, who is a doctor, accompanied me to help with any medical attention needed and to serve as a confidant to my sister in Egypt as we worked through the various issues we faced once she was found. In addition, I provided a daily e-mail journal of the events in Egypt to my closest friends in Hong Kong,

Europe, and the U.S. This network of friends around the globe, through their direct guidance and assistance, or simply as confidants, served as a major support system while I struggled with the decisions and frustrations encountered during the trip. Each one in some way became a part of my journey and proved the many valuable friendships that I had developed over the years.

Lastly, this experience demonstrated to me my strength for building consensus. Before the trip, each family member held varying views on the goals of the trip. Much of the focus was on bringing them back to the U.S. These views did not consider my sister's original rationale for moving to Egypt and the possible desire on her part to remain there. Nor did the family's views match my priorities of simply ensuring my sister's and my nephews' safety and health. Meeting the challenges of this situation required consolidating and reaching a compromise among these three separate views, priorities, and values. My sister's, the family's, and my own views all needed to be in sync in order to effectively pool the resources of the family in this effort. Shaping the focus and objectives of the trip led to one common purpose – locating and re-establishing communication with my sister. Any other desires such as bringing them back to the U.S. would not be a focus of this trip and it would allow everyone to be sensitive to their wishes to remain or leave Egypt. As a result not only were we able to locate her, but based on my sister's and nephews' own desire to return to the U.S., we were also able to successfully relocate her and my nephews back to the States and reunite her with our family.

My experiences with my sister in Egypt left me with a perception of the world as a smaller, reachable place with more in common across cultures than differences or separators. Communication is the first step. As shown in our family, establishing a dialogue that finds the common ground is the activity needed to cross borders and influence and guide people of all cultures. The result is the development of a universality in one's ability to communicate with others. This experience was about family and made me aware of the real importance of family structure to myself and the world in general. My family has not only shaped my values and priorities, but has also provided me much of my strength, drive, and determination to succeed. As part of a family, I as well as others in the world, contribute to this life and leave something for future generations as well. The success of my journey has helped our family, which was disparate, pull together for a common good. There is now a more cohesive family and, through my nephews, a future beyond the present.

■ ■ ■

Candidate's biography: Tim is male, American, educated in the U.S.

Describe a personal achievement that has had a significant impact on your life. In addition to recounting this achievement, please analyze how the event has changed your understanding of yourself and how you perceive the world around you. (Wharton)

I have always believed in this work ethic principle – as long as someone puts forward their best effort, good results will always arrive at the end. As one expression goes, "*If you plant a melon seed you will get a melon, and if you plant a bean seed you will get a beanstalk.*" I have been told that persistence and effort are rewarded while laziness and complacence are punished. The equation has always been easy to understand and to follow for me. By investing the proper time and effort I have been able to attain a fine high school education, a solid college preparation experience, as well as an opportunity upon graduation to work for a prestigious consulting firm. I believe that everyone has equal opportunity, equal access, and an equal understanding of how to be successful in this world.

"Stouffer Boy" – my nickname throughout my college years – reminds me of a life experience that caused me to re-evaluate a personal belief. It was a period of my life in which my own values and "hard work" beliefs were being challenged over a length of time. Most people saw little value in why I chose to work there – a 30-hour per week job at Stouffer Dining, one of the main student dining halls at Penn. Not only am I now proud of the fact that I was able to partially finance my college education, but also proud of the experience that has given me a new perspective on the challenges that others faced where equal opportunities might not exist.

Despite the rigors of working in the dishroom, the dirty surroundings of the trash compactor, or the grueling task of cleaning up after students in the eating halls, I experienced and learned other things beyond the $8.50 an hour that Stouffer had to offer. I persisted in working at Stouffer for a few years and gained the well-rounded education that others did not value or see. My friends passing through the dining hall would jest at me and yell, "Stouffer Boy, what is the soup today?" They could not comprehend the reason why I was working there, "wasting" valuable time that could otherwise be spent hitting the books at Van Pelt. At Stouffer, students who *operated* the dining hall were different than the students who *ate* there. All of the student workers were not only bound together by the need of extra pocket money, but they also faced another level of adversity beyond the regular demands of school. While one fellow worker at New Jersey had divorced parents who could not support one penny in her education, another student from Texas had to send his wages back to support his family. I found that students under such pressures tend to develop a realistic, hardworking, and thankful perspective toward their education and their lives – something I had learned working side-by-side with them. For the student workers at Stouffer, the real challenge was not just getting admitted into Penn, but also balancing financial and academic requirements in order to stay and to succeed there.

Most people also did not see another opportunity I had at Stouffer – working closely, learning from, and building friendships with the local residents of West Philadelphia. Since Penn's environment is known to be quite hostile, many students in their four years at Philadelphia were afraid to interact closely with the people from the school's community. As I was promoted to be a Student Supervisor, I had to manage a team of seven to eight workers in one shift composed of both student workers and local workers. The local workers were varied in their backgrounds as well – some were lifelong union members in their 40s and 50s, while others were local high school students.

I felt initially that the local workers had an invisible wall separating themselves from the students. It was quite difficult at first to integrate the different groups and to understand clearly everyone's motivations and beliefs – many times I was even threatened by local workers as they did not like the assignments I gave them. However, I gradually learned how to gain their confidence through my work, and I was successful in breaking down some of their stereotypes of Ivy League students. They eventually changed their initial confrontational attitudes with me to a more cooperative one. As I got to know several of the local workers over longer periods of time, I even found that some of them were more diligent and conscientious than us Penn students. Through my interactions with them I slowly learned that my strongly-held work ethic belief does not always apply. Most of them came from an under-privileged environment in some way or form – not only financially, but also other factors such as coming from a single-parent family, a background of drug abuse, or an environment of constant harmful peer pressures. No matter how many news or books I have heard or read about inner-city problems, I could never have understood the tribulations they have gone through. I realized how difficult and how "unequal" their circumstances were.

It was interesting to also understand the local people's perspectives of the school – some were grateful of the school's contribution to the local economy, while many consider the students to be inconsiderate of the local people and the environment. Many of my younger fellow local workers were extremely smart but did not share the same opportunity to attend Penn, and often had stereotypes of the students. I felt that by leading through example, I changed some of their biases toward myself as I helped them to understand the school and the student body better. I invited some of them to several campus parties including our St. Patrick's Day party. They found the costumes to be extremely funny and they also found out that Penn students were fun, hardworking, and had interests similar to everyone else in West Philadelphia as well!

Working as a management consultant in Eastern U.S., clients and colleagues always seem to be surprised by the fact that I know how to fix a broken soda machine in a restaurant or how to operate a yogurt machine on-site at a client's cafeteria. They never guessed that I learned those skills at college. However, what I have carried forward in my life beyond graduation was not only a new set of finance, management, and dining hall operational knowledge, but a better understanding on the difficulties others faced and how greatly they differed from my own. I now believe that the traditional work ethic model, while still true, does not always guarantee success for everyone. Groups and individuals have their own unique set of circumstances and constraints to overcome, and people must be aware of those. There is simply no secret formula that applies to everyone. Today, the Students' Supervisor pin on my office desk serves as a symbol of "Stouffer Boy" days. It serves as a symbol of my persistence to defy popular beliefs and to see value in something where others did not.

WRITING THE "OVERCOMING DIFFICULT SITUATIONS" ESSAY

Any "ethical dilemma" or "failure" type question is really a sub-component of an "overcoming difficult situations" type essay question.

EXAMPLE

Describe an internal conflict (or difficult decision) that you have faced. How did you resolve the situation? What did you learn from this? (Harvard Business School)

Common mistakes

Some of the common mistakes applicants make when it comes to writing this kind of essay are:

- Not summarizing their writing so that the reader knows for sure what the "difficult situation" that they are talking about is.
- Not addressing the psychological aspects of the difficult situation.
- Not showing how one is a better person because of the difficult situation—what was learned?

Winning approaches

Applicants can try these approaches when dealing with "overcoming difficult situation" essays.

Tip #49: Make sure the reader can actually figure out what your difficult situation is. Don't wait until the end of the essay to summarize.

Of all the essay types, the overcoming the difficult situations type is probably the easiest for the reader to get lost. The writer may take too long describing a difficult situation, leaving the reader to wonder, "where's this all going?" You may want to summarize the whole essay into one sentence before you start to write. For example: "My ethical dilemma involved weighing the risks of fitting unsafe contact lenses with the benefits of incremental sales and profits."

🖎 **Tip #50:** **Consider using quotes from people as a way to help the reader understand what you or other people actually felt.**

Difficult situations almost always have a psychological or moral component that brings emotion into play. Things actually said or thoughts held during these times can be key ingredients for understanding them.

🖎 **Tip #51:** **In terms of describing your difficult situation and addressing what you have learned from the situation, a good rule-of-thumb weighting is: "two-thirds—describing" and "one-third—what you've learned."**

Nowadays most business schools have begun asking, "what have you learned from your situation?" In the past this was an implied question but one which was often overlooked by candidates. One closely related question is how much weight to give to describing the situation and how much weight to give to stating how much you learned from it. A good formula would be "two-thirds describing" and "one-third for what you've learned." It is not necessary to break the two parts down into a 50-50 proposition.

SAMPLE "OVERCOMING DIFFICULT SITUATIONS" ESSAYS

Candidate's biography: Omar is male, Jordanian, educated in Jordan

I could have in all probability managed to take a couple of computers into Russia without declaring them. All I would have needed to do is to lie on my declaration form and play ignorant with Russian customs officials. I was reluctant to do so for a few reasons. First, if I were caught, I might be fined and face an embarrassing situation. Moreover, if I succeeded I might be inundated by other requests to do the same for our other Russian colleagues. The dilemma I faced rested with my desire to want to help my colleagues – colleagues who continued to give me valuable assistance in my joint-venture negotiation and translation work. My relationship with them might hinge on doing them this favor. However, ethically I do not believe in trying to cheat government officials or in using my passport as a means of circumventing the law.

■ ■ ■

Candidate's biography: Shannon is female, American, educated in the U.S.

Recognizing that successful leaders are able to learn from failure, describe a situation in which you failed. Why did you fail? (Harvard)

One of the greatest assets of any company is its people. Therefore, I view the loss of a "valued" team member as my biggest on-the-job failure to date. While at Silicon Watch

Company, the Swiss watch manufacturer where I began my management career, our component purchaser resigned from her position. She had been with the company for six years and left only five months after I took over as her manager. She cited excessive workload and lack of support as the reasons for her departure.

As a first-time manager, I made several critical errors that actually led to her resignation. First, I imposed my own work ethic on her. I believed that everyone on my team should be willing to give 150 percent. I pushed her to finish urgent work before she left each day and held her accountable for giving timely feedback on production issues even when it meant working overtime. Her resignation showed me that not everyone's priorities are career-oriented and that sensitivity to my team's outside obligations is essential to being a good manager.

My second mistake was lack of communication. In an effort to learn more about our business, I met with some of our external suppliers individually. However, I did not properly communicate that in meetings with these vendors, I was not questioning my purchaser's abilities, but only trying to gain more insight into our product area. Since I did not make this clear to her, my purchaser misunderstood my intentions and felt that I was questioning her performance.

Fortunately, the next individual I hired for this position was actually much more dedicated. We were able to work together to decrease material costs and maintain a balanced work environment. Furthermore, I became much more aware of the work burdens on my team. Now, I do not hesitate to take action and provide relief when an employee is overloaded. However, I was only able to become a better manager through the process of losing my first purchaser due to my inexperience.

■ ■ ■

Candidate's biography: Marc is male, Caucasian, educated in the Netherlands

I faced a most difficult challenge in my work for a former senior accountant at Deloitte Touche Tohmatsu called Peter. Peter was known to be a bully to his subordinates. He earned his reputation for insulting subordinates' intellect, upbringing, capabilities, or personality. To make matters worse, since he was also a very demanding superior, he would seize upon any tiny mistake as an opportunity, in addition to the usual back-stabbing, to heap abuse upon colleagues.

Because of scheduling, I had to work for Peter on three assignments, stretching over a period of one-and-a-half years. Almost no day would pass without the two of us exchanging impressions of each other, and the whole department eventually got to know of our mutual disagreements. As I worked with him, I found out why he turned out to be such a "monster": he was very scared of losing our managers' confidence in his productivity. He abused other colleagues, both as a way to vent his anxiety and as a means to extract the highest level of productivity with fear as the "motivator".

Since then, I began to deal with Peter in two ways. First, I tried my best to avoid any mistake, and would ask him to clarify each time I was not crystal clear about the results he demanded. Second, I came to regard Peter as only a very difficult tutor, and told myself that he was here to make sure I would not commit the same errors I had made in front of him. I ensured that I would remain upbeat when I worked for him. Each time he started his routine abuses, I would turn his attention away from the abuses themselves to the factors he wanted me to pay attention.

I was not able to stop Peter from bullying other colleagues, but I found that Peter gradually reduced the frequency with which he abused me. Moreover, because I must pay extra attention when I worked with him, I learnt a lot more from him than from many other senior accountants, both in terms of the detailed requirements of our work and of how NOT to become a leader. Peter eventually departed in early 1997. To my surprise, before he left he actually mentioned to the managers about my attention to details and efficient execution of his order after clarifications as my good traits, something he had never done for anyone else.

■ ■ ■

Candidate's biography: Vivian is female, Hungarian-American, educated in the U.S.

Recognizing that successful leaders are able to learn from failure, describe a situation in which you failed. Why did you fail? (Harvard)

During my first managerial position at GE Lighting Europe, I faced the complex and diverse challenges of multi-cultural leadership. My efforts to foster an environment of cultural sensitivity and flexibility for my two Hungarian employees produced a dearth of direction and accountability. Ironically, it also brought a key cultural difference to the fore – Hungarians are often too proud to ask for directions or help. My plan of "empowerment" failed and left my staff without guidance. This lack of guidance caused our first project to veer irreparably off schedule.

My role as manager of the Western European Internal Audit Department was to create and lead comprehensive financial and business process audits for seven of our affiliate offices and three distribution centers. My team's first project in France did not go smoothly. The operational review of the business took twice as long as planned. Due to time constraints, our final report did not contain a complete balance sheet analysis.

When I hired my first Hungarian employee, Anita, I expected her to be a partner rather than a subordinate. Our deadlines were tight. We had two months to review both the financial accounts in the Paris affiliate and also audit the order-to-remittance process in the distribution center in Metz. This would necessitate us working not only on different reviews but also in different cities.

Although I anticipated that Anita might tackle her assignment from a different angle than I would have, I trusted her abilities and judgment. I wanted her to approach her work as she saw fit. Anita never called for advice or questions. Mistakenly, I never asked if she needed help. I interpreted her silence as affirmation that she knew what she was doing.

As an American, I took for granted that you ask for help if you have questions or are unclear about something. Only when an unplanned management request re-united us, did I realize we were over a month behind. Although I found that it is impossible to completely limit cultural misunderstanding, I did learn to better combine guidance and direction with cultural sensitivity.

■ ■ ■

Candidate's biography: Sabrina is female, French, educated in Luxembourg

Hundreds of people in the audience witnessed my failure on the memorable evening of December 29, 1995. Being 1 of 12 performers for the opening piece for the evening, I was granted the opportunity to dance on stage for the first time in my life. Although my part only lasted for about five minutes, those five minutes became significant moments in my life. Ever since rehearsals began two months prior to that evening, I had spent many hours practicing on my own in addition to the normal rehearsal sessions. Whether I was on the bus, waiting in a doctor's office, walking to work, I always had my CD player on, listening to the music and trying to go through the steps in my mind over and over again. I was determined to perform my very best. Despite my best preparation, my nervousness caused me to slip during the performance. All of a sudden, my mind went blank. I stood there, not knowing how to react to the music. Fifteen seconds seemed like fifteen hours in a normal day.

With music still ringing in my ears, it was my instinct and not my thoughts that thrust me forward into the line of other moving dancers who camouflaged my recovery. When the performance of the evening was all over, it was difficult to say if the audience fixated on the slip up, but I still lost the challenge to myself. The lesson I gained from that experience is the importance of staying calm and confident. Panicking in a crisis would only make the situation worse. Moreover, one should never give up. Persistence is the road to achievement. The only way to improve and learn from one's failures is to admit it with an open mind. It is more important to respond with an immediate solution and continue, than to be distressed about a past failure. As a result, the failure will become an insignificant yet integral factor to lead to overall success.

■ ■ ■

Candidate's biography: Peter is male, Chinese-American, educated in Australia

Discuss a non-academic personal failure. In what way were you disappointed in yourself? What did you learn from that experience? (Columbia)

Martial arts has been an important part of my life. I learned Tae Kwon Do for five years, obtaining my black belt and instructor's degree while at university in Australia. I have continued martial arts training and currently have the privilege of learning from one of

Hong Kong's most respected kung fu masters (Tam Hun Fan), who is from the same school where Bruce Lee began his martial arts career.

The personal failure that I would like to discuss involved a Tae Kwon Do tournament that I entered while I was still a student at the University of Melbourne. It was the State Championships and I qualified for the lightweight green belt division. Our club had ten or so entrants most of whom were exceptional fighters. In the months leading to the tournament, we all trained intensely and became very close friends. When the big day arrived we were all ready. The members of our school got off to a good start, and with the exception of two people, all progressed to the final of their respective divisions. I also made it to the final round of my division with a convincing victory over my semi-final opponent, gaining two knockdowns during the fight.

With all the final rounds completed and our club leading the trophy tally, one last match remained – mine. I was one of our instructor's favorite students. Before the fight he pulled me aside and said, "We want to finish this tournament with a big win from you. Do you think you can knock him out?" With my adrenaline pumping I thought I could do anything. He continued: "Look, I know I have taught all of you to go in hard as soon as the bell goes, but this time I want you to dance around the ring a bit and take a few hits. This will tire him out. After a minute passes, go in and knock him out."

The bell went off. The atmosphere was electric, reminiscent of a "Karate Kid" movie. I danced around the ring waiting for my opponent to tire so I could go for the big finish, but it did not progress as we had planned. My opponent kicked me in the face three times in quick succession. I was bleeding profusely from the nose and mouth. At this stage the referee stopped the fight and had a look at me; I wanted to continue, but he called off the fight. It was a tremendous anti-climax. It was lucky that the fight was called off at that moment because I found out the next day that my nose had been broken (I knew that something was wrong even before the X-ray. It had something to do with the green coloration of my nose).

What did I learn from this experience? Apart from learning that it is not healthy to be kicked in the face, this experience taught me that I should not be too greedy. If I had stuck to my normal technique I believe I would have beaten this opponent quite easily, but because I was over-ambitious I ended up not only not winning the division title, but suffering a painful loss. There is a Chinese saying that goes: *Qing Chu Yu Lan Er Sheng Yu Lan* (which literally means *indigo blue extracted from the indigo plant is bluer than the plant that it comes from*) which is sometimes translated as "the student surpasses the master". Before one can surpass the master he must master himself. And this means that one should have the confidence to follow one's own plan and not deviate from one's ability. In my case, I should have followed my original plan for a quick sure-win victory.

■ ■ ■

Candidate's biography: Steve is male, Irish, educated in the U.K.

Please comment on a situation where you failed to reach an objective and what you learned from it. (IMD)

I have paid dearly for a lesson when I chose to quit in my first marriage, which ended in September 1992.

I first got married in 1991 after six years of courtship. After a short and quiet while, trivial arguments often turned into big fights. Since both of us were young professionals and very righteous at that time, it was not long before we called it quits. It was a downhill journey from that point on and my first marriage had only lasted for a little more than one year. My life was shattered. I was deeply hurt and felt so ashamed to face people, especially those I knew before the marriage. Fortunately, I was able to recollect myself and focus on my career development.

I met my current wife, Elaine, in 1993. She was energetic, charming, and understanding and I knew she was the right one for me. However, I had difficulties shaking off my previous marriage experience and subconsciously I was driving her away. It was not until I became a Christian in late 1994 that I felt slightly more comfortable to accept my past and more ready to become someone's husband again. We eventually got married in March 1995.

I am not suggesting here that we have been living happily thereafter. But, with God's teaching through the Bible, we are able to establish a very important ground rule – "Quitting is not an option". This motto, together with vows we have pledged to each other, helps us through good times as well as bad times. We have the conviction that, with the help from our Lord, our relationship may be rocked but will never be broken.

■ ■ ■

Candidate's biography: John is male, American, educated in the U.S.

Discuss a failure. In what way were you disappointed in yourself? What did you learn from the experience? (Harvard)

My literature professor under whom I studied at Phillips Andover Academy inspired me in a subject that I previously had not shown a great interest. Relating to his straightforward and captivating teaching style and his ability to draw themes between literature and life, I chose English Literature as my college major.

My university experience was swarming with activities and events. I was a member of the varsity wrestling team and also held two different jobs, one with a local restaurant, the other in the Anheuser-Busch marketing department. I also had an active role in the Marine ROTC Semper Fi Club. Throughout university, I struggled to find a passion for my liberal arts courses. I persevered and battled my way through the literature courses with the belief that the result would help me to achieve my career goal. I believed that the number-oriented, business courses could wait until I completed my Marine Corps commitment and went to business school. It was a mistake to continue a course of study which I did not have a great enthusiasm for. I should have majored in business and taken literature courses as electives.

Despite this stumbling block, I believe that learning to think with a critical literature mindset has been and will continue to be very advantageous in my professional career. Reading and writing about great literature has greatly facilitated my written and verbal communication. In the military, it helped me quickly assess a situation, comprehend reports, and clearly and concisely communicate my operation plans and orders.

I have also enjoyed other benefits in the business world from the study of literature. I understand great writers and artists to be people who often test fringe ideas and concepts. As a reader of advanced literature, I learned to anticipate social issues arising from economic goals. For the greater part, based on my experiences to date, this is quite "optional" in the business world. Business leaders typically take the well planned, conservative routes as a means of achieving proven returns; they exhibit an ends-oriented, pragmatic thinking approach which typically does not entertain quixotic or figurative ways of thinking: the types of thinking that an artist, on the other hand, would feel comfortable entertaining. For example, not so long ago executives of large multi national companies such as Coca-Cola, Nike, or McDonald's would have considered it a strange idea that certain groups within the international local culture perceived such multi-national companies as unwelcomed perpetrators of American Culture and eroders of local culture. Although such issues have not been critical at this juncture of my career, I am at least able to acknowledge these types of situations, including the social issues (peripheral or pivotal) that they give rise to.

■ ■ ■

Candidate's biography: Alfred is male, Austrian, educated in the Netherlands

Recognizing that successful leaders are able to learn from failure, discuss a situation in which you failed and what you learned. (Harvard)

In my senior year of university I participated in the Tyrol Cup, a snowboard halfpipe contest, held in the "Axamer Lizum" a ski resort close to Innsbruck, Austria. It was my dream to participate in that contest, which attracted many of the region's best snowboarders. As an avid snowboarder for many years, with extensive experience in skateboarding and wakeboarding, I gave myself a high chance to be among the top five. However, in the end I ranked 24 out of 50 contestants.

Since I was young, I developed a passion for board sports and snowboarding became a must for me in winter. The feeling of gliding in a forest through deep powder snow, with the snow reaching my waist, became an addiction. When I signed up for the event, I had one month to prepare. To better train for the contest, I chose to practice in a halfpipe (channel constructed in the snow) that was considered extra difficult with a steep radius. I spent three to four days a week on the "Seegrube" (ski resort above Innsbruck) practicing all the tricks I wanted to perform. My highlights were two extra difficult airs, one a "Frontside 540 Indy Grab" (a 540° turn in the air grabbed with one hand and with a blind landing) and the other a "Backflip" (summersault in the air). To simulate the real conditions during the contest, I even practiced at night to adjust to the artificial light. I also went to the gym to strengthen my leg muscles and endurance.

On the night of the contest I was confident to get a top spot, given my rigorous and disciplined training. When I arrived at the site I was shocked to see that the halfpipe was very different from the "regular" ones. The radius was small and the half pipe was divided into two sections, which was combined by a flat section with a couple of small ramps. When it was my turn, I barely managed to do my tricks and I even fell once. It was a disaster and I was extremely disappointed. Although this setback seemed bigger at the time, it taught me a lesson. Practice and dedication are obviously important things but understanding the goal in terms of context is critical. This is the same whether it is sports or business. Today, for example, I would never just write a speech or prepare a report and get ready to present it unless I knew whom my audience was.

■ ■ ■

Candidate's biography: Maurice is male, Portuguese, educated in Spain

Describe a setback, disappointment, or occasion of failure that you have experienced. How did you manage the situation, and what did you learn from it? (Harvard)

I have never felt more disappointed in my life than in September 1997 when I did not voice out my opinion against my cousin's decision to have an abortion. It was a time I will always regret and a situation I have never spoken about. I had always thought that I would try to not only perform good Catholic deeds but also encourage others to do the same whenever possible. But when it came to a true test of faith, I let my complacency of "staying away from trouble" take over my moral beliefs.

When I was living with my cousin in Los Angeles, she inadvertently became pregnant from having sex with an acquaintance she had only known for a few weeks. We later discovered that her acquaintance already had a family of his own and that he had lied to her about several things including his education, wealth, and love for her. Emotional about her predicament, she turned to me, her older cousin, for guidance. Although I was against abortion, all I could do was console her since I was afraid to offer her any advice that would have lifetime ramifications. Before I knew it, she had turned to her family who surprisingly decided for her to have an abortion to avoid losing face because of a fatherless child.

This incident is not only about pro-life or pro-choice – it is about learning the consequences of inaction and taking responsibility for it. I will never know if I could have averted her from having an abortion had I decided to fight for what I believe in. This experience taught me to become more decisive and face personal challenges with conviction, not shy away from them. Since this incident, I have become more mature, realizing that I have an obligation to become more vocal and put my opinion forth. Only in this way can I be assured of being more "truthful" to myself and others.

WRITING THE "WILDCARD" ESSAY

"Wildcard" type essay questions are used by schools to get an idea of who you are and, to this extent, these questions take the place of the traditional "who are you?" essays. For example, the traits you admire and write about in describing another person become the traits a reviewer will see in you. On another level, these essays are open-ended and are meant to assess your creativity.

> **EXAMPLE**
>
> "If you could walk in someone else's shoes for a day, whose would you choose and why?" (University of Chicago)

What are "wildcard" type questions? The following are some examples.

- Name three persons living or dead whom you would like to invite to dinner and what you would talk about.
- If you were an animal what kind would you be and why?
- Mention one day you would like to relive and why?
- Propose a question that we, the admissions committee, should have asked and answer it.
- The admissions committee has just reviewed your application. Write what has been written in your file.
- Describe a teacher/mentor you admire and explain why you admire him or her.

Common mistakes

Below are two of the common mistakes made by applicants when writing "wildcard" essays.

- Not revealing enough of their personal characteristics through these essays.
- Not briefly summarizing their experience, or giving a brief answer to the question, before going into full-blown description.

Winning approaches

Here are two tips for writing "wildcard" essays.

✍️ **Tip #52:** **Reveal as much of your character and personal strengths as possible—personal, professional, motivations, spiritual, emotional, intellectual, latent potential, insights, likes and dislikes. These essay questions invite (and expect) you to get fancy and take chances.**

✍️ **Tip #53:** **Briefly summarize and directly answer the question at hand before getting fancy (and do it in two or three sentences).**

SAMPLE "WILDCARD" ESSAYS

In the sample essay that follows, William opens his essay with such a summary, "The three persons whom I would invite to this special dinner, would be Winston Churchill, Tang Tai Zong (the second emperor of the Tang dynasty of China), and my late father." In the sample essay written by Tiffany, her first sentence acts as an implied answer to the question of which her favorite fruit is, "An apple is a most versatile fruit."

Candidate's biography: William is male, Chinese-Canadian, educated in Canada

If you chose any three people who have ever lived to join you for dinner, whom would you invite and why? (London Business School)

The three persons whom I would invite to this special dinner, would be Winston Churchill, Tang Tai Zong (the second emperor of the Tang dynasty of China), and my late father.

Before being British Prime Minister, Winston Churchill warned about the ascent of Adolf Hitler in post-WWI years. Few people, even in his own country, believed in Churchill; he had even been ridiculed for his insight into the Fuhrer's ambitions. However, he never ceased to point out Hitler's true intentions and, when WWII finally broke out, he vindicated himself by leading the British Empire from the brink of defeat to victory. I would invite Winston Churchill to dinner, in order to be inspired by his decisiveness and strong leadership in the face of immense pressure.

When Emperor Tai Zong received the reign of the Tang dynasty from his father in A.D. 626, China was war-torn after more than three centuries of civil war and was vulnerable from invasion by the Turkish nomads in present-day Mongolia. He set out to recruit the best ministers he could find, built a team out of them, and with their conscientious counsels restored China's civil stability and military might. In A.D. 630, he started a campaign against the Turks which ended in the khanate's rout and westward migration. I would invite Tang Tai Zong to dinner because I want to learn how to recruit outstanding advisors, form a think-tank with them, and motivate them to give prudent counsel freely.

Unlike the first two, my late father was not a historically famous man. He was serving as the deputy chief engineer of a railway in China when the Communists were marching down south in 1949. He escaped to Hong Kong as a refugee, only with the clothes on his body and a few dollars in his pocket. But, my mother told me, he never lost hope and confidence. When the construction industry took off in Hong Kong, my father managed to have himself hired by a big local construction firm, and eventually worked his way up to become chief engineer before leaving to launch his own subcontracting business. I would invite my late father to dinner, to remember old times and to be influenced by his perseverance and optimism.

■ ■ ■

Candidate's biography: Tiffany is female, English, educated in South Africa

If you had to choose to be a type of vegetable or fruit, which would you choose and why? (Oxford)

An apple is a most versatile fruit. It can make cider or pie. As a raw liquid it is juice, as a cooked solid it is pie. Apples are a diverse lot. They can be described as red, green, yellow, tiny, large (reaching four pounds I believe), tart, or sweet. Famous names of apples include Delicious, Golden Delicious, Macintosh, Rome Beauty, Jonathan, Granny Smith, and there is even a Crab named Apple. Some companies have put apple in their names and grown as well. I am thinking of Apple Records before Apple Computers.

If I were an apple there would be many places I could visit and still feel at home. Apple is a truly pervasive fruit. It can be found on all continents and most countries including Canada and the U.S., China and Japan, France and Italy, Poland and Russia, Iran, Australia and New Zealand, and last but not least, South Africa. Apple is also a complementary fruit. According to the strict rules of juicing, only fruits can be mixed with fruits and vegetables mixed with vegetables. Apple is the exception. Apple and carrot are a winning combination.

Unlike a perishable peach or pear, an apple is durable and can stay for a while before getting too ripe to eat. An apple is an apple you might say. There is no mistaking its identity. A tomato, on the other hand, is caught in a strange dilemma. It can be either a fruit or vegetable. Botanically it is a fruit because it contains seeds, but horticulturally it is a vegetable because it grows on a vine.

The apple is a recognized symbol of health and prosperity. It is said that, "An apple a day, keeps the doctor away." And there are other sayings that adorn the apple. "An apple does not fall far from the tree" means (I guess) that we take on the characteristics of those around us or perhaps that we cannot escape our backgrounds and culture. Whatever! I'd rather be an apple on an orchard tree, basking in the warmth of a summer's day.

■ ■ ■

Candidate's biography: Kyle is male, American, educated in Canada

Which recent development, world event, or book has most influenced your thinking and why? (Oxford)

I studied the award wining book *Siddhartha* by author Hermann Hesse during my philosophy course as an undergraduate. At first read, I thought this small novel was only about Buddhism. But when I examined it more closely for the purpose of writing a book critique I could see many interesting things. Since I was majoring in business, I began thinking about how this book might be similar to business and wrote some thoughts in my journal. In order to answer this question, I have restudied the book and read through my journal and would like to mention how the book has most influenced me.

Siddhartha is foremost a story of objectivity. Where would the story have gone if Siddhartha had stayed in the palace and never questioned anything or had the courage to go out alone? His struggle is like that of a true entrepreneur who must pursue a dream and follow a tough "path" in his quest for accomplishment.

The story is about how Siddhartha (the prince) gets an idea, tests that idea, receives feedback, tests that idea out again, and finally reaches his goal. Each time he runs into problems, he must reevaluate what he is doing and how he will next proceed. For example, Siddhartha first believes that the way to live is to be a Brahman. He lives a life but is not satisfied. He reevaluates. Is the answer over there? So Siddhartha pursues a another pasture – he joins the Samanas and is still searching. With the pursuit of Gotama, he thinks he has found a place, but realizes he must reject this and travel yet again. Along any one of these paths Siddhartha is actually successful. Through constant reevaluation he is able to make his experiences internal ("alone in the forest") and then go on to pursue a life in a village as a businessman for Kamaswami and confidant of Kamala. Each step of the way, he reevaluates his "success" and sets out again. Later he finds himself at the river learning from Vasudeva. Eventually he leaves to find his ultimate goal.

The story is also a study of perseverance. To some the story might seem like the ramblings of a philosopher. But it must be agreed that it is a story about a guy who gets dirty. It is about sweat. Siddhartha follows a grueling path toward the goal he seeks. His perseverance is interwoven with purpose: a purpose that is like a whip that has no mercy. Along the road to success are temptations and distractions. Some of these distractions almost lead to his death. He lives on the edge. He is a maverick. This experience could be translated to the story of a top notch business person, a Steve Jobs or a Bill Gates, fighting with feelings of self-doubt before the world knows them for who they can be.

Perseverance requires courage and bravery. Even without vision or a purpose the journey would have been wasted if efforts were not fully used. Siddhartha has talent and intelligence but he also has courage. His courage – his spirit – it is a bird that can never die.

Lastly, *Siddhartha* is a story of appreciation. Appreciation is an offshoot of both objectivity and perseverance. How many times does Siddhartha think he has it figured things out only to be back on the drawing chart? We can't help but wonder how many times he will have to think again. The process of anticipating thinking again is what I call appreciation. The process of seeing *two* where there was previously only *one* is another sign of appreciation. Siddhartha does not become cynical by his experiences. He remains appreciative and balanced.

Siddhartha also holds strategic lessons in terms of understanding the roles of leader vs. manager. Siddhartha played the role of manager when he worked alongside Kamaswami. As a manager Siddhartha confronted what it was like to be responsible for people and the daily operations of a business. This is a characteristic that most distinguishes a manager. A manager is responsible. The characteristic that most distinguishes a leader is a sense of vision or purpose. A leader is creative and doesn't always lead through words or instructions but often through emotions or feelings or inspirations. Siddhartha leads Govinda in this way. Not all the things he communicates to Govinda can be read, spoken, or heard. A leader exercises non-verbal communication. Siddhartha is all a worker, manager, leader, and individualist.

This book continues to have an effect on me because it shows me how there are many lessons to apply to business that come from places outside of business. If a person can use the mind fully, the ability to find lessons in one area of life and transfer them to other areas is a most useful tool.

WRITING THE "ANALYZE A BUSINESS SITUATION" ESSAY

"Business situation" questions cover great latitude, and therefore it is difficult to comment on all possible types in a specific way. This type of question appears to be gaining in popularity in recent years among business school admissions officers.

EXAMPLE

At Wharton, the Learning Team, which consists of approximately five first-year students, is often assigned group projects and class presentations. Imagine that, one year from now, your Learning Team has a marketing class assignment due at 9 a.m. on Monday morning. It is now 10 p.m. on Sunday night; time is short, tension builds and your team has reached an impasse. What role would you take in such a situation? How would you enable the team to meet your deadline? (Note: The specific nature of the assignment is not as important here as the team dynamics.) Feel free to draw on previous experiences, if applicable, in order to illustrate your approach. (University of Pennsylvania [Wharton])

Common mistakes

Common mistakes made by applicants when writing "analyze a business situation" essays are:

- Not thinking about all aspects of a problem as required by an all-round thinking process.
- Not breaking the essay into distinct sub-components as required by an analytical approach to problem solving.

Winning approaches

Two of the winning ways to tackle such essays are:

Tip #54: Consider scenario analysis.

Consider as many aspects of a business problem as possible. Occasionally, scenario planning is required if asked what might happen or what might be the problem and/or solution. One approach is to say that there are three potential problem areas and, therefore, three potential solutions to complement each problem. In the case where you are required to sketch a business plan, do not forget to mention each of these major components: summary, product, people, market and customer, competition, and financing.

In situations where you have an open-ended essay which does not specify a particular company, product, or person, you may want to center your discussion on a fictitious company, product, or person. The upcoming essay, written by Caroline, illustrates this technique through her use of a hypothetical employee named "David".

Tip #55: Signpost your discussion using enumeration.

Refer to Chapter 10: *Packaging Your MBA Essays and Application* for a description of this technique.

SAMPLE "ANALYZE A BUSINESS SITUATION" ESSAYS

Candidate's biography: Caroline is female, Jewish, educated in Israel

As a graduate of the Stern MBA program, you are a successful manager and responsible for hiring people in your department. It now appears you may have made a mistake. An employee you selected six months ago is not performing at an acceptable level. You have confronted this person, reviewed performance expectations, and given constructive suggestions for improvement. However, the employee's performance has not improved and you have decided this cannot continue. How will you handle the situation? (New York University)

Let us take a hypothetical scenario in which I am sales director of ABC Co. who has made the mistake of hiring "David" for my department. Although David has not performed to an acceptable level by meeting sales goals in the past three months, I have decided to give him another chance. Given that I am a compassionate person with good interpersonal skills, I see three options to consider in resolving this dilemma:

1. Keep him in my department but assign him to a different position; or
2. Transfer him to another department but keep him in our company; or
3. Terminate his employment.

First, my preferred action would be to give David another chance at another position within my department, provided he has the rudimentary skill-set. In my current job as a human resource consultant, one of the lessons I learned is that different people have different motivational levels. An intense line position with profit and loss responsibilities is more suitable for an ambitious achiever as opposed to a behind-the-scenes staff position. David may perform better in a support function with a base salary rather than in a sales position with a commission-based salary. He may not be as financially motivated as he is motivated by job stability.

Secondly, I would consider transferring David from my department to another department if his skill-sets are suitable to another department. Through my interactions with many department managers, I have found that because an employee cannot perform in one department does not mean he cannot excel in another department. In the case of David, perhaps his strong analytical skills are more attuned to finance models than to the marketing world.

As a last resort, if David is not responsive to my suggestions to stay within the company, then I will terminate his employment. I will suggest that he go to personnel for a career skills assessment test. It may be that he would be effective in a different industry and may not realize it. His failure in his job might be a blessing in disguise. I may have helped David save some time by encouraging him to find a job he can excel in.

■ ■ ■

Candidate's biography: Rodriquez is male, Brazilian, educated in the U.S.

At Wharton, the Learning Team, which consists of approximately five first-year students, is often assigned group projects and class presentations. Imagine that, one year from now, your Learning Team has a marketing class assignment due at 9 a.m. on Monday morning. It is now 10 p.m. on Sunday night, time is short, tension builds and your team has reached an impasse. What role would you take in such a situation? How would you enable the team to meet your deadline? Feel free to draw on previous experience, if applicable, in order to illustrate your approach. (The University of Pennsylvania [Wharton])

Teamwork is my "specialty". Although I am not always a person who can draw insightful theories about teamwork, I am a team player who can always make significant contributions to the efficiency and effectiveness of the team. My understanding of team dynamics was strengthened by my experience in organizing activities in university, preparing team assignments during my Masters of Accounting degree program, and coordinating financing proposals at Credit Suisse First Boston (CSFB).

I see five steps involved in a team project. The steps are *problem identification*, *data gathering, solution planning, implementation, and evaluation.* As Wharton students are usually highly motivated individuals, by 10 p.m. on Sunday night, I assume that we would have at least gathered the necessary data and would be about to start our third stage, *solution planning.*

Given the time constraint, I see three potential scenarios that would overcome such an impasse. I would play a different role in each scenario to facilitate timely completion. The three scenarios are:

  i)   We have the same solution. ☺
  ii) We have different solutions. ☺
  iii) We have no solution at all. ☹

In the **first scenario**, I would play the role of a *coordinator*. This is the most common situation that I face in the investment banking industry. At CSFB, we often already know the financing solution for a client company. However, the greatest challenge is often "tying up" our credentials, views, and methodologies together under immense time pressure. Based on my experience, once the solution is identified, there are four sub-steps in the *implementation* and *evaluation* process. First, I would suggest that my team outline the project. Once we agree upon the outline, we would first determine which part of the project is the most critical. The critical part would be done with priority and given most attention.

Second, each part would be drafted primarily by one person, and the most critical part would be drafted by two or more persons. We would also agree on the deadline for the first draft of each part, for example, by 4 a.m. Third, once we have the first draft (combined or not), each person would orally present his/her part and receive feedback from other team members. Each member would then further modify his/her own part to incorporate the additional suggestions. Finally, at around 6:30 a.m., we would circulate the second draft and finalize any changes if needed. From putting numerous proposals together under a tight deadline, I learned that time management and polishing the critical parts or key messages are most critical to the success of any project.

In the **second scenario**, I would play the role of a *moderator*. With two different solutions under time constraint, we could first continue to debate the solution indefinitely and end up putting minimal effort into actual implementation of the solutions, or even miss the deadline at 9 a.m. Clearly, the outcome is not acceptable. Second, we could impose a deadline for determining a solution, for example, by 2 a.m. From my experience in my Masters of Accounting program, we often had to determine the accounting treatment of many unusual activities. Although there is no one rule that specifically defined the situation, there are many conceptual statements or related pronouncements that would hint at the correct solution. My experience tells me that when there are different solutions, it is optimal to break down the solutions into different components. Understanding that each member has his/her own *rationale*, I would suggest that the team members present their ideas to other members. After examining and understanding the source of differences, we should either slowly narrow them down to one solution, or more likely, we should be able to integrate the best parts of different solutions and subsequently create a better approach to the problem.

However, if there is still no consensus by 2 a.m., we would then have to pick the two alternative routes. First, given the diverse background of my Learning Team, we can create a self-imposed hierarchy in the team and allow the person with the most relevant experience and background to determine the solution and drive the entire process. For example, assuming it is a marketing project about introducing new vehicles to Japan, our group member named "Keio", a Japanese who worked for Toyota as a sales manager, will become our team leader. Second, if there is no such person, we should simply take a *vote* and the majority would rule and drive the entire process.

In the **third scenario**, I would play the role of a *leader*. With no solution on hand, the deadline could be easily missed. In such a situation, there would be two options. First, I would impose the deadline for a solution at, for example, 2 a.m. Before the deadline, I would lead the team to attack the problem using an "analytical approach". I would take the lead to break down the project into as many little components as possible, and analyze the approach to each component separately. It is similar to my experience as the president of the Hong Kong USC Students' Club. As a newly-elected president, one of my goals was to promote memberships. I also had no solution initially. However, once I broke down the problem into many components affecting memberships, for example, membership fees, nature of activities, club image and profile, and effectiveness of organizational structure, etc., I tackled each component separately. As a result, membership tripled to over 200 under my leadership. Therefore, I believe, the "analytical approach" should at least enable us to identify partial solutions to the project. Second, if we cannot identify a solution by 2 a.m., I would find one based on our partial results and our best estimates. As long as we can carefully explain our rationale, we should be able to get credit for our educated estimates. The bottom line is "something is always better than nothing."

In any scenario, effective communications, mutual understanding, commitment to hard work, and cohesiveness are key factors for successful teamwork. I am confident that I could contribute positively to those aspects of my Learning Team at the Wharton School.

■ ■ ■

Candidate's biography: Alice is female, Hong Kong-Chinese, educated in the U.S.

(Dartmouth, Tuck) A well-known, multinational company has a long-term contract to extract previous metals in an impoverished region in a developing country. Over the past decade, the operation has proven very profitable to the company. Recently, there have been peaceful, but highly disruptive, demonstrations by members of communities adjacent to the company's property. The ruling military dictatorship has been unresponsive in meeting the local communities' needs. The local communities are now demanding a share of the mining operation's profits in the form of approximately US$8 million to provide clean water and basic sanitation for the surrounding villages.

You have recently been promoted and sent to this country as the expatriate general manager responsible for the operation. The mine is assessed US$20 million in annual taxes by the government. This year you will show a US$50 million after-tax profit if you elect not to address the request of the local community. Your team has worked very hard this year. A US$50 million profit is the minimum level to ensure that your team meets its bonus plan.

Provide an analysis of your options.

Describe what you would do.

Discuss the rationale for your choice.

Address your plan to communicate with any constituent affected by your decision.

The case is a classic management dilemma of achieving profits while caring for the local communities. On one hand, our company must guarantee at least US$50 million after-tax profit to fulfill the bonus plan of my diligent team. On the other hand, we must promptly address the local needs to maintain the privileges of conducting business in the country.

To seek an effective resolution, we must first understand the three critical success factors of our mining operation:

1. The revenue drivers are rates of output and productivity. Therefore, our company's profitability relies heavily upon free access to abundant precious metals and cheap local labor.
2. We must skillfully balance the interests of all stakeholders: our operation, our employees, the local communities, and the ruling military dictatorship.
3. As we help settle the unrest by addressing the public's concerns, we will also build goodwill toward our brand.

After thorough analysis, as the operation's new expatriate general manager, I have identified and evaluated three options as follows:

Option (1): Maintain the US$50 million after-tax profit so as to fulfill the team's bonus plan.

This option is consistent with the objective function of commercial enterprises in a capitalistic world. As my team has worked hard, they are entitled to receive the financial rewards for their fruitful labor. However, this option prioritizes the short-term financial interests of our operation and our employees above the long-term well-being of the local communities. Therefore, Option (1) fails to address the needs of the local communities, and would cause the local military dictatorship to endure continuous public protests. As a result, this is a win-lose option.

Option (2): Recognize the concerns of the local communities and donate a portion of the profit to environmental projects.

This option prioritizes the long-term well-being of the local communities above the short-term financial interests of our operation and our employees. The donation would help improve the living conditions of the surrounding villages, and benefit the dictatorship by avoiding further disruptive public unrest while still maintaining the stipulated tax income. However, we would forsake the team's bonus plan and risk dampening their morale and our company's future performance. As a result, this is also a win-lose option.

Option (3): Jointly raise the US$8 million with the local communities, and establish a new profit-sharing plan for long-term community development. This represents a win-win situation and is the recommended course of action.

This option aims at attaining the long-term well-being of the local communities as well as the long-term financial health of our operation and our employees, through a new profit-sharing plan. The essence of the new plan is to bond the interests of, and share risks among all key stakeholders.

Under the new plan, our company would first establish a shared goal among employees and the local communities to enhance our productivity and develop innovative mining methods to increase output. The objective of enhanced collaboration is to achieve higher, sustainable profitability for our mining operation that would help fund local community projects in the long run. With the improved profitability, our company would donate, from after-tax profit in excess of US$50 million, up to US$8 million in the first year to provide clean water and sanitation facilities. Meanwhile, employee bonuses for this year would be paid out from the US$50 million after-tax profit. In the next five years, our company would donate five percent of the excess to community projects. We would distribute another five percent as additional bonuses to employees, while retaining the remainder for internal operations. At the same time, we would petition the government for tax credits on the ground that our plan has channeled the energy of a potentially large-scale social unrest, which would destabilize the business and political environment, to benefiting the development of the local communities.

This is a win-win option that balances the interests of all stakeholders. Our company would achieve a higher profitability while fulfilling its greater social responsibility toward the local communities. Our employees would benefit as the new plan promises additional bonuses, while their morale would also be boosted as a result of the public goodwill generated. The local communities would not only receive the donation required for providing clean water and sanitation facilities, but also take an active role in maintaining a healthy environment through participation in our plan. Finally, the local government would avoid unnecessary public protests.

Furthermore, Option (3) would also allow our company to build a solid foundation for long-term growth and profitability in the country along three dimensions:

1. *Developing corporate citizenship.* Externally, the plan is a bold expression of our commitment to the well-being of the local communities. Through sharing our profits, we would demonstrate our pledge to grow with the communities. Internally, the plan would help develop future generations of employees who can appreciate and shoulder corporate responsibility.

2. *Establishing regional industry leadership early on.* The plan would open new avenues for deepening our existing relationships with the local government and communities. It would also help us achieve competitive advantage over our competitors by establishing our regional industry leadership early on.

3. *Achieving long-term economic viability.* By drawing public interest to our success, the plan would enable us to leverage local manpower and expertise in exploring opportunities to streamline operations, increase productivity, and achieve long-term profitability.

At the execution level, I would propose a three-tiered communication approach targeting all stakeholders:

■ *Communication to employees.* This first-tier level of communication will solicit company-wide support and feedback. In forms of corporate memo and discussion forums, this communication will detail the rationales and policies of the new plan, and emphasize its important role in the long-term financial success of our company and our employees.

■ *Communication to the government.* This second-tier level of communication will petition government support of and contribution to the plan. It will be conducted through face-to-face meetings with key government officials, since government cooperation is critical to ensure our smooth transition into the new plan.

■ *Communication to the local communities.* This third-tier level of communication will formally announce details of the plan while soliciting public support. Conducted through press conference and advertising campaigns, this communication will also reinforce the primary objective of the plan: Help develop the local communities while furthering our growth.

CHAPTER 5

Essay Writing Part III:
Optional Essay Entries

"Don't view your essay as an academic article or a business memo, but as a human interest story about yourself."

Linda Abraham, Admissions Consultant

INTRODUCTION

Below is an example of an optional or "blank" question.

EXAMPLE

The Admissions Committee would like to know if you wish to address anything not mentioned in your essays or application. Please feel free to leave this area blank if you feel you have adequately presented your case.

The questions below are answered often, and sometimes only, through use of the blank question.

- How do you show diversity of character?
- How do you truly differentiate yourself from other candidates?
- Where do you address an anticipated weakness in your application?
- How do you show you are an interesting person?
- Where do you elaborate on your work experience?
- How do you further show your ability to handle detail and creative challenges?
- How do you illustrate your insight and intelligence?
- How do you embellish your strengths?
- ???

TIPS FOR WRITING OPTIONAL ESSAYS

A real secret to putting together a first-class application lies in taking advantage of the optional or "blank" question. The blank question is probably the most under-utilized area of business school applications. It is estimated that only ten percent of business school applicants address this question. And when candidates choose to do so, it is generally only used to address an anticipated *weakness* in their applications, in particular, "Why I have a lower than average GMAT score or GPA?" But there are many more dimensions to the optional question. In fact it is as much an opportunity to embellish your strengths as it is a place to address weaknesses.

A few well-developed optional essay entries can add a whole new dimension to your application. There are many things in your background—hobbies, interests, sports, awards, recognition, service projects, work projects, mentors, and virtually anything you feel is important—that could be the topic of an optional essay. Do not let something that you feel passionate about get reduced to just a single sentence or a one-line entry hidden away in your essay, employment record, or list of extracurricular and community activities. There may be no other place to draw attention to your piece and this may be just the kind of thing that could help your application catch fire enroute to acceptance.

Even in terms of academic strengths, do not think that everything can be read from your academic transcripts or that the whole of your academic experience comes down to a single grade point average. You may want to help the reader understand what the full significance of your academic experience is. If you have a high GPA, take half a page in the blank question area and say exactly what it means to you and why it is important. You might mention some habits or ideas you picked up along the way that spelled success in the academic arena. At a minimum you might say how you committed yourself to your studies and how commitment is the key to your future business success. Perhaps you do not have a high GPA but were a double major or perhaps you wrote a particularly interesting senior thesis or research paper.

Business schools want diverse, intelligent, and compassionate people to fill their classes. Your main essays alone are generally an insufficient medium to present yourself as a unique and creative individual. In all likelihood, no business school application can really explore all the attributes of a complex and unique individual. The optional question provides you with an opportunity to explore some different areas. When you finish writing your standard application essays for a given school, ask yourself: "Do my essays, employment record, and extracurricular activities really describe me?" If your answer is, "Yes", stop. If your answer is, "No, they do not describe me in a complete way", then you may need to address your untouched attributes through additional entries. It is recommended that all business school applicants consider creating at least two optional question entries. Possible topics follow in this chapter.

Most candidates will not put serious effort into the optional application questions, and admissions committee members cannot help but be impressed by a candidate who knocks him- or herself out in preparing the application. They will believe you think very highly of their particular school because you put so much effort into the application.

Tip #56: Readability is of paramount importance. Try to keep each entry to a single page. You must make every effort to help the committee get through your optional questions. Think of the reviewer as skimming through your additional information.

Make your entries well-organized and of high quality and the admissions committee will perceive you as a well-organized professional who produces high-quality work. The most common argument for not including anything in the optional area is: "Why should I do anything extra? The admissions committee must consist of busy people, they do not have time to read this stuff." While it is true that admissions officers are very busy, they do have an allotted amount of time to spend on reviewing your application. Moreover, experienced admissions people develop a sixth sense for what is in an application. They know whether things are in order and whether there is substance to the application. Even if the admissions committee does not have time to read through all of your material, they can still go away with a favorable impression of what you choose to present.

Be extra brief and be hyper-sensitive about making it easy for the reviewer to get through your work. Unlike your essays and other required application components, "blank" questions are, after all, optional. You should definitely consider including a table of contents when including three or more items, and be sure to use headings on each page. Also, use one or more stylistic or readability tools for clarity—bolds, italics, indentations, enumerations, font sizes, shadings, as well as short sentences (see Chapter 10, *Packaging Your MBA Essays and Application*). Lastly, keep individual entries to three pages or less in length. Keeping each entry to *one page* (if possible) has the advantage of being psychologically manageable for the reader because everything is right in front of him or her.

All American business schools have an optional question. In fact, so does every single American undergraduate college. This is one of the hallmarks of American education. You are given every opportunity to express yourself and demonstrate your individuality.

The optional question must however, be viewed in the context of the business school to which you are applying. Different business schools have different degrees of tolerance toward the amount of material you include with your application. Harvard for example is said to not like much extra material. Try to add no more than one page if applying to Harvard Business School. But other American business schools such as Yale, Michigan, Northwestern, Stanford, and Chicago seem to look favorably at an applicant's attempt to go the extra distance and express his or her individuality. European business schools are at best intrigued, and at worse, indifferent toward use of the blank question. INSEAD gives candidates only 15 lines. A few other European schools even go as far as to say "do not include anything extra". But overall, for over 95 percent of the world's business schools, the blank question is exactly that—blank and wide open to use as you see fit.

> 🖎 **Tip #57: View the optional area as having five possible uses. Determine which of the five uses or combination of these will best serve you.**

The five uses of the optional area include: (1) clarifying issues and addressing weaknesses, (2) summarizing the strengths of your candidacy, (3) showing diversity of background and character, (4) showing evidence of solid work experience, and (5) elaborating on reasons for wanting to go to a particular business school.

THE FIVE USES OF THE OPTIONAL QUESTION

✔ Use #1 – Clarifying issues and addressing weaknesses

Points which serve to support your current application may include a discussion of anticipated application weaknesses, e.g., "I have a low GPA or GMAT score" or may include a discussion to clarify an issue, for example, "You may wonder whether my three-year undergraduate degree is equivalent to a four-year U.S. degree—let me explain."

☑ Use #2 – Summarizing the strengths of your candidacy

An optional question entry might be used to summarize your whole application as if you were doing the work of an admissions officer. It can be a powerful and persuasive tool to get the committee to make a favorable admissions decision. Make your assessment impressive and the admissions officer may adopt your summary as his or hers.

☑ Use #3 – Showing diversity of background and character

Concentrate on those things which serve to show your versatility and uniqueness of character. These may include reference to your favorite hobby, travel experience, cultural background, unusual experience, community service, volunteer work, art work, creative writing sample, etc.

☑ Use #4 – Showing evidence of solid work experience

Concentrate on those things which serve to support your solid work experience. These may include on-the-job projects, tasks, or assignments which show either breadth (variety) or depth (intensity) of experience. Your experience should highlight professional abilities, such as your decision-making skills, business acumen, integrity, character, or dedication.

☑ Use #5 – Elaborating on reasons for wanting to go to a particular business school

As covered in the "Why XYZ School Question" (Chapter 3), it is prudent advice to sell a school on your reasons for wanting them in particular, rather than the MBA in general. If you feel, for any reason, that you have not been able to fully articulate this, then err on the side of writing more, not less.

WHAT ARE SOME OPTIONAL TOPICS YOU CAN WRITE ABOUT?

☑ Use #1 – Clarifying issues and addressing weaknesses

- lower than average undergraduate GPA
- lower than average GMAT score
- why a particular three-year college degree is equivalent to a four-year degree
- why I cannot get a recommendation from my current employer
- overcoming difficult situations, handicaps, illness, accidents, or tragedy

✔ Use #2 – Summarizing the strengths of your candidacy

- high GPA
- good work experience
- high test scores
- interesting cultural background
- unusual achievements
- special research completed
- impressive work titles
- significant on-the-job achievements
- community service awards
- unique hobbies or interests
- business vision
- personal experience dealing with a social problem
- athletic achievements
- articles written
- books published
- difficult situations overcome
- international travel

✔ Use #3 – Showing diversity of background and character

- what being from country X means to me
- my favorite hobby, sport, or outside interest
- the challenges of an interracial marriage or relationship
- a copy of an important speech
- plot summary of a book in progress
- excerpt from a published work
- a special award or recognition
- time spent as an exchange student
- a community service project
- proposed research project you want to undertake while at business school

✔ Use #4 – Showing evidence of solid work experience

- my most challenging work project
- my most difficult customer
- sample analysis of a business situation
- where my chosen company or industry is headed
- a brochure containing information on my startup business venture or hobby

✔ Use #5 – Elaborating on reasons for wanting to go to a particular business school

See Chapter 3, *Writing the "Why XYZ School?" Essay* and *Ten Tips for Writing the "Why XYZ School?" Essay* on pages 62–66.

MAKING OPTIONAL ESSAY ENTRIES

Sample entry—"The five Chinese elements"

The easiest way to make an optional essay entry is to simply borrow a single essay that you wrote as a standard essay for another school. That is, if you have completed a particularly interesting essay as part of an application for another school then, by all means, include it as an optional essay entry for your current school. Try to limit your optional essays to one or two pages in length, single spaced. In the case of Candidate #1, Audrey's optional essay appearing here is essentially a condensed version of her seven-page long Stanford Essay A viewed in Chapter 3. The idea of using five Chinese elements—metal, wood, water, earth, fire—as representative of her life worked well for her. Therefore, for schools other than Stanford she submitted the following essay, single spaced, as an optional piece.

Candidate's biography: Audrey is female, Chinese-American, educated in the U.S.

Introduction

Throughout history, mankind has tried to explain the events and situations encountered in life through philosophical and mystical means. The Chinese have a unique way to explain their lives and their world through an understanding of the five elements which comprise all matter: *metal*, *wood*, *water*, *earth*, and *fire*. In the same way that these elements can characterize all matter, they can metaphorically characterize each of our lives, our health, and destiny, not to mention how we interact in society, how we affect others and our immediate surroundings and vice-versa, and ultimately, how we affect the world. These elements, collectively, produce both a creative and a destructive cycle, eventually bringing balance and harmony in our lives. Through a review of the symbolism of each of these elements, I would like to explain the influences of how the people, events, and situations in my life have shaped who I am today.

Metal

Metal symbolizes my chosen profession in the field of architecture. Architecture has been influential in my life as an art form that integrates multiple disciplines in both its academic approach as well as professional application. Through my undergraduate studies and working career, I have infused the disciplines of analytical skills, scientific knowledge of physics, environmental science, geology, mathematics, and art for the constant experimentation of architectural forms, into daily use in the form of critical analysis, strategic thinking, and creative problem solving.

Wood

Wood is symbolic of my artistic and creative abilities. As the source material for all paper products, wood symbolizes a relevant point in my childhood. At age eight, I was the youngest person at that time to have exhibited a piece of artwork at the Oakland Museum. In my third grade class, I had produced entirely from mental images and my hands, a papier-mâché Thai elephant which was so realistic in its effect that my teacher, Mrs O'Neill, presented it to the school principal. The school principal suggested and arranged for it to be exhibited at the Oakland Museum to encourage program support for art studies at the elementary school level. After the exhibition was over, my father proudly featured my elephant on his desk in his private den. Throughout my life, it proved as a constant reminder to me that I had creative skills which set me apart from most other people and encouraged the artistic development of my young mind. The elephant papier-mâché project saw the beginning of my artistic and creative aspiration, which has been a common thread in my life, whether this talent is applied toward my work, my hobbies, or my perceptions and appreciation for aesthetic values in life.

Water

The element water is representative of my Chinese cultural and international background. The Pacific Ocean is the body of water that connects East to West, or my ancestral home of China with my physical home in the U.S. This waterway has had a profound influence on my life in many ways, including insight and admiration for other cultures in the world and the ability to learn multiple languages. From the time I was an infant, I had traveled back and forth from Asia to the States, first as a necessity while my father was serving in the U.S. Army as a medical officer, then later to visit my grandparents and other family members who live in China and Hong Kong, and recently as I have been working in Hong Kong. The travel experienced when I was younger most profoundly influenced me in my language abilities. As a four-year-old going to kindergarten in Hong Kong, I was compelled to speak, read, and write Chinese, although I only knew how to speak English at the time. By the time I had begun to learn and understand some Chinese, my family moved to Seoul, Korea where my father served in the U.S. Army as a medical officer. There, at the International School, I was taught in English but also was exposed to the Korean language. A year later, we moved again, this time back to the States to Monterey, California. My struggles with languages and as a result, identity, had initially provided me with challenges as a child but subsequently, with strength in knowing I can accomplish whatever goals I set.

Earth

In its elemental form, earth symbolizes my well-grounded belief systems. As an earthquake tests the stability of the ground, so have my belief systems been tested by the professional endeavors I have undertaken. Last year, I reported a case of bribery arising from one of our business dealings to my manager who in turn reported it to the director of our client company. Subsequent to this situation being remedied, I have not again personally encountered a similar situation since. However, I find myself in touch with peers and other members of my industry who are confronted with such decisions with increasing frequency. My advice to them is to do their best to discourage the development of such behavior and to uphold the principles by which our industry has traditionally thrived.

Fire

On the morning of October 20, 1991, our family home of 20 years was engulfed by fire. It was the most devastating event of our lives, the loss of our home to the fire that raged through the Oakland and Berkeley Hills burning down thousands of homes, destroying a once-beautiful tree-nestled hillside community in the East Bay. I was home that morning of the fire and was the first in my family to notice the dark gray clouds of smoke amidst the clear blue skies of the Indian summer's day in northern California. My mother, my little brother, and I were the only ones home that Sunday morning as my father was on-call at the hospital and my sister was still away at law school. We were given 15 minutes to evacuate our home and in the hustle of packing two cars with our life's possessions, we had forgotten our family photographs. To this day and forever forward, we will only cherish those images in our minds as those precious photos are gone forever. I will never forget the sight of the charred and smoldering land where our family home once stood when, two days after the fire, my mother and I were finally allowed to view the damages in person. Chinese TV Channel 26 apparently was in the area filming some of the damage and caught on film my mother and I as we collapsed at the brick footsteps of our previous home which had become a mountain of hot ashes. I learned a valuable lesson from the whole experience. I learned that nothing is more important to me than the safety and togetherness of my family. We had survived the drastic event together and it no longer mattered to me that I lost forever all my yearbooks, family heirlooms and valuables, mementos from our past, and even the papier-mâché elephant which made my father so proud.

■ ■ ■

Sample entry – "Chess versus *Go*"

Since you are applying to business school, suppose that you want to create something for the blank question area—something creative, impressive, different—but you are not sure what it should be. You can:

- **First, pick a topic.** Start with your *hobbies* or *interests*. Say, for example, that you have had a long-standing interest in the game of chess and as a result of your being stationed in Asia—Korea, Japan, China or the like—you have taken to the game of *Go*, Asia's version of the Western game of chess.

- **Secondly, force a question.** One day you wonder, "Are these games just randomly different or is there some meaning behind the difference between chess and *Go* that reflect Eastern and Western cultural differences?" You also wonder if there might be some way these two games hint at understanding modern business strategy in each respective region of the world.
- **Thirdly, sketch.** To sketch things out, choose a grid-like diagram.

Game	Differences
Chess	? ? ?
Go	? ? ?

- **Fourthly, add structure.** Thinking a little more, you come up with three major differences between these games based on the different kinds of playing pieces, the different types of moves possible, and the objectives of each game.

Game	Differences	Interpretation
Chess	⇒ Playing pieces ⇒ Moves ⇒ Each game's objectives	? ? ?
Go	⇒ Playing pieces ⇒ Moves ⇒ Each game's objectives	? ? ?

- **Fifthly, fill in.** Filling things in, eventually an outline emerges. You might present it exactly as it appears below, or recraft it in written narrative form. Better yet, you may turn to concentrate on one aspect of the original question: "Do these games reflect modern business strategy?" See Exhibit 5–1 for a comparison between chess and *Go*.

Exhibit 5–1   Creating optional entries – Chess versus *Go*

Game	Differences	Interpretation
Chess	■ **Playing pieces** – called chess men. • diversity of individual playing pieces. • different pieces, i.e., King Queen, Bishop, Knight, Rook, Pawn; individually carved pieces. ■ **Movement** – varied and "uninhibited" directional movements based on the identity of a given chess piece. ■ **Objective** – to remove players from the board and to bring into checkmate (capture, surrender) the opponent's King – symbol of the most important piece in the game.	■ Belief in the individuality of inputs and the acknowledgment of human character and uniqueness. ■ Ability to make varied moves of surprising capacity and significant consequence signifying the dynamics of individual input. ■ Chess is a connected "individualistic" game. Why, because chess pieces generally remain in close proximity to one another during the game but look different in appearance (retain individual characteristics) and share unequal values. Chess signifies the idea of hierarchy and progression to the top, as there is only one King and one Queen – they stand higher than the other smaller pieces who exist to serve and protect them. Chess indicates the importance of individuality as well as the Western concept of annihilation and conquest.
Go	■ **Playing pieces** – called stones. • uniformity of individual playing pieces. • identical small button-like objects. • set colors: black or white. ■ **Movement** – simple forward movements are restricted to one space per move as analogous to pawns in the game of chess. ■ **Objective** – to control the board by capturing the greatest amount of space on the playing surface and, secondarily, to remove pieces (stones) to achieve this objective.	■ Belief in the expendability of resources and the intrinsic parity of all pieces. ■ Simple directional moves show limitations of individual stones but their ability to be placed in open "uncharted" regions which later become pivotal is the hallmark of long-term thinking. ■ *Go* is a disconnected "collective" game. Why? Because *Go* pieces need not be placed in close proximity of one another on the board but always look equal in appearance and share equal value. ■ *Go* signifies the Eastern concept of space and expendability of human or state property; space is the most valuable possession; pieces show parity of status and submission to the grand scheme; uniformity of pieces implies there is even more power in the holder of power – be it emperor, zaibatsu, company, etc.

SAMPLE OPTIONAL ESSAY ENTRIES FOR THE FIVE USES

☑ Use #1 – Clarifying issues and addressing weaknesses
Candidate's biography: Camilla is female, Danish, educated in Denmark

The purpose for this entry is to explain why the candidate's three-year degree from Denmark is equivalent to and/or perhaps substitutable for a four-year U.S. degree. It is appropriate for candidates to address this type of clarifying issue through the optional question.

Essay title: The equivalency of my three-year undergraduate degree

I am aware that XYZ school normally requires a four-year bachelor's degree in order to meet entrance qualification for your MBA studies. Therefore, I would like to take this opportunity to explain to the committee why my bachelor's degree is a three-year degree and also why I still believe I am at a sufficient academic level to qualify and succeed in your program.

The Copenhagen Business School, my undergraduate school, only offers three-year bachelor's degrees. A four-year bachelor's degree is not an option. In addition to my undergraduate studies, I studied one year in France and three months in a graduate school in the U.S., which further add to my academic skills and my belief that I will be qualified to complete your program successfully.

The level of education in Denmark is high and I am confident that my academic level is equivalent to those who hold a four-year bachelor's degree from other countries. This opinion is supported by the PIER report "Denmark, A Study of the Educational System of Denmark and Guide to the Academic Placement of Students in Educational Institutions in the United States" published by the American Association of Collegiate Registrars and Admissions Officers, NAFSA. This report, conducted by Valeria A. Woolston, Director of International Education Services, University of Maryland at College Park and Karlene N. Dickey, Associate Dean of Graduate Studies Emerita, Stanford University, recommends American schools accept the Danish bachelor's degree as an equivalent to the American four-year bachelor's degree.

■ ■ ■

The following entry is to explain why the candidate could not obtain a recommendation from his current employer as is often requested by business schools. Since many business schools specifically request a recommendation from your current boss, candidates nowadays are generally required to write responses like the one that follows on the next page.

Candidate's biography: Conrad is male, American, educated in the U.S.

Essay title: No professional recommendation from my current employer

I was unable to ask for a letter of reference from my current employer, because if I did, my chances of obtaining a future promotion or pay raise would greatly diminish. I talked to Ms Jennifer Merle of your admissions office by phone on October 11 about this matter. I conveyed to her the difficulty of securing three professional reference letters, as I have had only two jobs since graduating from university, and asked her if I could substitute with a non-professional letter of reference from a member of the American Chamber of Commerce here in Brussels. She conferred and said it was the best option next to submitting a professional letter of reference.

■ ■ ■

What do you do if you have a "low" GMAT score and you think it will hurt your chances for admission? Why not address your lower than average GMAT score so that the admissions committee will not think you are underestimating the importance of the GMAT. You can also minimize the exam's effect on your overall application if you cite other cases where you have succeeded in your quantitative (numbers) and/or qualitative (verbal) endeavors. Also, refer to Chapter 2, *Most Frequently Asked MBA Admissions Questions,* question #8.

Candidate's biography: Bernadette is female, Swiss, educated in France

Essay title: My lower than average GMAT score

My recent GMAT score of 550 falls below your average GMAT score of 650 as published in your admissions brochure for last year's entering class. My GMAT score also falls below my expectations because on my most recent practice tests taken under timed conditions, I achieved scores of 570 and 620.

I must admit to having some anxiety toward taking this kind of standardized test because these tests are unknown in the French education system. In addition, my extended overseas business trip just before the exam did not help either. However, rather than try to retake the test and miss your deadline for the second round, I have decided to apply with my 550 score. Upon examination, my math score component of the exam was 490 while my verbal score was 630. Regrettably, my undergraduate major of sociology did not provide the chance for me to take many courses in mathematical subjects. Of the few courses I took while at university, I received grades of B in Operational Statistics and A in Quantitative Decision-Making. Moreover, I am well versed in using computers as a result of preparing computer and financial spreadsheets for my current boss. In order to be ready for fall business school classes, I am planning on enrolling in a spring session math skills refresher course offered through our community's continuing education service as well as a calculus course during the upcoming summer.

■ ■ ■

✔ Use #2 – Summarizing the strengths of your candidacy

Candidate's biography: Josephine is female, Singaporean-Chinese, educated in Singapore

A young lady from Singapore as part of her application to INSEAD submitted the short essay below. The INSEAD Business School Application contains the following optional question: "Is there anything that you have not mentioned in the above essays that you would like the Admissions Committee to know?" (15-line limit). INSEAD has notoriously short essay questions with their recommended length for each response limited to 15 lines! Most candidates figure that 15 lines are not worth doing anything with and that the application ends here—but why leave the space blank? The strategy employed here is to use the blank question to sum up her whole application and to tell the admissions committee in a nutshell why she should be admitted. In this concise essay, we get an idea of her title, professional experience, vision and goals, as well as her academic qualifications, her linguistic ability, and her reasons for wanting to study in Europe, along with how she might contribute to the INSEAD community.

Essay title: Summary of my candidacy

My career goal of becoming an executive in the payment services industry in Asia would be strengthened with an MBA from INSEAD. Credit card "chip" technology is becoming a mass phenomenon, but it is in the European marketplace that we see the opportunity to learn from customization. I believe that the ability to understand European payment services holds the key to understanding diversity (marketing) in the future Asian context. At present, I have achieved top associate level position at "ABC credit card company" in Hong Kong (title: Members Relations Representative, Asia-Pacific region) and have received the mentorship and support of Ian Johnson, the region's CEO. My solid academic preparation includes an honors degree from the competitive National University of Singapore and a GMAT score of 700 (96th percentile). I am also fluent in Cantonese, Mandarin, and English. As an Asian female (Singaporean citizenship) with my mentioned career objective, my goal would be best advanced by the opportunity to study at INSEAD because I see it has the most international business program in the world. Furthermore, my flexible and energetic nature would help me build strong relationships with fellow students at INSEAD.

✔ Use #3 – Showing diversity of background and character

Candidate's biography: Camilla is female, Danish, educated in Denmark

Essay title: What my Danish nationality means to me

My Danish nationality and upbringing are clearly reflected in my personality. Having being born and having grown up in a small country in Northern Europe of approximately five million inhabitants makes me different from many people in a number of ways. Therefore I would like to tell the committee a little bit about my home country.

Denmark is one of the relatively few racially homogeneous countries in the Western world. We have a long history and a constitutional monarchy dating back to A.D. 900, and we do not have a long record of mixed cultures. Furthermore, Denmark is one of the few countries that really practices the welfare system. We have a high standard of social security and public services, including a high-quality educational sector. This means we do not have a big gap between poor and rich which is the case in many other countries. All this makes the Danes quite uniform and this is reflected in the average Dane's values and mindset. An example of a uniform belief is the Danes' belief in "The Jante Law", an unspoken law stating that you should not emphasize your own achievements over those of others.

Denmark is not only a small country in regard to population but also in area – 44,000 sq. km. Sixty-five percent of the country is farmland, which gives everybody the opportunity to go for a Sunday walk in the fields, and nowhere in Denmark is a person farther than 52 km. from the sea, which means that every child and adult has the unmistakable distinction of having been for a swim in the sea.

Denmark is governed by a democratically elected government and a parliament in a multiparty system. The Danes in general take interest in political issues and the rate of participation in elections is very high. This interest in politics concerns domestic as well as international matters. Recently, during the situation involving French nuclear testing, a group of Danes got on their bikes and rode all the way to France to speak their opinion.

Since I started traveling around the world my awareness of what it is to be Danish has become much clearer to me. I am probably more Danish now than when I was living in Denmark. And yet I appreciate so many other cultures and adapt some of these traits to my own. Although I do not applaud everything about Denmark and the Danish people, I am proud of my nationality.

■ ■ ■

Candidate's biography: Ben is male, American, educated in the U.S.

Many applicants think that it is necessary to write on an obscure topic in order to have an interesting piece of writing. This is not so. The following piece is written on an apparently simple topic but is nonetheless memorable.

Essay title: Either with friends or alone

One of the activities I enjoy most outside of the work environment is travel, either with friends or alone. I have found that when traveling with friends, the opportunity to see them outside of their everyday environment reveals facets of their personality which I would not have seen otherwise. There is also a certain camaraderie shared while traveling that transcends the barriers put up in everyday life. And since the conveniences of home are not readily available, there is a sense of urgency that accompanies the need to work together as a team. This need for teamwork seems to be especially important while traveling overseas. When I was working in Venezuela, I spent my weekends traveling with a group of Canadian consultants. We found that we needed to pool our resources, both physical and linguistic, to get where we needed to go, but had a fantastic time in the process – climbing in the jungles north of Caracas, canoeing to Angel Falls and scuba diving off the western coast near Maracaibo. What I especially enjoyed about the group was their strong sense of adventure and their willingness to be experimental.

I also enjoy traveling on my own. For occasional periods, it can be lonely; however, the brief periods of loneliness are far outweighed by the benefits of getting to know a country and its people on a less superficial level. One time, I went up into the hills of northern Italy near the village of Asiago. I saw an interesting looking elderly man and sat down on the bench beside him. We had a two-hour discussion on what things were like before the war which few friends of mine would have the patience to bear. No doubt they would want to move on to see the "real sights", but discussions such as the one I had help me to understand the personality of a country with more depth than I can from just reading or visiting without interaction. For that reason, I sometimes travel on my own. Traveling on my own also has a few other benefits; on a one-month trip to Europe in 1990 I received invitations to stay with new friends from over 30 countries.

■ ■ ■

Candidate's biography: Soyoung is female, Korean, educated in South Korea
Essay title: Tear gas and molotov cocktails

Tear gas and molotov cocktails take up a large part of my memory of my college years. The 1980s was the era of an authoritarian military regime in Korea. My aunt and my cousin were both massacred during the protest staged by Korean students and civilians against the Chun Do Hwan regime in the Kwanju massacre in 1980. In spite of the howling 2,000 deaths during that massacre, no government officials were brought to account. No media could justly report the terrifying scene.

As I entered college, like many of the students at the time, I felt a strong moral obligation to fight against the government and bring democracy to Korea. My daily life during the first two years of college centered around the National Organization of Students and inter-school groups to discuss the alternative curricula or so-called leftist books. The anger and injustice we students felt toward our government would almost always end up in staging a demonstration, whether violent or not. After two years spent in blind outburst, I began to doubt the effectiveness of violence of any sort. Coincidentally, I became acquainted with a student at Yonsei who also shared my thoughts. He was involved in the student movement but started to seek other routes to sending the message to the students and the public. And because he was involved with the drama team at

Yonsei School of Politics, we decided to work on a play toward delivering our thoughts. It took 30 members and a period of over a year from the initial meeting to write, produce, and stage a play. The subject of the play was how two men from the lowest-paid working class viewed the world and despite their feeling of injustice, how they became immune to it by finding a niche within that crooked society. It was a small stage with only a little over 200 students seeing the play over two nights.

Looking back, I do not regret spending my earlier youth for a just cause. The student movement together with the worker association is what after all brought democracy to Korea. But what I conceive as failure is that I was not mature enough to play the "tune" in harmony with society. The very people I thought I was fighting for were hurt along the way. I also realize the price I paid for losing a balance of reality. Instead of focusing on my main duty as a student, I failed to grasp the full benefit of an academic college education. After all is done I know that there are more effective and sensible ways to change the society. No one is completely free from his/her past. But it is how you look at it and grow from it that makes that difference. Now I understand that no one will view you with respect, let alone listen to you, if you neglect your primary duty. In the future, I intend to succeed in the field I choose. I understand that by doing this I will be able to return more to my society and my country.

■ ■ ■

Candidate's biography: Leilani is female, Filipino, educated in the U.S.

Essay title: My Filipino-Chinese heritage

I have had a lifetime of understanding and reconciling cultural differences. As a Filipino-Chinese, conflict of identity is an issue I have had to contend with all my life. I take pride in both the ancestries and cultures that comprise my being. However, coming to terms with this mixture has been made difficult by the stereotypes and biases I have had to overcome. Learning to accept all of who I am has taken me through a journey of self-discovery, one that has helped me strike a balance between my two halves and celebrate the merits of my Filipino-Chinese heritage.

Filipinos have made many sacrifices to alleviate the difficult conditions in which they live. The past decade has seen millions of residents leave the country to seek better opportunities elsewhere. Many of these people secure employment as menial workers. Women in particular have generally filled jobs as domestic helpers. They have inundated the international market for domestics to such an extent that the word "Filipina" has become synonymous with maid-servant. This generalization has given rise to many biases internationally, as well as fueled the discrimination that exists between the Chinese and Filipino in my country.

On the other hand, the value of being Chinese in the Philippines is very clear. Together, the Chinese comprise 70 percent of the business community while only totaling 1.5 percent of the country's population. The large, profitable enterprises they have established is evidence of the entrepreneurial genius that has helped them gain a position of relative affluence in society. For many Chinese, however, this standing has made them wary of associating with Filipinos due in part to heightened concerns for their own security. Because of the contrast in economic status, Filipinos are widely suspected of operating kidnap and extortion rings targeted at the Chinese community resulting in a mistrust that further aggravates the problem of intolerance.

While my family does not fall into the extremes of these Filipino and Chinese stereotypes, we are affected by them. As a businessman, my father saw the advantages of maintaining ties with the Chinese and decided to send my siblings and me to Chinese school from the age of 4 to 17. This experience illustrates how difficult it was for me to cope with the social implications of my Filipino lineage. Belonging to the minority of students that was not pure Chinese, I was exposed to virtually all aspects and manifestations of prejudice. Children were discouraged from playing with me because I was too dark-skinned; personal relationships were restricted. Prejudice against Filipinos was so strong that most children of mixed Chinese-Filipino descent disavowed their Filipino ancestry in an effort to fit in.

Being placed in the awkward situation of choosing one of my halves forced me to look closely at my identity. While I would not have had much difficulty blending into the Chinese community because of my physical appearance and language ability, the same did not apply for other members of my family. Both my parents did not speak Chinese and one of my brothers possessed the dark Malay features of a true Filipino. Because of this, denying my Filipino bloodline never even came to mind. I was, and still am very proud of my family and of the Filipino values with which I was brought up.

Through the years, I have struck a balance between my two sides through knowledge and appreciation of the language and culture of both. By surrounding myself with Chinese and Filipino friends, I have learned to mediate differing viewpoints and deal with intolerance through patience, persistence, and understanding. In addition, it has helped me establish what I admired most in both races. I attribute my success in coping with discrimination to the inherent Filipino traits of kindness, forbearance, and good humor. Filipino values have also helped me become adaptable and spiritual. Immersion in Chinese culture, however, inspires me to improve my entrepreneurial skills and work values. Observance of their resourcefulness, ingenuity, and unwavering determination motivates me to apply the same to my own pursuits.

Establishing my identity has given me a firm sense of who I am and where I belong, which makes me stronger. But at the same time, I also keep in mind the Filipino saying, *"Ang taong hindi lumingon sa kanyang pananggalingan ay hindi mararating ang kanyang paroroonan"* which translates into, "the person who does not look back to where he came from will never get to where he is going." To me, this means remembering the difficult lessons I have gleaned from my past and applying them to improve myself today. As I travel from place to place, I endeavor to maintain the tolerance, open-mindedness, and adaptability that have greatly contributed to the richness of my life.

■ ■ ■

Candidate's biography: Marie is female, Hispanic-American, educated in Hawaii

Essay title: Rainbow without a beginning

My life is like a rainbow without a beginning. Just as dark clouds gather to produce the rain needed to create a rainbow, inexplicable events had occurred which led to my abandonment as a baby in front of an orphanage. I grew up in Hawaii and still vividly remember seeing single and double rainbows frequently during the tropical rainy season. Like so many people, I consider seeing a rainbow as a lucky sign, but I can never forget that rainbows can only occur as a result of dark clouds and rain. I now feel fortunate to be able to return to Latin America as a successful businesswoman. My life is full of colors and each color has a symbolic relationship to the different influences which shaped me at an early age.

RED is the color of Mayan clay and it represents my Guatemalan heritage. The official records only state that I was found as a four–six week old infant, at the door of the El Pablo Babies' Home, near the Honduras border in Guatemala, one September morning in 1968. Although I cannot be absolutely sure, I have always assumed that I was born in Guatemala or Honduras. This was a year when tens of thousands of homeless and starving Guatemalan refugees were fleeing across the border into Honduras. Many babies were found abandoned in Guatemala during those turbulent times from the late sixties to the early seventies. Although I have long since come to feel at peace with the possibility that my birth parents may have been killed or forced to abandon me, I continue to wonder who they were and if they were among these refugees. I can only thank my birth parents for creating me and giving me a chance to live, if only in an orphanage, at a time when untold thousands of Guatemalans perished during the political instability and fighting in Guatemala caused by military extremists groups and the communist resurgencies.

ORANGE is like a sunrise. It symbolizes how I rose from being an orphan in underdeveloped Central America to becoming an infant adoptee in the USA. Unable to rely on my birth family, an important traditional source of comfort and protection, I had to become adaptable and self-reliant from the time I was just a few months old. For example, babies only a few months old had to quickly learn how to drink from a cup instead of a nursing bottle. This was because the chronic shortage of orphanage staff meant that it was more efficient for one staff member to sit six babies close together and feed them all at once by holding three cups of milk formula in each hand and tipping the nourishing liquid simultaneously into six hungry mouths. With dozens of babies requiring five daily feedings, there was simply no time for the staff members to take each baby in their arms and use a bottle to feed him or her.

When I was adopted by my Spanish-American parents in Hawaii at the age of 18 months, they told me that I was so overwhelmed by my new environment that I did not utter a sound for one whole week. Because I did not even cry, my mother and father were surprised when their family doctor said that there was nothing wrong with my vocal chords. Eventually, I did regain my vocal ability after another week in my new home, but my deepest psyche would be permanently scarred by the early loss of my birth parents, and sudden separation from my homeland.

YELLOW is part of the sun itself. This color represents how I was influenced by growing up in rural Hawaii, because this color brings the brightness and warmth of the *Aloha* spirit to my mind. Although I did not know it at the time, going to public school in Hawaii was an invaluable cross-cultural experience. My elementary school classes were composed of ethnic Japanese, Filipino, Hawaiian, Portuguese, Samoan, Chinese, English-Irish, and Korean children. As part of my crash course in social conditioning, I learned to speak fluent Pidgin to communicate with so many different ethnic groups, despite my mother's constant encouragement for me to speak standard Spanish and English. With its unique history as a former Polynesian kingdom which closely allied itself with European royalty and its predominantly ethnic Asian population living as U.S. citizens, Hawaii became the site of some the world's first truly integrated, multi-racial societies. I was raised at an early age to feel comfortable and confident while communicating with people from diverse cultural, social, religious and economic backgrounds because of my real life experience of growing up among people of diverse backgrounds.

My life is like a rainbow without a beginning. Because I survived a traumatic early life, my parents wanted to give me a name that would remind me that I was one of the chosen ones, almost as if reborn while still alive. My Guatemalan name is the poetic word combination "Lora Mournel," literally meaning the brightness after darkness or the first glow of the morning sun, a new beginning. When my *Aloha* spirit meets my industrious side, the result is helping myself and others to find new beginnings. This includes using my knowledge of medicine to promote the well-being of others. Where do I get the strength to help others? The source of this strength is the joy that I get knowing that life is like a rainbow, full of color – a chance occurrence – which springs forth in a mighty arc and propels each of us forcefully into the future.

■ ■ ■

Candidate's biography: Claudio is male, Italian, educated in Switzerland
Essay title: Experiencing the culture shock of a sky burial

International living has played an important part in my personal and professional development. Living in a place like Geneva, encountering an abundance of cultural differences constitutes the norm. But one of the most significant cultural shocks I have ever encountered occurred when I saw a "sky burial" in Tibet.

Sky burial is a rather unique Tibetan cultural practice, which involves shredding the flesh of the deceased into pieces and feeding it to the birds of prey. When a commoner dies, the corpse is first bound in a piece of white cloth and left for a three- to five-day mourning period. The body is then transported to a sky burial site in the mountain where the Tibetan monks go through the process of flesh shredding and bone crushing. The eagles and vultures, which inhabit the area, devour the remains. I felt nauseous after watching the process, and lost my appetite until well into the next day. I wondered how such a barbaric habit could be practiced today. The question remained in my mind until the origin and necessity of this practice was explained to me.

I was made to realize that such a practice evolved over a period of time and was in fact a reaction to physical conditions and resource restrictions. In Tibet, where the climate is cold and dry, it is difficult for a corpse to decompose through land burial. It is also costly to cremate a body because of the scarcity of wood and the low concentrate of oxygen in the higher altitudes. Consequently the practice of sky burial makes perfect sense when viewed from the perspective of the local situation.

As a result of this incident, I developed a better understanding of different cultures, their motivations, and practices. Above all, I became determined to attempt to objectively understand other cultures from their own perspective rather than to judge them based upon my own culture. This habit has enabled me to develop a deeper understanding of others and assist me in improving my communication skills with people from different societies and cultures.

■ ■ ■

Candidate's biography: Brad is male, Canadian-Caucasian, educated in the U.S.

The following example illustrates how one candidate expressed his creativity by use of an optional essay entry. It acts as support for the idea that he is a creative person, something that may otherwise be difficult to illustrate. Also it serves to impress the reader—how many people can find the time or the talent to create their own quotations?

Essay title: Original quotations submitted to *Reader's Digest* magazine.

Words are my oil wells.

Wit is the invisible knife that carves humor from language.

To know "not what to do" is a "knot" one must undo.

Chemistry starts a relationship, congeneality carries it.

Life's greatest misfortunes lie not in the opportunities that we lose but in the talents that we fail to use.

The building of a strong life is like the building of a house: intellect best draws the blueprint but only passion can dig the foundation.

To the scientist, reason is everything; to the hunter, instinct is the thing; to a child – *sight, sound, smell, taste, touch* – these compare to anything.

Jealousy is like the sound of a dripping faucet; it can drive us crazy.

Life's lessons are like books on a shelf – storing them is one thing, remembering to use them is another.

Theory without practice grows timid;
Practice without theory grows reckless.

The S.U.C.C.E.S.S. acronym:

Super effort.
Unusual drive.
Copy what works,
  Change what doesn't.
    Exercise now and cut out excess.
      Save a little more, spend a little less.
        Start all over again the very next day.

✔ Use #4 – Showing evidence of solid work experience

Candidate's biography: Eva is female, American, educated in Sweden

The following essay is written by a candidate who portrays a strong record of employment despite having only one or two years of full-time work experience. The essay serves the purpose of plugging an anticipated application weak point by making her short, one-year of work experience seem as impressive as someone's two or three years of experience.

Essay title: My intensive investment banking experience

I realize that many of INSEAD's applicants have several years of professional experience. Although I have only worked a short time, my professional experience has been immensely valuable. I am an analyst in a boutique investment bank, Pacific Rim Capital Asia Limited, based in Hong Kong and founded in 1995. We now have three professionals as well as working partners in the U.S. and Hong Kong. Our work involves strategic advisory, mergers and acquisitions, and corporate finance, mostly private equity placements from Asian corporations to international institutional investors. Our firm is currently billing US$40–50,000 in retainers per month plus another US$15–25,000 in monthly expenses. We are presently working on over US$100 million worth of deals with potential success fees of over US$5 million, in addition to equity linked compensation.

Working for an entrepreneurial investment bank in Hong Kong is very intensive, not only because of the intensity of Hong Kong itself or the fast-paced nature of investment banking, but because I am working for a family business which my brother started a little over a year ago. Working for a family member means working around the clock, and is amazingly stimulating. Because of my brother's confidence in my ability and judgement, I have been able to take part in major negotiations and have gained exposure to top executives in major investment banks and merging companies. My responsibilities include all aspects of the business, from managing client relations and working with the team to pitch for new business, to creating financial models, market research, investment presentations, and selling documents for clients and investors. I am currently working with clients in Hong Kong, China, New York, and Germany as well as with investors and strategic partners from around the globe.

As a member of a small entrepreneurial firm, I have by necessity become involved with every aspect of our business including corporate registration, securities regulation, employee and partnership agreements, accounting systems, and other organizational matters in addition to my work with and for our clients. I have quickly come to appreciate the importance of both high-level professional activities such as pitching for new deals and the seemingly more mundane tasks of collecting accounts receivable and managing cash flows on a day-to-day basis. The combination of the small size of our professional team and the critical nature of the projects and dollar amounts with which we are dealing, has given me a level of responsibility in our organization beyond that of my peers in larger investment banks. I am playing a critical role in several of our transactions, including two "live" deals expected to bring us approximately US$3 million in fees over the next 90 days.

■ ■ ■

Candidate's biography: Kevin is male, New Zealander, educated in New Zealand

Many candidates do not fully capitalize on their major work accomplishments. The resume (or employment record) can only tell so much. Furthermore, most candidates have had reasonably substantial work experience before applying to business school. If you have worked on a memorable project, then elaborate on it in a page or two. The applicant below highlights a short-term project he was involved with in Mexico City.

Essay title: Working on consulting assignment in Mexico

My first consulting experience unfolded in the volatile Mexican marketplace. I was familiar with computers but *not* with Mexico. A southern California venture capital firm had taken an equity stake in a quickly-expanding Mexico City computer operation (B & T Company, S.A. de C.V.), and a long-time friend of mine from university with experience in Latin American business was assigned to go to Mexico to assist in its daily operation.

My friend, Scott, requested that I be hired to help him with various accounting applications. All we really knew before leaving was that there were little to no accounting controls in place. The Mexican principal, who had been in charge of daily operations, was a shoot-from-the-hip entrepreneur. He had little work structure but was reputed to be a fantastic salesman and eventually was nominated for entrepreneur of the year award in Mexico City. Our job was to add structure to the operation. My job was to put accounting controls in place in order to make sure the company was processing its paper properly and could produce reliable financial information. Scott's job was to concentrate on marketing and administration. Cash flow and margins were both our concerns. I continually thought about how different this situation was from my joint-venture auditing experience gained with Coopers and Lybrand when auditing companies like Kraft. Such companies had no real cash flow problems and received solid support from their U.S.-based parent companies. With no uniform company manuals in Mexico, every daily activity was subject to the vagaries of the moment – it was as if everything was happening for the first time, happening by chance. The experience really shook me up. It was a lesson in total decentralization.

I spent June, July, and August of 1992 in Mexico City. From this experience, I came away with an appreciation of the difficulty of doing business in the Mexican business arena. I learned to double-check everything and employ astute guesswork to figure out what is happening around me. What people say is not what they do. I found this to be true in Mexico where spoken words are suggestions rather than absolutes – in Mexico, what is said verbally is not meant to be taken verbatim and would likely not carry as much weight as it might in the U.S. or Canada. Conversely, things written down in black and white seem to carry even more weight in Mexico than they would back home, assuming of course they are actually read!

■ ■ ■

Candidate's biography: Caroline is female, Jewish, educated in Israel

The following essay adds a nice touch to the candidate's application package. The essay is personable and tells us a little more about her insights into the world of executive search.

Essay title: Diamonds in the rough

As mentioned in my essays, my career goal includes obtaining an MBA and becoming a leader in the executive search field. Therefore, I would like to include a few insights that I have developed as a result of my current work in this field in Asia.

I have the good fortune of working for England's most successful headhunter, Ryan Portier. He has been written up in many news articles and has been quoted as saying, "Two things that make a good journalist and a great headhunter are the love of information and a love of people."

A love of information is important in order to locate a candidate once an assignment has been confirmed. How do you go about finding the "perfect" match? For sure, search takes a good deal of initiative and creativity. I have to very quickly review information in books, magazines, newspapers, on-line searches, and by word of mouth. I am a cross between an investigative reporter, management consultant, and sales person. I must know the industry, the people, the market dynamics, and be able to sell a potential candidate on the new "idea".

It is true that my boss is extremely charismatic, but I really feel it is his passion for people that enables him to focus on what is best for the search candidate. Top search executives know that there is a difference between the best candidate and the right fit. It is not whether we have the best candidate but the right candidate. The right candidate may not be the best candidate; the right candidate will fit the organization like a glove.

A search executive must be able to identify possibilities. The first step is to view the long term. Certain corporate persons, unknown today, may become the stars of the future. The headhunting process is like finding diamonds in the rough. It may be true that you will occasionally work with a star candidate and place this person outright. But more often it will be true that you must place a candidate into a position that makes he or she a star. We must have a sixth sense about people and market opportunities. We must realize that diamonds do not look like diamonds in their raw state but rather are disguised as clumps of coal. By analogy, many of tomorrow's leaders of industry will remain disguised until we seek them out and match their talents with market opportunities.

■ ■ ■

Candidate's biography: Camilla is female, Danish, educated in Denmark

If you are working for a family-run company or are a self-employed individual, you may want to think of comparing your current company to that of a present day corporate leader. The strategy here is to imply that you and your company will be a market leader in ten or more years. It is a little like saying, "Look over there, that is where we will be tomorrow." This is likely to create a positive impression on the committee members and increase a candidate's chances of acceptance to highly competitive business programs. Admissions officers of major business schools desire to avoid rejecting applicants who may one day be giants in their respective fields. In the following example, a young lady compares her family-run company in the women's accessory business with that of Benetton because of Benetton's initial success in Europe and subsequent late entry in the U.S. market.

Essay title: Evita Peroni – The next Benetton?

Basically all my practical experience is in our family fashion business Evita Peroni and it is in this context that I am pursuing my long-term career goal – to become CEO. Therefore I would like to present the committee with more detailed information about our company. Although we are represented in 38 countries, we are not represented in the U.S. and therefore you may not be familiar with our brand. The strategy of Evita Peroni has been first to build up a good and stable business in Europe and Asia before reaching for the U.S. market. We have side-stepped the U.S. market deliberately but now feel that we are ready and we are at the initial stages of making our market entry.

Introduction to Evita Peroni

Under the brand Evita Peroni, our company has specialized in design, manufacture, and marketing of ladies accessories in particular hair-accessories, scarves, sunglasses, and brushes in 38 countries around the world. The company has its origin in Copenhagen, Denmark where the founder, my father, started the accessory business in 1963. Today, 33 years later, Evita Peroni's main office is in Hong Kong with the research and development office in Copenhagen, the design studio in Los Angeles, and the international marketing in London, England.

How and where Evita Peroni is sold?

Evita Peroni is sold through franchise distributors in 38 countries around the world with Europe comprising 50 percent of our total turnover and Asia (including Japan) comprising 30 percent. The remaining business is spread over the Middle East, Australia, South America, South Africa, and recently the U.S.

Evita Peroni is mainly sold in medium to high-level department stores, such as Galleries Lafayette in France, Breuninger in Germany, Central Department Stores in Thailand, and Sony Plaza in Japan just to mention a few. An average size department store like Zen

Department Store in Bangkok has a yearly turnover of US$330,000 (retail) on a 40-foot-long wall display. Evita Peroni is also sold in perfumeries, specialty stores, duty-free stores, and in exclusive Evita Peroni shops. In 1994 Evita Peroni was awarded the Most Dynamic Beauty Supplier in France in competition with brands like Estee Lauder and Lancome.

My vision about Evita Peroni

My vision is that Evita Peroni will be the next Benetton within ladies accessories. We are the only truly international brand within hair-accessories, which is our present field of expertise and we are gaining good ground in the field of sunglasses, scarves, and brushes. The total concept of Evita Peroni has proved its success by already being accepted in 38 countries. Furthermore Evita Peroni benefits from brand recognition by consumers as well as retailers and wholesalers, and we are contacted frequently by parties from all over the world who want to do business with us. I believe we are where Benetton was a few decades ago. We have firmly established ourselves in Europe prior to looking at the U.S. market. My vision is to make Evita Peroni one of the international leading brands within ladies accessories. I believe Evita Peroni has what it takes and I believe we will make it!

Use #5 – Elaborating on reasons for wanting to go to a particular business school

In the sample essay excerpt below, note how the applicant finds a fresh voice. The best applicants find ways to push the limits in order to rise above the crowd. Try to write one level of detail beyond what the average informed candidate will write—be specific and be personal.

Sample essay excerpt

The GSB campus would be an ideal place to spend two years. Its open walkways and shared courtyards speak to the collaborative atmosphere of the school. After four years living in high-rises of the urban jungle, the figure "8,000 acres" reads like a keyword for freedom! It must have been the vast acreage that inspired the Stanford motto: "The wind of freedom blows." I imagine tree-lined Palm Drive is actually the secret entrance to a Spanish-tiled cultural haven. One of my favorite artists, Richard Diebenkorn, occupies the galleries of the new Cantor Center. His sun-drenched abstract landscapes, painted in swaths of heat-colored vistas, are a reason to apply to Stanford GSB unto themselves. The new wing of the Cantor Center was designed by the same firm behind the Pequot Museum in Mashantucket, Connecticut, and the Rose Center at the American Museum of Natural History: my two favorite museums on the East Coast. I am excited to see the new Cantor wing's curved walls, cast in the high-finish concrete pioneered by my favorite architect, Louis Kahn. I plan to study by Maya Lin's new "Timetable" sculpture outside the Packard Engineering Building, the same way I relaxed to the murmur of her "Women's Table" water sculpture at Yale. Set among such cultural riches, Stanford GSB provides an ideal environment to study.

Sample essay excerpt

> I have met a number of INSEAD grads who have told me of their unbelievably positive experiences including one-and-a-half page emails bragging about the diversity of the school – classrooms of more than 20 nationalities, study teams of half a dozen people who can speak 12 or more languages collectively, and students choosing between living in a flat in the center of town and a real castle 18 kilometers from the school!

■ ■ ■

In the two essays that follow, each candidate creates a sense of excitement, preparation and anticipation.

Candidate's biography: Alice is female, Hong Kong-Chinese, educated in the U.S.

I would like to take this opportunity to further elaborate on my reasons for choosing the Tuck School of Business.

My six years in the consulting industry, both in North America and South America, reflect a constant pursuit to mold myself into a distinctive management consultant, who has outstanding character and a broad yet balanced range of professional qualities and competence. Over the years, I have successfully transitioned from implementing tactical IT solutions to formulating strategic management game plans for top executives. As a former IT consultant at PricewaterhouseCoopers and IBM, I led transnational organizations to implement state-of-the-art IT solutions. Since joining McKinsey as a junior associate, I have re-shaped top CEO agendas, led Latin and South American companies to tackle their most burning business and technology issues, and shifted the fundamental way that businesses have been run.

Each successive career move has honed my professional qualities and competence: to master business and technology issues of broader implications to a corporation's competitiveness; to conduct fact-based and penetrating analysis with a strong sense of logic; to be imaginative and resourceful in developing original solutions to management problems; and to be a trusted team player. I have also learned to leverage important aspects of my character, including trustworthiness, honesty, and integrity, to deepening my relationships with client and team members.

Like that of any other distinctive consulting company, the future of McKinsey depends on the basic qualities, skills, and knowledge of its people. We need superior people with superior minds. In turn, the key to my future success at McKinsey depends on enhancing my management and leadership abilities. To achieve my goal, I require Tuck's inter-disciplinary and pragmatic MBA education that effectively capitalizes on the intellectual capital and resources of a distinctive community to help me build sound management and leadership abilities. My recent visit to Tuck offered me a direct opportunity to experience your distinctiveness beyond the Tuck MBA brochures. The Tuck MBA program will help me achieve my goal in three fundamental ways:

Rigorous general management curriculum. To become an outstanding consultant, I must acquire strong management fundamentals that include the basic managing process, and the interdependence and interactions of various managing elements. Tuck excels in this area by systematically breaking down its management education into a set of functionally driven yet strategically coherent studies. I am particularly excited about the general management forum, where I would apply the concepts and skills I learned about economics and technology systems, toward developing a real-life project, such as IT-enabled productivity improvements in developing countries. Meanwhile, I would be exposed to an intense training on analytical thinking and innovative problem-solving, as I strive to develop recom-mendations that would be valuable to target organizations and executives.

Collaborative learning approach. From intimate class sizes to study groups, the Tuck approach to collaborative learning would allow me to capitalize on the diverse experiences and viewpoints of students at a personal level. It would also enhance my ability to understand others' perspectives. Everyone I met at Tuck, from the admissions officers to student hosts, demonstrated a high level of enthusiasm and passion toward building the community. Meanwhile, Professor Amy Hutton's accounting class, which challenged students to go beyond memorization of textbook principles to strategic analysis of ac-counting statements, reflected Tuck's commitment to superior teaching quality. What could be more satisfying than to be engaged in a learning environment, where every capacity or talent one may have is expanded, every lesson one may have is used, and every value one cares about is furthered? As your MBA student, Anne Heung, summed it up best, "Tuck has been an amazing experience so far. Tuckies are just the smartest, nicest, and most fun bunch of people I have been around."

Balanced leadership training. Tuck's commitment to providing balanced leadership training is exemplified in your weekly announcement of a variety of exciting extra-curricular activities and social events. Given my background in women's issues, I am particularly keen on joining the Tuck Women in Business Club and Consulting Club to foster the next generation of female leaders in the consulting industry. These experiences would allow me to explore my enduring passions while cultivating in me strong funda-mentals for a lifetime of caring leadership for the community. Furthermore, the daily visits by high-level executives, the breath and depth of topics covered, and the opportunity for up-close and personal discussions would allow me to stay abreast of the latest management thinking.

A premier education institution like Tuck requires committed students to advance its legacy of academic excellence and rich tradition of collegiality. Given my multi-cultural upbringing and diverse professional background, I will help inject greater cultural diversity to the Tuck community and stronger international focus to classroom studies. Specifically, I was raised and educated in three different countries through which I have honed my multi-language skills and appreciation for cultural differences. As an international consultant, I have traveled to and worked in numerous countries to serve a diversified portfolio of clients on strategic and management issues. Coupling my global experience with my capability to relate to people on a personal level, by speaking their languages and understanding their unique cultural challenges, I will add valuable inputs and context to classroom learning and student interactions at Tuck. Furthermore, I will leverage the extensive business network that I have cultivated over the years with the business communities and governments in Asia to further the global reach of Tuck's alumni circle and strengthen Tuck's representation in the global business community. Finally, my passion in volunteer work will help expand the horizon of the student life at Tuck.

■ ■ ■

Candidate's biography: Amar is male, American, educated in the U.S.

During the course of the past year, when I first became interested in attending a graduate program in business administration, I had the privilege of attending a number of presentations by top U.S. business schools. All of the presenters were informative and portrayed their respective schools in a positive manner. However, their information, in conjunction with my own research, led me to the conclusion that there were only a few business schools that could help me achieve the goals that I had set for myself.

As a business professional and an aspiring student, my goals are straightforward: (1) To further develop the technical, financial, and intellectual skills that will enhance the techniques I have already gained from working in the credit markets of New York and Hong Kong; (2) To study under innovative scholars such as Gary Becker in order to solidify the academic knowledge that I gained at Vassar and the London School of Economics; (3) To prepare for work in the international arena and bolster my chances of becoming a development finance professional at an international organization such as the World Bank or the Inter-Americas Development Bank.

For the last three years, I have learned the business of credit analysis and the debt capital markets in an "on the job" basis or in hurried training seminars. To my firm's and my colleagues' credit, I have learned a great deal about high yield bonds, the leveraged loan markets, mergers and acquisitions, credit analysis and, most recently, emerging markets. However, I am certain that there are gaps in my professional knowledge that need to be filled if I am ever to be a productive participant in the financial markets. I do not think these gaps can be filled by on-the-job training or the knowledge-sharing of my everyday work environment. I strongly believe that a rigorous academic setting that provides access to both the theoretical and practical issues is important to the development of a young professional.

I see the University of Chicago as the ultimate intellectual platform. First, the university is revered as a "graduate school". Only one out of every three students on campus is an undergraduate; two out of every three students on campus are either graduate students or PHD students. Second, the influence of Nobel Laureates on the university as a whole is astounding. Elaborating on the fact that the University of Chicago has won more nobel prizes than any other university in the world, a school administrator put it in a memorable light: "If the University of Chicago were a country, it would be ranked number three in the world in terms of the number of Nobel Prizes received. In first place would be the United States of which the University is a part of; in second place would be England, and in third place would be the University of Chicago." Third, the reputation of Chicago grads among employers is noteworthy. There is a saying: "if you don't know an answer, go ask a Chicago grad."

The second major reason for choosing Chicago as my first choice is my desire to study with scholars of the GSB. During my senior year at Vassar College, I had the opportunity to study advanced labor economics. During the course of that year I was able to study the work of Gary Becker, George Borjas and Jake Mintzer and their important contributions in understanding the consequences of labor policy. Taking part in a class that Gary Becker teaches at the GSB would allow me to take part in what I anticipate would be a unique academic experience. Students rarely have the opportunity to study under any scholar who helped lay the foundation of modern labor economics theory. I work in an environment filled with the sophisticated concepts of trading, risk management and deal execution. However, despite the sophistication of today's financial markets, labor market issues still manage to be of critical importance in driving or hindering economic growth and policy. *IG Metal* still has a powerful voice in German industrial organization, newly-laid state workers in China protest the growing "rustbelt" in the northwest provinces and pension obligations have crippled U.S. steel companies despite newly-installed tariffs. Structural rigidities or, conversely, a lack of social protection have been detrimental to the European, Asian and, to a lesser degree, the U.S. markets.

At institutions like the IFC within the World Bank, one has the opportunity to use the knowledge gained in both financial markets and labor economics to assist still-developing economies overcome illiquid financial markets and structural weaknesses. I have been fortunate in seeking my professional experiences and in finding mentors during my career. I was able to be an intern economist during my LSE Masters program at JP Morgan in London during the Euro's first year in existence. I was able to serve in UBS Warburg in New York as a credit advisory analyst during one of the most trying credit cycles in a generation, and I have had the opportunity to help rebuild Asian financial institutions as they struggle to shed the legacy of 1997. The GSB offers the opportunity to deepen these experiences, particularly in the international arena. Tackling new studies, developing new perspectives, participating in lectures and group work, talking with fellow classmates, and making new friends, who will be partners in the future, are all essential ingredients in making this happen.

CHAPTER 6

Resume or Employment Record

*"Your resume is ready when your mother looks at it and
doesn't recognize who it is."*

Unknown

INTRODUCTION

How will your work experience be evaluated?

The admissions committee will rate your work experience in two ways: the depth and the breadth of your work experience. The depth or intensity reflects the amount of time you have worked and your accomplishments. Depth of work experience is sometimes evaluated from looking at your job titles, job responsibilities, job accomplishments, promotions, and/or salary increases. Breadth or variety of work experience, on the other hand, largely reflects the number of different tasks or job functions you have performed or have been exposed to in the workplace. Breadth of work experience may also refer to your ability to acquire people (i.e., team building) skills as opposed to technical skills, although there usually exists some degree of trade-off between acquiring depth or breadth of work experience. It is unclear whether it is more important to have depth or breadth of work experience. It is also unclear whether it is better to work for one company for, say, four years, or two different companies for two years each. However, it is not well regarded if you work for four different companies each for a single year.

What is the difference between a resume and an employment record?

Business schools generally require that you submit an employment record as part of your completed application. Sometimes your resume (Exhibits 6–1 and 6–2) or CV (curriculum vitae) is required in addition to your employment record. The employment record, as required by business schools, differs in three basic ways from a standard resume. The first is format, the second is length, and the third is content. In terms of format, think of an employment record as a "reformatted" resume. A resume is broken into "lateral" thirds: (1) education, (2) work experience, and (3) extracurriculars. An employment record is usually broken into "vertical" thirds: (1) company or organization placed in the first column, (2) places and dates in the second column, and (3) job responsibilities and/or accomplishments placed in the third column.

In terms of length, a resume is typically one page in length whereas an employment record is usually three to five pages in length. This added length results from the format of the employment record, which necessitates placing the bulk of job description and work accomplishments into the third right-hand column.

In terms of content, both a resume and an employment record contain five standard pieces of information regarding each job experience. These include: (1) name of company or organization, (2) title or position, (3) geographical location of company or organization, (4) dates of employment, and (5) job responsibilities and/or accomplishments. However, employment records usually include two additional pieces of data, namely starting and ending salaries for each position and reasons for leaving each job. Candidates sometimes wonder why schools ask for beginning and ending salary. In the words of one admissions director, "When times are good, salaries move but titles don't. When times are bad, titles

Exhibit 6–1 Sample resume: Todd A. Gillman

Author's note: This is a standard resume format with dates placed on the left-hand side.

TODD A. GILLMAN
Apt 22B, Exchange Towers, 64 Grant Street, Hartford, CT, USA 06501
Bus/Tel: (203) 782-4200 Res/Tel & Fax: (203) 785-1717

EDUCATION

BOSTON UNIVERSITY, Boston, Massachusetts
Bachelor of Science in Business Administration, May 1990
Concentration in Accounting, GPA 3.65, Cum Laude

PROFESSIONAL
EXPERIENCE

1993–1995   **BANK OF AMERICA**, Hartford, Connecticut
Associate and Financial Analyst
- Analyzed branch performance and devised new strategies to improve regional market share. Formulated two-year marketing plan for two branches.
- Developed new commission system and assisted in implementation.
- Devised tax-saving strategies and advised principal clients on investment portfolio compositions.

Use consistent verb tenses?

Any result? Was it effective?

1991–1993   *Financial Analyst*
- Evaluated clients' corporate credit ratings based on credit history, performance, and financial ratios. Developed structure of interest rate, loan maturity, and payment schedule to ensure maximum net income.
- Managed foreign exchange transactions involving U.S. dollar and Japanese yen. Served as consultant to corporate clients on foreign exchange transactions by predicting short-term exchange rate fluctuations and suggesting appropriate time to engage in transaction.
- Issued, confirmed, and negotiated letters of credit and authorized issuance of official import and export licenses on behalf of the U.S. government.

How many? How large? Try to quantify accomplishments

1990–1991   KRESTER and JONES, New Haven, Connecticut
Tax & Audit Staff
- Prepared consolidated financial statements for medium-sized companies.
- Prepared tax returns for individuals, corporations, and partnerships.
- Resolved tax matters with IRS and CA Franchise Tax Board for clients.
- Tested and analyzed new accounting and audit software.

Achievements: Passed all four parts of the November 1991 CPA exam in one sitting. National Association of Accountants Scholastic Achievement Award. Membership to Beta Alpha Psi and Beta Gamma Sigma Honorary Society.

Skills: Excel, Lotus 123, Word, WordPerfect, Platinum, MAS 90, and tax and audit software. Fluent in Spanish.

Interests: Translator and guide at International Exposition in San Paulo, Brazil. Enjoy skiing, tennis, mountain biking, and weight training.

Dates?

Exhibit 6–2 Sample resume: Sonia Khan

> Author's note: This is another standard resume format with dates placed on the right-hand side.

> Sonia quantifies her work accomplishments by using numbers where possible and thinking in terms of the overall impact of her experiences.

SONIA KHAN

Current Address:
House 22, Belgravia Square
London, England SW114DG
Tel: (4471) 917-8754

Permanent Address:
5B Sunita, Ridge Road
Karachi 6, Pakistan
Tel: 91-22-366-1635

EDUCATION

INDIAN INSTITUTE OF TECHNOLOGY, New Delhi, India

Degree/Concentration:	B.Sc. in Electrical Engineering, May 1992
Academic Distinction:	High Honors Graduate; McEnery Scholarship Recipient
Extracurricular Activities:	Captain, Women's Field Hockey; Recreational Cricket

PROFESSIONAL EXPERIENCE

ANDERSEN CONSULTING
Consultant, Business Process Design

London, England
January 1994 to present [1997]

- Conducted comparative studies on existing marketing strategies and tools utilized by leading Fortune 1000 Office Automation companies. Project results were subsequently sold to 12 companies.
- Re-engineered a local client's sales billing system to empower sales representatives, increase customer service, and reduce cost. Resulted in 23 percent increase in sales and 34 percent reduction in costs.
- Helped lead seven-member team in designing and developing a system to automate a shipping process through an on-line software package with centralized data repository.
- Presented seminar *Logistics in Action* to 400 persons at London Exhibition and Trade Center.

INTEL CORPORATION
Technical Marketing Support Liaison

Bombay, India
August 1992 to December 1993

- Worked on team of ten engineers, technicians, and college interns in providing technical and marketing support for i486 and Pentium processors to South Asian client base.
- Promoted from Grade 3 to Grade 5 for outstanding project management of pre-Pentium processors.
- Received *Intel Recognition Award for Results Orientation* – for meeting tight deadline in developing test procedures and validating client motherboards, which were displayed in ROMDEX, the biggest computer show in India.
- Received *Intel Recognition Award for Customer Service* – for creating documents for on-line tools which resulted in increased client downloads by 30 percent.

OTHERS

- Worked part-time while pursuing full-time study; earned 40 percent of university expenses.
- Junior Achievement – (1991) Taught algebra weekly to eight grade class during university. Encouraged students to learn geometry by seeing practical application of these skills.
- Public Relations Representative – (1993) Arranged lectures for Intel Senior Management, coordinated philanthropic activities; set up recreational trips for 200-plus members.
- Fluent in English, Hindi, Punjabi, and Urdu. Enrolled in intermediate level French course.

move but salaries don't. In an era where titles do not mean as much as they once did, salaries give an added indication of responsibility level.

Consistent with Tip #62 in this book, you are also encouraged to consider including commentaries in the form of brief summaries or anecdotes to highlight what you found significant or meaningful about your work experiences. Resumes do not include such summaries.

A resume also includes a summary of an individual's educational history and extracurricular involvement but these items are not included in the employment record. Business schools require separate forms to be completed with regard to educational institutions attended and extracurricular activities undertaken.

The basics of the employment record do not vary but different schools have slightly different formats, so you will need to adapt your formats as required. Sample resumes appear on the following two pages. They are included to familiarize candidates with standard formats and presentation.

SEVEN TIPS FOR A MORE IMPRESSIVE EMPLOYMENT RECORD

The following seven tips can help you make your work experience look more impressive:

☞ Tip #58: Use corporate descriptions, especially if your company or organization is not well-known.

Corporate descriptions are essential if a company is *not* well-known. Adding descriptions helps the reviewer clarify immediately what industry a company is in. Say, for example, your resume or record of employment contains the company name, Goliath Industries, Inc. The reviewer will have to guess at the nature of the industry that this company operates in. Providing a corporate description will clear up the confusion.

> **EXAMPLE**
>
> Goliath Industries, Inc. is a Vancouver Stock Exchange public-listed company which trades under the symbol GOL. The company specializes in oil and gas and mining ventures. Its subsidiary, Goliath Mining South America, is currently involved in gold mining operations in Bolivia.

To be consistent, consider adding corporate descriptions for all companies even if the companies are well-known.

> **EXAMPLE**
>
> PricewaterhouseCoopers is a U.S.-based international "big four" accounting firm specializing in audit, tax, consulting, search, and investigative work.

Tip #59: Use bullet points to start each line of your resume when highlighting a description of your work experience and use an equal or greater number of bullet points when listing your most recent job experience, compared with previous jobs held.

Putting more bullet points under your latest piece of work experience, will give the reviewer the impression that you are gaining more and more experience and responsibility. This is an especially good technique if you have worked for your current company for less than one year.

Tip #60: Use verbs and consistent verb tenses to begin each line of the resume when highlighting your work experience (i.e., responsibilities and/or accomplishments).

Each line of a resume or employment record will typically begin with a bullet point followed by a verb expressed in the past tense. Verbs in the past tense usually end in "ed". Examples include the verbs "achieved", "maintained", or "counseled". The one exception occurs with your current job in which you have the choice of beginning each line using a verb in the "ing" form (i.e., an "ing" verb) or a verb in the past tense (i.e., an "ed" verb).

Tip #61: Quantify your work-related accomplishments with number-based modifiers to avoid overly general descriptions.

When listing your responsibilities and accomplishments on your employment record (or resume), begin each entry with a verb and, when possible, list a quantitative measure of your accomplishment. Some of the examples are as follows:

- Work_ed_ on project Y, which increased company revenues by _10 percent_ while decreasing expenses by _5 percent_.
- Install_ed_ a new computer system and trained _two_ employees.
- Involv_ed_ in a deal-making process that resulted in a _10-million share_ initial public offering (IPO).
- Organiz_ed_ a company picnic for _700_ employees.

Concentrate on your work accomplishments, not simply a description of your experience, and do not overlook what may be accomplishments, for example, using less time, limiting expenses, increasing safety, bolstering corporate reputation, or raising employee morale.

In evaluating work accomplishments, it is meaningful to distinguish achievements from responsibilities. Responsibilities are the tasks or duties a person is required to perform as part of his or her position. Responsibilities are typically detailed in a job description. Achievements, on the other hand, are results accomplished on the job. For example, "managed the company's sales force in San Antonio" is a responsibility; a "20 percent annual growth in sales for five consecutive years" is an achievement.

✍ **Tip #62: Add "employment summaries" to explain what you found significant about each of your work experiences.**

Company or organization	Location and dates	Responsibilities/accomplishments
PricewaterhouseCoopers *Junior Consultant* (PricewaterhouseCoopers is a U.S.-based international "big four" accounting firm specializing in audit, tax, consulting, search, and investigative work.)	Chicago, IL June '00 – May '02	**Responsibilities:** • Worked … • Installed … • Involved … **Summary:** "I learned to … "

Company names and job titles do not necessarily tell the whole story. They mean a lot more when accompanied by a reason *why* the candidate thinks his or her work experience is important or significant. The headings "Summary" or "What I Learned" or "Why this is Significant" are used in upcoming examples to signal use of such summaries. Ideally, if your summary is well-phrased, the reviewer may adopt your comments as his or her own. If nothing else, they will serve as well-organized and purposeful summaries. It is an excellent idea to mention why your job activities were important or significant and what work themes arose from your employment opportunities. Employment themes are discussed in the next section.

Tip #63: Review employment themes as the basis of writing meaningful "employment summaries".

Thinking about how to summarize your work experience is an important part of the business school process. You need to think about what your employment record means and strategize about how it impacts your whole application. Your resume directly and indirectly impacts the quality of your letters of recommendation, application essays, and interview sessions. *Work summaries* help to show the meaningfulness of your work experience. Work summaries can also help show that your career has developed in a systematic and coherent way. Give the reviewer the impression that everything about your experiences is linked together—that it has a rhyme and reason. Your previous work experiences must be viewed in terms of your ultimate career goal. A major problem many candidates have is not insufficient experience, but the inability to explain why their job experiences are meaningful, particularly in the light of their evolving career paths. Show off the richness of your work experience, not only by citing your accomplishments, but also by mentioning your work themes.

There are three potential groupings of work themes: (1) working across different job functions or across different departments, (2) working across different industries or sectors, and (3) working across different geographic or international settings.

Working across different job functions or across different departments. In terms of job functions or skill-sets, there are several key ones including accounting and financing, marketing and selling, manufacturing, and engineering or researching. In days gone by, people used to refer to work in one of three ways—you could "make, sell, or count". In other words, you were effectively a factory worker, a sales person, or an accountant. In terms of departments, the major departments within companies include administrative (including management, legal, personnel), marketing (and sales), finance (and accounting), production (including engineering, technical), and research and development.

- **Example:** "As a bond trader, I gained exposure to the different product areas of bond sales, trading, and research."

- **Example:** "We anticipate conflicts to take place between the finance and marketing departments, but not between the marketing and sales departments. As a brand manager, I see the brand as the company's most important long-term asset. Salespersons, on the other hand, are motivated by short-term objectives, (e.g., price discounts), which may or may not be beneficial to overall brand management."

Another way to view work themes according to job functions or departments is in terms of scope or job responsibility. For example, draw attention to some combination of experience you have as a specialist or generalist, manager or technical person, line-person or support person, self-employed individual or corporate employee.

- **Example:** "I have worked as an investment specialist for a retail bank and as a self-employed individual. Working as my own boss in my own small business helped me see all areas of a business. I was responsible for writing checks, drafting proposals, and soliciting clients. It was an opportunity to see a complete business cycle which includes paying for expenses and supplies, selling a product or service, and collecting the money."

- **Example:** "I learned, first hand, the difference between being a financial controller and a financial stock market analyst. While the former sees things from an operational point of view, the latter sees things from a financial market point of view, and I learned of the different things that a corporate manager feels are important in running a successful business versus the kinds of things that a stock market analyst views as important in evaluating a public-listed company."

- **Example:** "I found that 'leadership by command' was useful and necessary for leading our sales team, but 'leadership by example' worked best for motivating our company's research scientists."

Working across different industries or across different sectors. If you have held a variety of different jobs prior to applying to business school, this is your opportunity to emphasize the diverse nature of your work experience. If you have worked steadily for one company prior to attending business school, look at diversity in terms of work in different industries or departments, or projects or clients you have served. For example, consultants often work across many different industries. Have you worked in different industries (e.g., marketing versus finance, manufacturing versus wholesaling or retailing), or in different sectors (e.g., private versus public or government)?

- **Example:** "My legal background helps me to set up businesses within a legal context whereas my banking experience helps me evaluate whether a business deal makes economic sense."

- **Example:** "As a member of the asset management team, I was able to better understand how individuals or companies operating in different industries measure the key drivers of performance. As an example of this, retailers measure profitability by sales per square foot whereas leveraged buy-out firms measure profitability by internal rates of return."

Working across different geographical or international settings. If you have worked overseas, this is your chance to emphasize the value of your international experience. On the other hand, it is still possible to have gained considerable exposure to international business without having left your home country, particularly if you have worked for a multinational company. In short, draw attention to the fact that you have a combination of international versus domestic experience, or national versus regional experience (e.g., east versus west, north versus south).

- **Example:** "I have worked in three geographically diverse continents of the world, namely Europe, North America, and Asia."

- **Example:** "I have worked in both developed and developing countries, and gained exposure to doing business in both free market and socialist-based economies."

Tip #64: Anticipate strengths and weaknesses in your employment record.

In terms of the number of companies or organizations you have worked for (from the time you left college up until the time you apply to business school), you will fall into one of three categories:

1. You have worked for one single company or organization.
2. You have worked for exactly two companies or organizations.
3. You have worked for three or more companies or organizations.

The average MBA applicant works approximately three to five years before applying to business school. In the event that you have worked for three or four different companies within a three- or four-year period, you will likely be faced with the problem of "weaving" your experiences together into a cohesive whole. You must address the otherwise implicit question of why you have worked for, say, four companies each for a single year rather than one company for an entire four years. Unless you address it, this problem will make you look unfocused. The solution is to weave your three or four experiences together and make them look connected. Try to compose an "employment analysis summary sheet" (Exhibit 6–3) in which you summarize your employment experiences as if you were preparing a cover sheet. In fact, in the era of paper-based application this would in fact be an optional cover page to help summarize your employment for the reviewer.

An "employment analysis summary sheet" can show employment themes resulting from diversity in terms of work over differing geographical, industrial, or functional areas. In the particular case of consultants, a cover page can work marvelously for highlighting diverse work endeavors gained from working on different projects or for different clients.

The following section includes the employment records of two MBA candidates.

Candidate A—Kevin
Candidate B—Vivian

These two employment records are very much juxtaposed. Whereas Kevin has worked for three different companies in five years, Vivian has worked for one single company for seven years. Kevin benefits from an "employment analysis summary sheet" in order to consolidate his experiences and sell the admissions committee on the merits of his work diversity. His strategy is to say, "Hey, three different jobs in three different industries is the best thing that has ever happened to me." His career objective to be a fund manager potentially benefits from his eclectic work background. Vivian also benefits from an "employment analysis summary sheet", de facto cover sheet, because her seven pages of otherwise impressive work experience might simply blend together in the eyes of the reviewer. Note also how the use of employment summaries or anecdotes helps both candidates in making their experiences more personable and meaningful. These appear in single or double quotation marks in the responsibilities column. Lastly, in terms of presentation, Kevin uses a landscape (horizontal) format; Vivian uses a portrait (vertical) format. Nowadays this distinction is irrelevant due to the advent of on-line applications in which information is fed into data fields ("data boxes").

Exhibit 6-3   Sample employment analysis summary sheet: Kevin

Employment Analysis Summary Sheet

Application to XYZ MBA School for Fall 1998

My career objective is to take a leadership role in the *fund management industry*. Business people working in the fund industries need to be well acquainted with broad-ranging issues and disciplines, such as finance, legal, marketing, etc. My work experience has helped me to gain broad exposures in a short period of time. Only as a result of these diverse experiences, I now feel that I am best prepared for an MBA education and subsequently to focus on a career in Fund Management. The following is a brief summary of my employment record.

Full-time employment

From	Company	Nature	Categories of experience
Apr '95 – Present* [Dec 1997]	Nedcor Asia Limited	Banking	Financial analysis
Mar '93 – Mar '95	Shougang Concord Steel	Steel business	China trading
Sept '91 – Feb '93	Decor Field Corporation	Import/export	Trading/entrepreneurship

Summer/part-time/internship employment

From	Company	Nature	Categories of experience
Jun '91 – Aug '91	Decor Field Corporation (summer)	Import/export	Trading/entrepreneurship
Sept '90 – May '91	University of San Francisco (part-time)	Teaching	Education
Jun '90 – Aug '90	Decor Field Corporation (summer)	Import/export	Trading/entrepreneurship

Page 1 of 3

Exhibit 6-4 Sample employment record: Kevin

EMPLOYMENT RECORD (FULL-TIME)

Company	Location & dates	Responsibilities
NEDCOR ASIA LIMITED (This company is a restricted license bank [restricted license limits the bank in certain aspects, such as the ratio of capital to loan, nature and amount of deposit, etc.] wholly owned by Nedbank, South Africa. It has a client portfolio of about 220 accounts and annual turnover of over US$240 million each year from 1995 to 1997. There is about 70 staff in the Macau office.) **Credit Department** *Credit Officer –* *Financial Analyst*	Macau Apr '95 to Dec '97 Min. 50 hrs/wk	• Evaluated and wrote comments on corporate credit ratings of existing and prospective accounts based on clients' credit history and financial ratios. Minimized problem loans by reducing about one account per month. • Developed new financial packages to encourage clients' utilization of credit lines. The aggregate utilization rate was improved from 65 percent to 83 percent after implementation. • Designed new operation procedures to re-engineer the existing operating system. This helped to simplify and standardize work flows. • Developed a system to delegate daily operational duties to respective departments. Supervised to ensure the smooth handover of tasks. This restated the credit department's function in risk assessments and strategic duties. • Assisted in managerial duties to prepare credit agenda and credit reports for credit manager's presentation in the weekly credit meetings and annual board meetings. "I took up the role of a financial analyst to analyze, assess, and restructure over an average of 20 new review proposals each month together with approving and administering over 120 applications each month. We are interacting with 11 marketing staff who continue to expand their portfolios by either increasing the number of clients or making larger volume of loans to clients. In such a fast-paced environment, my credit analyzing skill is growing at the same horizon."
SHOUGANG CONCORD STEEL INTERNATIONAL TRADING COMPANY LIMITED (Shougang Concord Group is a public-listed red-chip steel enterprise in Hong Kong. Its parent company, Shougang was the No. 1 state-owned steel production plant in Beijing, China. The average annual turnover was over US$600 million. The plant in Beijing, China has over 60,000 staff. The Macau office has about 100 staff.) *Marketing Executive &* *Assistant Manager*	Macau Mar '93 – Mar '95 Min. 50 hrs/wk	• Designed shipment, conversion, and repayment schedules in the form of barter trade for 30,000 tons of iron from the iron mine in South America to China. • Placed purchase order on basis of marketing trend and performed sales analysis to avoid overstock. Resulted in 15 percent decrease in expenses in stocking of steel products. • Participated in infrastructure tender in China and serviced a portfolio of active clients. The income contributed to the group by the tender projects was about US$300,000. My previous portfolio of clients constituted 15 percent of the group's turnover. "Our trading department contributed over 40 percent (= US$379 million) to the group's turnover in 1993 and 1994, representing over 14 percent profit contribution (= US$4.5 million). As the second staff to join the department, I played a critical role in many of those transactions. This job has given me solid China trade experience and specialized marketing and operational management, applicable to a career in global economy." Reasons for leaving: to establish my career in the finance field – banking. After gaining some China trade experience at the two former jobs, I aim to lay a foundation in my career objectives.

Page 2 of 3

Exhibit 6-4   (cont'd)

EMPLOYMENT RECORD (FULL-TIME)

Company	Location & dates	Responsibilities
DECOR FIELD CORPORATION (Decor Field Corporation is a family-owned trading company specializing in the trading of sundry products, such as artificial plants, ceiling fans, photo frames, and Christmas decorations. It is a small company with 10 staff. The annual turnover was about US$7 million.) *Assistant to General Manager*	Macau Sept '91 – Feb '93 Min. 60 hrs/wk	• Responsible for account functions – prepared tax returns, handled account entries, and reconciled bank statements. • Established a computerized accounting system, ACCPAC and trained two staff to operate the system. Resulted in 15 percent reduction of expenses. • Promoted a new item, photo frame. Duties included organized exhibitions and negotiated contracts with clients and suppliers. Contributed 8 percent to sales turnover in four months. "Assisting the general manager in a family-owned business translated to working unlimited overtime. Yet, this was the best way to learn about entrepreneurship in a real-life experience. The training from opening a bank account to negotiating business gave me solid experience in managing small businesses." Reasons for leaving: to seek China trade experience in preparing myself for the future business world.

(SUMMER/PART-TIME/INTERNSHIP)

Company	Location & dates	Responsibilities
DECOR FIELD CORPORATION [A family-owned trading company.] *Management Trainee*	Macau Jun '91 – Aug '91 Jun '90 – Aug '90 Min. 40 hrs/wk	• Handled full set of shipping documents • Responsible for daily account entry • Replied all in-coming business correspondence from clients, manufacturers, shipping companies, and other trading agents
UNIVERSITY OF SAN FRANCISCO Mathematics Department *Teaching Assistant*	San Francisco, CA Sept '90 – May '91 Min. 20 hrs/wk	• Tutored students in calculus classes • Corrected students' homework and examinations in calculus classes

Exhibit 6–5 Sample employment record: Vivian

PROFESSIONAL EXPERIENCE SUMMARY (EMPLOYMENT ANALYSIS SUMMARY SHEET)

The following career goal and cover sheet serve to summarize my professional work experience.

Career Goal

All of my work experience has taken place under the umbrella of General Electric. I have worked in both European and Asian markets; this includes experience in financial management, internal auditing, and investment analysis. I feel that the depth and variety of these experiences will play an integral role in preparing me for my ultimate career goal: Becoming a leading **Business Ethics/Corporate Citizenship Consultant**.

Company & position	Dates	Location	Page no.
NATIONAL BROADCASTING COMPANY ASIA (NBC Asia) Manager, News Finance and special projects	Feb '96 – *[Jan '98] * present	Hong Kong, China	2
GENERAL ELECTRIC LIGHTING EUROPE Manager, Western European Internal Audit Department	Nov '94 – Feb '96	Based in Hungary (extensive Western European travel 2–3 wks/mth)	3
GENERAL ELECTRIC LIGHTING EUROPE Investment Analyst, Incandescent and Halogen Lighting Product Lines	Sept '93 – Nov '94	Budapest, Hungary (monthly travel to the U.K.)	4
GENERAL ELECTRIC LIGHTING EUROPE Cost Analyst, Budapest Light Source Factory (6-month Financial Management Program [FMP] Rotation)	Apr '93 – Sept '93	Budapest, Hungary	5
GENERAL ELECTRIC LIGHTING EUROPE Financial Analyst, Financial Planning and Analysis (FMP Rotation)	Jul '92 – Apr '93	Budapest, Hungary	6
GENERAL ELECTRIC LIGHTING EUROPE Financial Analyst, Technology Finance (FMP Rotation)	Feb '92 – Jul '92	Budapest, Hungary	7
GENERAL ELECTRIC LIGHTING EUROPE Financial Analyst, Sales and Marketing Finance (FMP Rotation)	Jun '91 – Feb '92	Budapest, Hungary	8

Page 1 of 8

Exhibit 6–5 (cont'd)

Dates	Firm name:	**NATIONAL BROADCASTING COMPANY (NBC ASIA)**
From: 02/96	Firm size:	Appr. 298 employees; 1997 revenue US$4 million
To: Present	Nature of business:	Broadcasting company
	Job location:	Chaiwan, Hong Kong

Job title:	Starting annual	Current annual
Manager, News Finance and Special Projects	base salary: US$42,000	base salary: US$45,300
	Additional: Location premium US$28,000	Additional: Location premium US$30,000

List and description of responsibilities:

- CNBC Asia Business News Channel's *first* financial manager.
- Working closely with CNBC Asia management to develop annual business and operating plans for channel and establish monthly and quarterly budgets.
- Tracking and reporting expenditures and providing variance analysis versus budget on a weekly, monthly, and quarterly basis to CNBC Asia management and quarterly results and analysis to NBC NY headquarters.
- Performing monthly internal closings of *all* CNBC Asia accounts and account reconciliations and reconciling inter-company expense and liability accounts for purchased programming with NBC NY headquarters and NBC Super Channel in the U.K.
- Responsible for approving *all* CNBC Asia expenditures and performing various financial analysis for the channel.
- Responsible for NBC Asia's total headcount reporting to NBC NY headquarters.
- Working closely with NBC Asia technical staff to create budget and track over US$35 million of annual expenditures for satellites and link charges for company. Providing variance analysis versus budget on a monthly basis to local management and quarterly results and analysis to NBC NY headquarters. Performing monthly internal closings of *all* satellite and link accounts and account reconciliations.
- Providing financial support to legal department and helping to negotiate contracts with suppliers such as stringers, newswire agencies, and production houses.

Most significant challenge of this position:

- "I am responsible for controlling spending and redirecting resources to opportunities in line with CNBC Asia's goals. At the same time, I have to maintain a good working relationship with CNBC Asia's management as the channel's *first* financial manager."

Reason for leaving:

- N/A

Exhibit 6–5 (cont'd)

Dates From: 11/94 To: 2/96	Firm name: Firm size: Nature of business: Job location:	**GENERAL ELECTRIC LIGHTING EUROPE** 9,000 employees; US$700 million in revenue Manufacturing; lighting industry Based in Budapest, Hungary; extensive Western European travel 2 to 3 weeks per month
Job title: **Manager, Western European Internal Audit Department**	Starting annual base salary: US$37,100 Additional: Cost of living & location premium & home leave adj. US$32,000	Ending annual base salary: US$37,800 Additional: Cost of living & location premium & home leave adj. US$38,000

List and description of responsibilities:

- Created *new* organization. Led and managed two employees.
- Planned, organized, and headed *all* financial and business process audits at GELE sales offices in France, Spain, England, and Hungary.
- Audited office's financial statements for accuracy and adherence to generally accepted accounting principles (GAAP).
- Interviewed employees, process mapped office's activities, and conducted transactions tests to verify routines and controls.
- Conducted compliance audits with management and key staff to ensure knowledge of and adherence to GE Spirit & Letter Integrity Policies.
- Audited information system security and deleted unnecessary and/or conflicting system access of staff.
- Presented findings and made recommendations on issues uncovered to local and upper management.
- Worked in multicultural teams to resolve issues and implement recommendations.
- Provided financial analysis as member of a cross-functional team set up to reduce excess inventory in the incandescent product line.

Most significant challenge of this position:

- "Although the job description and responsibilities were vague, I was able to create a new organization, quickly identify major business issues, and successfully incorporate business goals into the audit program."

Reason for leaving:

- Promoted to Manager, News Finance and Special Projects at NBC Asia in Hong Kong

Exhibit 6–5 (*cont'd*)

Dates From: 9/93 To: 11/94	Firm name: Job location:	**GENERAL ELECTRIC LIGHTING EUROPE** Budapest, Hungary; Monthly travel to the U.K.
Job title: **Investment Analyst,** **Incandescent and** **Halogen Lighting** **Product Lines**	Starting annual base salary: US$32,700	Ending annual base salary: US$37,100
	Additional: Cost of living & location premium & home leave adj. US$14,000	Additional: Cost of living & location premium & home leave adj. US$32,000

List and description of responsibilities:

- Responsible for analyzing, approving, and tracking of over 90 projects totaling US$6 million in capital investment in Hungary and the U.K for the incandescent and halogen lighting product lines.
- Conducted financial analysis of proposed capital investments using DCRR, NPV, IRR, and financial modeling techniques. Worked in cross-functional and multicultural teams to gather financial and operational information to perform analysis and made recommendations to management based on results.
- Financial representative for GELE's *first* major rationalization project, coordinating pan-European information gathering, analysis, and tracking of US$5 million of fixed assets transferred from the U.K. to Hungary as a result of plant shutdowns.

Most significant challenge of this position:

- "I was able to successfully gather and analyze financial and operational information in an environment where data was scarce and project team members were located in different plants throughout the U.K. and Hungary and had conflicting objectives."

Reason for leaving:

- Promoted to manager of Western European Internal Audit Department

Exhibit 6–5 (cont'd)

Dates From: 4/93 To: 9/93	Firm name: Job location:	**GENERAL ELECTRIC LIGHTING EUROPE** Budapest, Hungary
Job title: **Cost Analyst, Budapest Light Source Factory (6 month FMP Rotation)**	Starting annual base salary: US$32,700	Ending annual base salary: US$32,700
	Additional: Cost of living & location premium & home leave adj. US$14,000	Additional: Cost of living & location premium & home leave adj. US$14,000

List and description of responsibilities:

- Prepared investment analysis for *new* incandescent manufacturing line in Budapest Light Source Factory using DCRR, NPV, IRR, and financial modeling techniques. Worked in cross-functional teams to gather financial and operational information to perform analysis.
- Audited routines and controls for movement and sale of scrap lamps and components from factory. Made recommendations to change process involving use of environmentally hazardous materials in order to ensure greater safety.
- Financial representative for GELE Asset Committee – a cross-functional team set up to dispose of buildings and houses owned by Tungsram in Hungary. Responsible for the financial analysis of the rental and disposal of this property. Helped committee members negotiate with real estate agents and company representatives for the sale and rental of buildings/houses.

Most significant challenge of this position:

- "I was accepted by the Budapest Light Source Factory plant management and employees and gained their trust to accurately complete investment analysis."

Reason for leaving:

- Promoted to off-program position as investment analyst for GELE's incandescent and halogen lighting product lines

Exhibit 6–5 (cont'd)

Dates	Firm name:	**GENERAL ELECTRIC LIGHTING EUROPE**
From: 7/92	Job location:	Budapest, Hungary
To: 4/93		

Job title:	Starting annual	Ending annual
Financial Analyst,	base salary:	base salary:
Financial Planning	US$31,400	US$32,700
and Analysis		
(6-month FMP		
Rotation)		
	Additional:	Additional:
	Cost of living &	Cost of living &
	location premium	location premium &
	& home leave adj.	home leave adj.
	US$14,000	US$14,000

List and description of responsibilities:

- Responsible for the information retrieval, tracking, and reporting of US$65 million worth of Purchase Accounting (PA) expenditures. Personal investigation yielded US$1.6 million of previously undiscovered PA.
- Conducted an in-depth investigation into an entire system of passenger transportation at Tungsram. Recommendations were used as basis for management decisions.

Most significant challenge of this position:

- "I had to communicate regulations and proper accounting methods of Purchase Accounting, a complex GAAP procedure, to a group of non-English speaking factory accountants who were unfamiliar with U.S. accounting standards and practices."

Reason for leaving:

- Six-month FMP rotation (General Electric's Financial Management Program)

Exhibit 6–5   (cont'd)

Dates From: 2/92 To: 7/92	Firm name: Job location:	**GENERAL ELECTRIC LIGHTING EUROPE** Budapest, Hungary
Job title: **Financial Analyst, Technology Finance (Six-month FMP Rotation)**	Starting annual base salary: US$30,500	Ending annual base salary: US$31,400
	Additional: Cost of living & location premium & home leave adj. US$8,600	Additional: Cost of living & location premium & home leave adj. US$14,000

List and description of responsibilities:

- Successfully implemented GE Lighting Tungsram's *first* fixed asset investment tracking system (RKP) tracking US$44 million worth of capital investment and program expenditure.
- Trained and instructed all users of system.

Most significant challenge of this position:

- "I was responsible for implementing a complicated information system under a tight deadline without the support of the designing team (an FMP and information systems consultant who left the project)."

Reason for leaving:

- Six-month FMP rotation (General Electric's Financial Management Program)

Exhibit 6–5 *(cont'd)*

Dates From: 6/91 To: 2/92	Firm name: Job location:	**GENERAL ELECTRIC LIGHTING EUROPE** Budapest, Hungary

Job title: **Financial Analyst, Sales and Marketing Finance (Six-month FMP Rotation)**	Starting annual base salary: US$30,500	Ending annual base salary: US$30,500
	Additional: Cost of living & location premium adj. US$8,600	Additional: Cost of living & location premium adj. US$8,600

List and description of responsibilities:

- Responsible for the *first ever* detailed analysis of pricing and profitability by Lighting product line and for recommendations for price increases.
- Created a transportation spreadsheet program to calculate per product transportation cost by product line and destination.

Most significant challenge of this position:

- "I generated incremental margin through pricing increases despite internal resistance from the local sales and marketing personnel and lack of reliable sales and contribution margin information."

Reason for leaving:

- Six-month FMP rotation (General Electric's Financial Management Program)

CHAPTER 7
Letters of Recommendation

"I always know when candidates write recommendations themselves. They never brag about themselves in the way a recommender would."

Admissions officer of a leading business school

INTRODUCTION

How many recommendations do you need?

You are generally required to obtain between two and three recommendations in order to apply to business school. In the old days, it was common to get both recommendations from your college professors with a third or optional letter from your employer, if applicable. The reason for this was simply that graduate business students most often came directly from college and therefore academic recommendations were the norm. Nowadays the situation is reversed. Schools generally want both your recommendations to be work related, with ideally one written by your current boss. When a third recommendation is required, it may be professional, academic, or community service in nature.

A typical candidate will be required to submit two or three recommendations as follows:

1. Professional.
2. Professional.
3. Academic, professional, or community service in nature.

The rule of thumb is that unless your third recommendation is going to present another aspect of your work experience, and not merely repeat the first and second recommendations then you should go for *diversity* on your third recommendation. Think of a person who can write your recommendation who you have been associated with outside of work or school, particularly a person working in community service, or politics.

How are your letters of recommendation evaluated?

There are two dimensions along which letters of recommendation are evaluated. The first is the objectivity dimension: "Who says it?" The second is the content dimension: "What is said?" Both the objectivity and content dimensions combine to give a sense of credibility. The person "who says it" should be someone capable of observing your work or academics. The strength of "what is said" is ultimately linked to the examples (or lack thereof) used by the recommender to support what he or she says. Content will vary depending on the type of recommendation, namely professional, academic, or community service.

Regardless of whether a recommendation is professional, academic, or community service-oriented, the reviewer will look for evidence of a candidate's personal traits and qualities. Thus, a professional recommendation should ideally touch on those personal traits and qualities important to your career development. Likewise, an academic recommendation should ideally touch on those personal key traits to your intellectual development.

Exhibit 7–1 Generic Letter Method

(typed letter)

staple

Jan 17, 19xx

Admissions Director:

It is my pleasure to serve as a reference for Richard Tyler in his application for admission to your Graduate Business School. I have known Richard for 14 years; first as an associate of his father (we worked together in a large U.S. conglomerate from 1984 to 1991). Later Richard worked for me at Xerox Corporation as an accountant and financial analyst.

Richard demonstrated a high level of intelligence, strong technical skills, and a very effective and positive way of interacting with people. He gained quickly the respect and support of his peers and seniors. He made a substantial contribution at Xerox Corporation during his period of service. I would particularly like to cite his originality and desire to innovate new systems and procedures.

Another remarkable quality worthy of mention is Richard's wide range of interests – from the specific and exacting profession of accounting and quantitative analysis to the broad interests that took him to Japan for study and international experience. This is a unique range.

Based on my 32-year career in the financial management of high-tech companies, my own XYZ school MBA degree, and knowledge of many applicants and young graduates over the years, I would rank Richard in the top 10 percent of his peers now applying for admission.

Sincerely,

Frank B. Moore, Jr.

Frank B. Moore, Jr.
Vice President of Finance
and Chief Financial Officer
Xerox Systems of America

(back side of recommendation form)

Confidential Recommendation   MBA PROGRAM
The ANDERSON SCHOOL AT UCLA

5. Please rate the applicant on the qualities listed below, identifying here the group to which you are comparing the applicant: _____

	n/a	< 50%	> 50%	> 25%	> 10%	> 5%	> 2%
Ability to work with others						X	
Analytical/quantitative skills				X			
Intellectual ability						X	
Oral com. skills					X		
Written skills				X			
Motivation/initiative				X			
Leadership potential					X		
Maturity				X			
Sense of humor				X			
Respect from peers					X		X
Respect from management				X			
Potential for career advancement					X		

mender's signature *Frank B. Moore, Jr.*   Date Jan. 17, 19xx

Exhibit 7–2 Individual Question Method

(front side)

```
Confidential Recommendation _____

          MBA PROGRAM
     The ANDERSON SCHOOL AT UCLA
```

Name of Applicant _____

TO THE RECOMMENDER:

The person whose name appears above is applying for admission to The Anderson School MBA Program. The Admissions Committee values the direct contact you have had with the applicant and asks for your personal and candid assessment of his or her potential for senior management. The most helpful recommendations are those that present a balanced view and give detailed descriptions of an applicant's abilities.

Please answer the following questions on separate paper, either in letter form or by number as shown below. **Return this form and your recommendation to the applicant in a sealed envelope, with your signature across the seal. The candidate will submit the sealed envelope as part of the complete application package.** We will send you an acknowledgment card informing you that your recommendation has been received by our office.

Name of recommender _____ Telephone _____

Position/title _____ Firm/school _____

Address _____

1. How long have you known the applicant and in what context? Please comment on the frequency of your interaction.

2. What are the applicant's principal strengths and special talents?

3. In what areas can the applicant improve? Has he or she worked on these areas?

4. Compared to others with similar responsibilities in your organization, how would you rate the applicant? Why?

(back side)

```
Confidential Recommendation        MBA PROGRAM
                              The ANDERSON SCHOOL AT UCLA
```

Please rate the applicant on the qualities listed below, identifying here the group to which you are comparing the applicant: _____

	n/a	< 50%	> 50%	> 25%	> 10%	> 5%	> 2%
Ability to work with others							
Analytical/ quantitative skills							
Intellectual ability							
Oral com. skills							
Written skills							
Motivation/ initiative							
Leadership potential							
Maturity							
Sense of humor							
Respect from peers							
Respect from management							
Potential for career advancement							

Recommender's signature _____ Date _____

Two methods to complete recommendation letters

The first method involves having each recommender type a generic, all-purpose letter. The second method involves having each recommender answer all questions on each individual recommendation form.

Generic Letter Method. Again, here is how this method works. Recommenders type separate letters on their corporate letterhead, two-thirds of a page to one-and-a-half pages long, and staple a copy of each typed letter to the specific recommendation form of the school. Each recommender will still have to rate the candidate by checking the boxes directly on the recommendation form for each particular category. For example, communication skills—top 5 percent, top 10 percent, top 15 percent, etc. after which the recommender signs the recommendation form. The recommendation (signed and sealed) will either be mailed back to the candidate (or mailed directly to the school) or nowadays submitted on-line.

In practice, recommenders like the Generic Letter Method because they can type a single letter to be used by a candidate for all his or her schools. Consider the recommender who is assisting seven people apply to business school in a single year, in which each candidate is applying to seven schools. Can you imagine being burdened with filling in some 50 individual recommendation forms! Admissions officers understand this procedure and will not reject a candidate simply because he or she did not have recommenders fill in answers directly on each recommendation form.

Individual Question Method. In practice, schools prefer that recommenders follow the Individual Question Method. Occasionally a recommender will both type a letter and respond to individual questions per each recommendation form. If the recommender has the time, committee members will not object to the extra effort.

Get them to mention specifics

The biggest problem with recommendations is similar to that of application essays—namely superficiality and a lack of concrete examples to support what is being said. The recommendation written for you is, in part, only as good as the information you give to the recommender. Your objective is to get the recommender to mention specific things about you, in order to make what the recommender says both forceful and credible.

With a tad of cynicism thrown in, many recommendation letters sound like: "Johnny is a nice boy" or "Suzie is a good girl". In other words, the reader is left with no measure of how to judge the applicant's qualities and credentials. Superficiality stems from two sources:

- The recommender really does not know the candidate. This is very true of most recommendations received from CEOs and high political officials. They are referred to informally as "letters of support", rather than letters of recommendation.

- The recommender knows the candidate but cannot express it through his or her writing. This is often true of recommenders who are either unfamiliar with the MBA admissions process (or other graduate level undertaking) or who are less than proficient in the art of writing (more often true of recommenders whose first language is not English). Such letters lack concrete details and examples, and may be full of unsupported adjectives, pleasantries, etc.

The following letter was obtained by a candidate who apparently met the U.S. Vice President at an official government function.

Dear Admissions Committee:

I recommend this candidate for admission to your school. I met the applicant at an official function and he impressed me with his honest-looking face and firm handshake.

Sincerely,

Mr. Vice President of the United States

This letter has become part of the folklore of graduate school admissions. Unfortunately, the letter contributed more in terms of comic relief to overworked admissions personnel than in terms of substantive advancement of the applicant's application. Admission committee members were probably far more interested in knowing how the candidate talked the Vice President into writing a letter when the Vice President obviously did not know him well. Where is the detail and where is the support?

You should try to supply each recommender with the following:

- First, a copy of your resume or employment record. An employment record ("re-formatted resume") is generally required by each business school you are applying to. Ideally, it should include a summary of what you found significant about your work (see Chapter 6). The objective here is to get the recommender to reinforce those things which you believe are highlights of your work experience.

- Second, a personal letter (suggested length, two type-written pages). A personal letter is needed in order to highlight for the recommender what your career goals are, and to elaborate what *you* believe *your* unique personal traits and achievements are, why you want an MBA, unique personal details, etc. Hopefully, this will include a clear idea of your general career direction and strong personal characteristics. Again, the more quality information you give your recommender, the better chance you have of getting a "good" letter of recommendation. Sometimes candidates send their recommenders copies of their admissions essays which serve to give recommenders background information.

Based on a well-written personal letter, your recommenders have *specifics*—both professional and personal—to use in writing your recommendation letters or in filling out your recommendation forms. It is vital that you have your *goal statements* and *vision statements* (refer to Chapter 3) written before you ask recommenders to write recommendation letters for you. Do not let recommenders guess at your career goals; help them to figure out what you are doing. Most candidates send recommendation forms to their recommenders with only a resume attached. However, without a candidate first deciding on his or her post-MBA and long-term career goal, and subsequently communicating this to his or her recommender, the recommender is likely to be left feeling confused by not having a better idea of what the candidate expects to do with his or her MBA and where his or her career path is heading.

You ideally never want the admissions committee to think of you as a clueless applicant. Consider this last paragraph of an actual recommendation letter:

> Eric is a "good person". He is very intelligent, yet with an ego under control. He has principles and morals by which he lives by. I am not sure if he is fiercely ambitious and has a clear vision of what he wants to do with his life, but in a stimulating MBA program, I am sure that this will soon change.

SEVEN TIPS FOR GETTING GOOD LETTERS OF RECOMMENDATION

The following are tips on how to get good letters of recommendation.

Tip #65: **Prepare early by choosing your recommenders.**

Notify your recommenders that you will be applying to business school and that you will be requesting recommendation letters. Give your recommenders sufficient time to receive forms and/or type letters.

Tip #66: **Write a statement of your career goals to communicate to your recommenders where you feel your career is heading.**

This tip will serve to impress the recommender and give him or her the added confidence in writing you a recommendation letter.

✍ **Tip #67: Update your resume and/or employment record complete with summaries on what you feel you have learned or what you feel is significant about your experiences.**

Refer to employment themes discussed in Chapter 6.

✍ **Tip #68: Send your resume and/or employment record along with a personal letter to each recommender.**

Your personal letter should be approximately two pages and may be presented in point form. It should highlight your goals, and address your work achievements, key traits, and personal strengths and weaknesses. The more information the recommender has, the more detail your letter is likely to be.

✍ **Tip #69: If your recommender insists that you draft your own letter, then ask a friend to write it for you so as to disguise your writing style.**

Admissions officers frown upon the practice that occurs whenever applicants draft their own letters of recommendation. Recommenders who agree to write recommendations should fulfill their responsibilities and write the letters themselves. In reality, your recommender may, for reasons of overwork, unfamiliarity, or laziness, ask you to write your own letter to be presented to the recommender for modification and signing. For purposes of style and voice, if your recommender is female, then have a female friend draft the letter; if your recommender is male then have a male friend draft the letter for you.

✍ **Tip #70: Think detail. The goal is to get the recommender to write in a specific and concrete manner, often highlighting one or two major work accomplishments, one or two distinguishing personal traits, or one or two major strengths or weaknesses.**

If your recommender allows you to see a copy of your recommendation letter, and you do not see sufficient detail, you may want to ask your recommender to add more in the way of specifics. As diplomatically as you can, suggest to your recommender that you understand that top ranked business schools are looking, above all else, for written details to support what you have done. Here is an opportunity to coach your recommender. You might say, "I was reading in the application brochure (on the web) that admissions officers are looking for detail. It mentioned that the admissions process has become more competitive in recent years and that schools want specific examples to understand how a candidate excels as well as gets things done in the workplace."

Tip #71: Send a thank-you note (or email) to your recommenders.

Your recommenders have done some good work for you, which required time and effort. You may decide to apply to more schools at a later point in the application process, and you may need to approach your recommenders again. Moreover, you will likely submit the names of your recommenders as job references when looking for work both in and outside of business school. Develop and keep rapport.

THE MECHANICS OF A "GOOD" LETTER OF RECOMMENDATION

The following five things are generally present in high quality letter of recommendation:

1. The recommender mentions in what *context* he or she knows the applicant.
2. The recommender mentions what the applicant *accomplished*, on the job or in school.
3. The recommender mentions how the candidate *ranks* in comparison with others.
4. The recommender mentions what he or she believes are the applicant's best personal and professional *traits*.
5. The recommender mentions one area of perceived *weakness* or one area of needed professional, academic, or personal improvement.

SAMPLE LETTERS OF RECOMMENDATION

The following are examples of two fairly standard letters of recommendation as may be seen in the business school application process. A critique of both letters follows.

Exhibit 7–3   Sample recommendation letter: Frank B. Moore

Admissions Director:

It is my pleasure to serve as a reference for Richard Tyler in his application for admission to your Graduate Business School. I have known Richard for 14 years, first as an associate of his father (we worked together in a large U.S. conglomerate from 1984 to 1991). Later Richard worked for me at Xerox Corporation as an accountant and financial analyst.

context ✓

Richard demonstrated a high level of intelligence, strong technical skills, and a very effective and positive way of interacting with people. He gained quickly the respect and support of his peers and seniors. He made a substantial contribution at Xerox Corporation during his period of service. I would particularly like to cite his originality and desire to innovate new systems and procedures.

what were these?

Another remarkable quality worthy of mention is Richard's wide range of interests – from the specific and exacting profession of accounting and quantitative analysis to the broad interests that took him to Japan for study and international experience. This is a unique range.

Based on my 32-year career in the financial management of high-tech companies, my own *XYZ* school MBA degree, and knowledge of many applicants and young graduates over the years, I would rank Richard in the top 10 percent of his peers now applying for admission.

rating ✓

Sincerely,

Frank B. Moore, Jr.

Frank B. Moore, Jr.
Vice President of Finance
and Chief Financial Officer
Xerox Systems of America

Exhibit 7–4 Sample recommendation letter: Elizabeth Lee

Dear Admissions Committee:

I still remember the first time I met Judith Chan. She was a bit shy when she applied to work in our firm as a sales support person in March of 1994. As a sales representative at the newly opened branch of Avon Cosmetic Products in Hong Kong, she would be responsible for monitoring the phones and walk-in customers, answering their questions and helping them with whatever we could offer them. As this was a new center for Avon International and women's accessories was a brand new product area, it had to be adapted for Hong Kong and PRC consumers. Judith not only exceeded her sales quotas but also became our regional expert on how to adapt, modify, and package all our local products. When Avon headquarters decided to revamp Asian operations, they got Judith's input.

by how much?

Besides having a very special organizational ability, Judith also has a wonderful way with her co-workers and customers. Co-workers listen to her advice and customers continue to buy from her. Judith is always willing to put in that extra to get things right. We have all watched Judith develop her marketing and sales skills. If she were not planning on going to graduate school, we would have offered her the position of director of our Beijing Avon office where she would not only administrate but also train sales staff to open up the China market.

can you cite a quote?

As an XYZ school college grad myself who started the Avon Hong Kong office and hired Judith, I am most proud of "finding" her for our company. She is extremely talented, diligent, and innovative, and all without business school training. Although we hate to "lose" her, we know that she would gain so much from further studies at business school, as I know that I did. As a teacher and administrator myself, I have to admit that I have never met another person who has greater potential to be a truly great marketer. She already is our most valued one and will be greatly missed. Thus, I unreservedly and enthusiastically recommend her for your program. The school would be proud of such a graduate.

any weak areas?

Sincerely,

Elizabeth Lee

——————————————

Elizabeth Lee
Director, Avon Cosmetics (Hong Kong) Ltd.

Exhibit 7–5   Sample recommendation letter: Norman Kravics

Massachusetts Institute of Technology
Sloan School of Management
Master's Admissions Office, Room E52-101
50 Memorial Drive
Cambridge, MA 02142-1347

To Whom It May Concern:

At the request of Ms. Julie Munzer, I am writing this recommendation in strong support of her application for admission into your graduate program.

Julie has been reporting directly to me for the past two years as a financial analyst at Goldman Sachs in Australia. In my current role as the Regional Head of Utilities Research, Julie and I interact frequently on a daily basis. Significantly, Julie's performance and contributions to the team have been nothing short of outstanding.

Appropriately, she was promoted to associate analyst in August of this year, a position typically occupied by post-MBA graduates.

The ability to handle multiple projects and service widely varying end-customers (investment banking, corporate clients, institutional investors, sales and trading, or others) is a requirement for success in equity research. Along this metric, Julie is a superstar. In my estimation, her capacity for carrying heavy workloads for sustained periods of time is among the top 1 percent of all financial analysts I have worked with globally. Julie has been instrumental in helping to expand our research coverage universe roughly three-fold in the past 18 months. She developed and maintains ownership of the firm's Utilities Weekly research product. She has been a key coordinator of our annual Utilities Symposiums, the largest conference of its type in the region and one of the firm's most visible annual client events. On the investment banking support side, Julie has contributed research directly or indirectly in several major transactions, including Initial Public Offerings (IPOs), secondary stock offerings, block trade executions, convertible debt transactions, and mergers and acquisitions. I am convinced that Julie's resourcefulness and on-going contributions were an important factor in our utilities team being named to Institutional Investor magazine's All-Asia Research Team in 2000.

It has been personally gratifying to me watching Julie's analytical abilities mature since the time I have worked with her. I am entirely comfortable with having Julie meet with and interview company management teams when I am unavailable. She asks probing questions and has developed "an ear" for what is important and increasingly how to interpret various (and sometimes conflicting) data points. In our latest new coverage report (Symbiotic Industries), Julie constructed the basic financial models and projections, as well as a major portion of the written material and investment thesis. She handles herself flawlessly in working across geographic regions, as companies that we actively research include multi-billion dollar corporations in Taiwan, China, Singapore, and Korea. Perhaps the strongest endorsement of our confidence in Julie's analytical ability is the fact that she is slated to soon begin introducing her own research franchise and senior coverage of stocks. Again, senior or lead coverage of stocks is typically not mandated to new analysts until a year or more after graduate business school has been completed.

Earlier this year, I was asked to spend a few days in Japan with other Goldman Sachs analysts visiting major institutional clients as part of a global marketing initiative. Due to scheduling conflicts, I was unable to participate. Feeling that she was up for the assignment, I asked Julie to take my place. Although it was clear to me that she was somewhat intimated at first by this request – and with good reason, as to my knowledge, there had been no financial analyst at her level at the time that had assumed such a prominent role in a research marketing trip – she accepted the challenge without hesitation. For my part, any cautiousness I had came from the fact that Julie had historically spent most of her time performing grass roots research and interacting with company management, not doing face-to-face institutional investor meetings. Julie spent a good deal of time preparing for the trip, probing me with insightful questions and studying the art of "stock positioning" versus "company positioning." She prepared herself to market her stock ideas with a strong "bottoms-up" approach, focusing on competitive positions and valuations of companies within the region, driving our ultimate investment ideas. Needless to say, the trip was a great success, with some of the other senior analysts coming back to me with feedback about how impressed they were regarding her performance on the road show and accompanying luncheon presentations (one of which featured more than 100 attendees).

Julie works effectively and cooperatively in the team environment, one of the cornerstones of our organization. With regards to managers and supervisors, she may sometimes come off as a bit shy to those she does not know well. I believe that some of this may be cultural, as there is a degree of natural modesty about her. With regards to peers, Julie is very successful in nurturing cooperation and getting things done. For example, she maintains good relationships with counterparts in various departments (sales, strategy, economics, etc.) and was praised by others in international offices for her cooperation and timely sharing of news flow. With respect to subordinates, Julie has begun the task of mentoring two new financial analysts that joined the team in June of this year. With the best of intentions, I have asked her to "clone herself" in the training of our new teammates. She has taken the task to heart, providing daily guidance in everything from financial model building to networking around the firm. One of the new analysts has even moved his own chair into her office.

I rate Julie's leadership potential as high. Although she has spent most of her career with me in support of group initiatives, Julie has clearly demonstrated key traits that I believe are critical in leadership: focus, teamwork, responsibility, and integrity. As mentioned above, she has recently taken on a mentoring role, and I believe has been successful in integrating these new analysts into the team in a very short period of time.

Within the organization, Julie has been giving of her time on several fronts, including college campus recruiting (sometimes requiring her to fly to other countries, such as Taiwan where her language abilities are a major benefit for the firm's recruiting efforts). In addition, Goldman sponsors an on-going program called "Community Teamworks" where employees volunteer their time outside of work to help the local community in projects ranging from public cleanup initiatives to tutoring to construction programs. Julie is an active member of Community Teamworks and I trust will provide more details of the various projects she has been staffed on in her application.

In summary, I am in strong support of Julie's application for admission into MIT's Sloan School of Management. I believe she has given careful consideration of her plans to enroll in an MBA program, as we have talked about this subject on several occasions. To be quite frank, while I am less than thrilled about the prospect of losing her contributions to the team while she pursues a graduate degree, I believe her motivations are sincere. Additionally, I believe Julie will share a unique global perspective with other students in the classroom setting. I welcome the opportunity to speak directly to the admissions committee should you feel you require additional information on Ms. Julie Munzer.

Respectfully submitted,

Norman Kravics

Norman Kravics
Executive Director, Goldman Sachs

The following serve as critiques of the two previous letters of recommendation.

Recommendation #1 (Exhibit 7–3)

This recommendation letter follows a traditional format for a business school letter of recommendation. It cites at a minimum, the context in which the recommender knows the candidate and a quantifiable comparison is made of the candidate to others applying to business school. This letter constitutes a solid endorsement, the only criticism is that it misses on a few opportunities to cite details in support of things said. For example, the reviewer is likely to respond to the recommender's statement, "I would particularly like to cite his originality and desire to innovate new systems and procedures" by asking what these new systems and procedures were. Moreover, the best professional recommendations may also make mention of a candidate's career aspirations, as well as areas of needed development. Sometimes the recommender cites anecdotes or quotes that other persons have made about the applicant in order to support some of the comments made by the recommender.

Recommendation #2 (Exhibit 7–4)

This recommendation is another example of a good one, written in a lighter, more colloquial tone. It comes across as warm and personable. A criticism of this letter, similar to the preceding one, lies in the lack of concrete details to support the things stated by the recommender. For example, the reviewer may want to know how much Judith did exceed her sales quota—1 percent or 200 percent—and perhaps how much sales of the Hong Kong office have grown and how much of this growth may be the result of Judith's efforts. The recommender should give one example of how Judith adapted, modified, or packaged new products for the local market because the reviewer is no doubt interested. Perhaps the recommender could cite a quote from one of Judith's favorite customers. Lastly, the reviewer may want to know at least one area where Judith is weak in order to balance out the recommendation.

Recommendation #3 (Exhibit 7-5)

The recommendation per Exhibit 7–5 provides an example of a longer recommendation (i.e., ≥1000 words). Lengthy recommendations are more commonly found in the world of management consulting and investment banking because recommenders working in management consulting and investment banking (including private equity and venture capital) are usually more familiar with the writing of recommendation letters, more likely to be graduates of top-tier business schools themselves, and more likely to be writing recommendations for candidates applying to the most competitive business schools.

There is some truth to the idea that "more is better". In this respect a recommender who writes more is signaling to the reader (admissions reviewer) that the candidate is indeed "good" because the recommender is expending more time and effort to write the recommendation.

In the recommendation written for Julie Munzer, all five mechanics regarding a recommendation letter are present. The recommender mentions the context in which he knows her, her rank relative to others, her accomplishments, her best personal and professional traits, and one area of perceived weakness or area of needed improvement.

Note that, in general, if we step back and look at recommendations from a distance, we see that regardless of length, recommendations generally say two basic things: "The candidate has good technical (or leadership) skills; the candidate has good people (or communication) skills."

CHAPTER 8

Interviews

"Poised, confident, knowing."

Motto of the perfectly prepared interview candidate

INTRODUCTION

Interviews are a potential variable in the MBA application process. Interviews are, depending on the school, either required for admissions, encouraged but not required, or simply not part of the normal admissions process. Many schools, e.g., Northwestern, University of Virginia, Harvard, Columbia, Carnegie Mellon, INSEAD, and London Business School virtually require interviews in order for candidates to be accepted. A number of other schools, e.g., University of Chicago, Dartmouth, UCLA, AGSM, and Melbourne Business School, encourage candidates to interview but do not require it. Still other schools, for example, Thunderbird, Berkeley, and Wits Business School, do not interview, and any interview will be at the school's request, not yours. Refer to the table *Interview Policies at Leading Business Schools* (Table 8–2), for a summary of the different policies followed by schools.

Why do schools interview? It is the old story: Would you hire a person on his or her resume alone? Would you marry based merely upon biographical information? Sometimes the reason given for interviewing is, "to (try to) avoid false positives and false negatives." A false positive translates to: "We accepted you (positive) but when you arrived at the school and we met you, you're not the person we thought you were." A false negative translates to: "We rejected you (negative) but you turned out to be the businessman or businesswoman of the century." Both of these mistakes are embarrassing for a business school. In the latter case, rumors continue to circulate about how now famous businesspersons, once rejected by certain top business schools, went on to achieve remarkable things. In the non-business arena, one very famous example is the rejection of Steven Spielberg from the USC Film School. Now, many years later, this tidbit still circulates as cocktail fodder, and as a welcomed addition to the folklore of scholastic rejection.

Although the trend in MBA admissions is for schools to want to interview candidates, schools are favoring the policy of first reviewing candidate application packages and then offering interviews to a select group of "final round" applicants, say 30 percent to 50 percent of the applicant pool. Schools will then make a final review of an applicant's application package and interview results, and select approximately 50 percent of those final round applicants. Such a policy allows business schools to interview virtually everyone who is admitted since only selected applicants are granted interviews. The growing number of applicants is the major reason behind the growing popularity of this policy. Nowadays it is virtually impossible for schools to allow every prospective student who applies for admissions to be interviewed.

Do not forget to schedule your interview well in advance (in the case that the interview is optional), by contacting the admissions office of your selected schools, especially if you are working overseas. Waiting until the last minute will only help delay your application. Also, as a general strategy, try to interview first at schools that are not your first or second choice—"best schools second, lesser schools first"—as you will inevitably get better at interviewing through practice. Remember to send thank you letters to your interviewers.

Should I interview?

Given the option, the decision to interview pivots on whether you feel you can favorably advance your overall application for admission. If you do not feel you can present yourself as a stronger applicant compared with the application package you have sent or are sending to a school, then it may be best not to interview. In this case, sit at home and let your application do the work for you. If you feel, however, that your "paper" application is weaker than you—the person behind that application—and you can articulate this, then by all means get out and get an interview and make an additional "application" to the school you are applying to.

Where do interviews take place?

Interviews, when required or encouraged by a school, may take place on campus, off-campus, or even over the phone. Off-campus interviews are carried out by alumni of each respective business school. This is true of interviews in international locales, where the interviewer is not only an alumni of the school in question, but also a member of the local business community. Occasionally, over-the-phone interviews are given but usually only in cases where it is impossible to schedule actual person-to-person interviews.

How are interviews structured?

Interviews may follow either a structured or an unstructured format. Business schools may have strict guidelines for interviewers to follow during the interview, as is the case when the admissions office makes a strong effort to obtain information that can be used to compare one candidate to another. Exhibit 8–1, for example, is modeled on an actual interview evaluation form used by one top school. It requires their interviewers to fill out an interview form by rating the interviewee from 1 (low) to 5 (high) over five categories including personal presentation, maturity, motivation, self-confidence, and communication skills. Some schools, like INSEAD, may actually require the interviewee to complete a short written and/or oral French test during the interview.

Regardless of the structure of the interview, the ultimate question from the perspective of an alumni interviewer is: "Would I like this person to have the same degree from the same school as I do?"

Here are some do's and don'ts

Five interviewing points worth adhering to are as follows:

- Do be on time for your interview
- Do dress conservatively
- Do not smoke (but do not stop your interviewer from smoking either)

Exhibit 8–1   Sample interview evaluation form

Confidential Interview Report	*MBA PROGRAM* *XYZ School of Business Administration*

Date: _____

Name of Applicant: _____

Name of Interviewer: _____ Class of: _____

Interviewer: Please supply short answers to each of the following questions based on your interview. Grade the candidate on a 1 to 5 scale with one being the lowest and five being the highest.

1. **Personal presentation and punctuality**   Rank _____ 5 _____
    Interviewee (candidate) was on time, neatly dressed, and professional in appearance.

2. **Career motivation/energy/maturity**   Rank _____ 4 _____
    A lot of energy. I have the impression she gets things done quickly and with flair. Quite mature. I think she needs to think more deeply about her career development. She stumbled somewhat on the "where do you see yourself in 10 years' time?" question. Good raw ingredients. B-School should prove helpful in refining career objectives.

3. **Communication skills**   Rank _____ 5 _____
    (If applicant is not a native English speaker please comment on spoken English ability)
    Confident speaker. Clear and concise. Astute in fielding different types of questions asked. Sharp with some wit.

4. **Fit with our business school**   Rank _____ 3 _____
    The candidate cited International Finance as her proposed area of academic concentration at XYZ Business School. However, she seemed a little unfamiliar with the details of our international program offering. This is probably the result of not reading closely the brochure.

5. **Other points noted including possible red flags**
    None cited. No red flags.

6. **Overall recommendation**   Rank _____ 4 _____
    A solid candidate. I think her strong sales and marketing experience will contribute nicely to the program. Very outgoing and thoughtful. My criteria is: First, does she have the background and second, is she an interesting person. Answer: A strong "yes."

- Do not tell jokes (but it is okay to laugh at them)
- Do not get opinionated (remember the interviewer is always right)

SEVEN THINGS TO DO FOR YOUR BUSINESS SCHOOL INTERVIEWS

What seven things do you need to do to prepare for your business school interviews? Different schools look for different things, and individual interviewers may use different interviewing techniques. In general though, you, as an interviewee, need to have a good handle on what your career goals are and why you want an MBA and why the particular business school you are interviewing for is a good match for you.

1. Review the school's brochure/website.
2. Review your own application including your work experience.
3. Know your career goal and your vision statements.
4. Anticipate mock interview type questions.
5. Relax and be yourself.
6. Have questions for the interviewer.
7. Send a thank-you note (or email).

✎ Tip #72: Review the school's brochure.

Learn as much as you can about the school's business program you are applying to—its academic and program specialties, professors, course offerings, geographical location, internship opportunities, special programs, etc. Some of these special programs include leadership classes, new product laboratories, and overseas or independent study opportunities. In short, why is this particular business school right for you? If you are perceived as an informed candidate, you will impress your interviewer. Certain information can be gleamed from contacting alumni of the university who can give you their own personal insights about their school and the business school process or visiting the website. But a great deal of information can be obtained simply by reading the brochure. Schools spend time, money, and effort to produce application materials and information that aim to be comprehensive and meaningful.

✎ Tip #73: Be able to defend every line of your resume (or employment record).

Review your application (if completed) and know the details of your resume or employment record. Be able to defend or explain each line of your resume. This means you should be able to answer questions regarding the responsibilities or accomplishments covered in any line or bullet point listed in your resume. There are two reasons why people cannot always defend each "line" of their resume. Either they are not used to giving a detailed, analytical account of their accomplishments, or they have simply forgotten about earlier jobs due to the passing of time. Should the interviewer focus on one of these previous jobs, they may struggle to recall past details. The good news is that the ability to defend each line of your resume is a skill needed to prepare for job interviews (summer internship positions and full-time positions) which take place during your first year in business school.

Lastly, be able to explain what your work experience means to you apart from your responsibilities and accomplishments as listed on your resume. This was covered under Chapter 6, *Resume or Employment Record* and, in particular, by Tip #63: *Review employment themes as the basis of writing meaningful employment summaries.*

✍ Tip #74: Articulate your career goals and your vision statements.

Do not assume that the interviewer has seen your application. In fact, due to the confidential nature of your application, schools will not release an entire application package to any interviewer, unless of course the interviewer works in the admissions office. And even if the interviewer has seen your resume, there is no way you can be certain that he or she can remember details of your background. Bring a copy of your resume just in case.

Mention early in the interview your clear goal statements covering both the long term and the short term. Ideally these should be tied to your vision statements. This is an excellent opportunity to dazzle the interviewer. Few candidates will supply vision—that idea of where their chosen industry is headed and how they will contribute or capitalize on this knowledge.

✍ Tip #75: Anticipate mock interview type questions.

One way to think about the interview is that the interview exists to find out things about yourself that are not necessarily mentioned in your application.

Mock interview questions can be used to prepare you for your interviews. They are used extensively by the job placement centers and career service centers of major universities to prepare candidates for their job interviews. Most people find mock interview questions tough, which is why practice is needed in order to be able to field such questions during a regular interview situation. Remember the adage: "If you want to interview without thinking, you must think when not interviewing."

The following are examples of possible interview questions. You should practice answering these as part of a mock interview.

- Tell me something about yourself.
- Why did you choose to attend XYZ college or university?
- Why did you choose X major as the focus of your undergraduate study?
- Where do you see yourself in your career in five years from now?
- Why in particular do you like XYZ business school?

- What do you see as your three biggest accomplishments?
- What are your strengths and weaknesses?
- What do you like or dislike about your current job?
- Why did you leave a particular job?
- What do you do in your free time? What are your hobbies?
- What do think is the world's most pressing problem and why? Any solution?
- Who are your heroes, historical or contemporary?
- If you could change something about yourself, what would it be?
- On a scale of one to ten, one being technical skills and ten being people skills, how would you rate yourself?
- How would you define the word leadership?
- Can you give an example of leadership both on and off the job?
- Give an example of how you use people skills?
- What movies have you seen lately?
- What is your favorite book, and why?
- What magazines and/or newspaper do you read regularly?
- What other schools are you applying to?
- Do you have any questions for me (as asked by the interviewer)?
- What else would you like the admissions committee to know about you that has not been covered in your application?

Sometimes interview questions are used by an interviewer to confirm or deny stereotypes stemming from job functions or occupations. Without becoming preoccupied with this idea of job stereotypes, review the list (Table 8–1) in light of your own background, recognizing that the interviewer may choose some questions in order to test your perceived strengths and weaknesses. Your goal is to emphasize your strengths while minimizing your perceived weaknesses.

Tip #76: Relax and be yourself.

Remember the motto of the perfectly prepared interview candidate: "Poised, confident, knowing."

Tip #77: Answer questions in a succinct manner. Don't waffle.

We all have experienced the rambling conversationalist. We struggle between mustering the boldness to cut them off and the courteousness to let them keep speaking. We listen but secretly wonder where this is all going. We want to say, *what's the point?*

Just because a listener listens without physically stopping you, it does not mean he or she is not annoyed. Keep your responses shorter, rather than longer. Rest assured the listener will probe for more. Observe a leading talk show host like Larry King. He has an ability to redirect and cut conversations with relative ease. And the reason he has to do this with a majority of guests is because they ramble. Most people like to say more rather than less. The person who can make a point and have the confidence and control to wait for the follow-up response will definitely chalk up points with the interviewer.

Tip #78: Have questions for the interviewer.

Candidate:	I am here for an interview.
Associate director:	Yes, I am the associate director of admissions and I am in charge of your interview. What would you like to tell me?
Candidate:	Yes … well….
Associate director:	Can I ask if you have any specific questions for me?
Candidate:	Well….

Toward the end of the interview, the interviewer will customarily ask, "Do you have any questions for me?" Your answer may say a lot about how prepared you are. If you say, "no", this may impact you unfavorably. As one headhunter remarked, "If a candidate has no questions for the job interviewer, then this is perhaps the worst sign of all." For your business school interviews, prepare at least one question ahead of time in the event that one does not arise in the natural course of the interview.

The following is a list of some questions you may choose to ask of the interviewer:

- Why did you choose to attend XYZ business school? How did you narrow down your choices? (Assuming the interviewer was accepted at one or more top business schools.)
- If you had to do your MBA all over again, would you choose the same MBA program?
- What aspect of doing an MBA do you feel is most helpful in your current work? In your current life endeavors?
- How does the placement office help students find summer internships and/or full-time employment opportunities?
- What were your favorite MBA courses? Least favorite courses? Favorite professors?
- What one thing did you not like about doing an MBA? What one weak point would you cite about XYZ business school?
- How is the social life at XYZ business school?
- How strong is the alumni organization in XYZ city?
- How can I get the most out of business school?
- What advice could you give me for my future interviews?

Table 8-1 Perceived strengths and weaknesses of interview candidates

	Perceived strengths	Perceived weaknesses
1. Accountant	• Good technical, quantitative skills • Good at reality checks	• Not dynamic; not a leader • Lacks big picture view despite exposure to different industries
2. Administrative/ Personnel	• Organized; detail minded • Trained to take care of people; team player	• Does not know how to build a business • Stuck on rules and procedures
3. Artist	• Flexible mindset; creative • Unique viewpoint	• Not quantitatively skilled • Does not know how to manage people
4. Computer/Internet geek	• Quantitatively skilled • Understands technology and uses hands-on approach	• Lacks people skills • Lacks big picture view
5. Consultant	• Can think outside the box; good business sense • Articulate; smart	• Does not care about detail • Too theoretical; too much style at the expense of substance
6. Engineer	• Methodical; hardworking • Quantitatively and technologically skilled	• Myopic; cannot see the forest for the trees • Lacks communication skills
7. Entrepreneur	• Dynamic; high energy level • Hands on; real doer	• Chaotic; disorganized; bored easily; impatient • Aversion to academic study
8. Investment banker	• Savvy; resourceful; knows the bottom line; good networker • Facility with numbers	• Callous; uncaring; arrogant • Focuses on the "ends", at the expense of the "means"
9. Lawyer	• Smart; clever communicator • Well trained; good organizational skills	• Works alone; set in his/her ways • Not quantitatively skilled
10. Marketer/Salesperson	• Strong personality; self-confident • Understands the consumer	• Lacks number sense • Does not see value in theory or book learning
11. Military	• Obeys rules; disciplined • Team player	• Commercial misfit • Too executional; not enough vision
12. Scientist	• Intelligent; unique viewpoint • Quantitatively skilled	• Lacks business sense; inhibited • Cannot "bullshit"; unwilling to develop soft skills

Tip #79: Send a thank-you letter (or email).

This is a courtesy, but it can also be a strategy. Say, for example, you did not feel your interview went well. The interviewer may have caught you off guard with a series of more detailed questions than you anticipated. The wording of your thank-you note could still help to influence the interviewer before he or she writes, types, or emails a response to the admissions office for inclusion in your application file.

The following short letter was written by an applicant as a follow-up to his interview. Although he thought his business school interview was so-so, he was later accepted to Harvard Business School. This letter may well have resulted in the interviewer writing a more favorable response.

Dear Mr Alumni:

Thank you for taking valuable time from your busy schedule to interview me. I feel that our interview not only provided me with insightful information about the Harvard Business School, but also provided me with a learning experience. Your many detailed questions made me think in real depth about the particulars of my own business and the changes taking place in the marketplace. If my business school education could help me develop a similar mindset, I know it would make a striking difference in my future business endeavors.

Sincerely,

Candidate Hopeful

INTERVIEW POLICIES AT LEADING BUSINESS SCHOOLS

Table 8–2 summarizes the interview policies followed by today's leading business schools.

Table 8–2 Interview policies at leading business schools

	Interview is required	Interview is encouraged but not required	Interview is not required (not part of the normal admissions process)
U.S. Business Schools:			
American Graduate School of International Management (Thunderbird)			X
Berkeley (Haas), University of California–			X
Carnegie Mellon University		X	
Chicago, University of		X	
Columbia University	X		
Cornell University (Johnson)	X		
Dartmouth College (Amos Tuck)		X	
Duke University (Fuqua)		X	
Harvard Business School	X		
Massachusetts Institute of Technology (Sloan)	X		
Michigan–Ann Arbor, University of	X		
New York University (Stern)		X	
North Carolina–Chapel Hill (Kenan-Flagler), University of	X		
Northwestern University (Kellogg)	X		
Pennsylvania (Wharton), University of	X		
Stanford University	X		
Texas–Austin (McCombs), University of	X		
University of California–Los Angeles (Anderson)		X	
Virginia (Darden), University of	X		
Yale University	X		
Canadian Business Schools:			
McGill University	X		
Queen's University	X		
Toronto (Rotman), University of	X		
Western Ontario (Ivey), University of	X		
York University (Schulich)	X		
European Business Schools:			
IESE [Spain]	X		
IMD [Switzerland]	X		
INSEAD [France]	X		
London Business School [England]	X		
Rotterdam School of Management (Erasmus) [Netherlands]	X		

Table 8–2   (cont'd)

	Interview is required	Interview is encouraged but not required	Interview is not required (not part of the normal admissions process)
Australian Business Schools:			
Australian Graduate School of Management (AGSM)		X	
Melbourne Business School (MBS)		X	
Asia-Pacific Business Schools:			
Asian Institute of Management (AIM), Manila	X		
Chinese University of Hong Kong (CUHK)	X		
Chulalongkorn University, Bangkok (Sasin)	X		
Hong Kong University of Science and Technology (HKUST)	X		
Indian Institute of Management, Ahmedabad (IIMA)	X		
International University of Japan (IUJ), Niigata		X	
Nanyang Technological University (NTU), Singapore	X		
National University of Singapore (NUS)		X	
South African Business Schools:			
Cape Town, University of	X		
The Wits Business School			X

In cases where the interview is required, most schools follow the policy of offering interviews to a pre-selected number of applicants based on an initial review of their application packages.

CHAPTER 9

Presenting Your Extracurricular Activities/Awards and Recognition/Community Service

"You don't need to have done something really exotic or esoteric to stand out in the pool, and that's what I want applicants to understand. There are a lot of people we admit who haven't done anything out of the ordinary, but the passion they bring to the job and to other activities is something that's going to carry over to the community here and really inspire others."

Marie Mookini, former Director of Admissions, Stanford Business School

INTRODUCTION

When applying to business school, you will be asked in the application to chronicle your extracurricular involvement. Extracurricular involvement may be thought of as a composite of any of the following three things: (1) your extracurricular involvement while in college, (2) your community service, either during college or on the job, and (3) your awards or recognition. In the case of your awards and recognition, you may go way back, and include things that occurred in your childhood, if significant, for example, "grade school national guitar finalist".

The generic format followed in business school applications is shown in Table 9–1. Actual on-line applications require that such information be placed in fields.

Table 9–1 Generic format for presenting extracurricular activities

Extracurricular and community activities
List in reverse chronological order your major extracurricular and community activities in college and since graduation:

Dates	Activity	Office Held	Distinctions, Honors, and Awards

Leading business schools view favorably candidates who show all-roundness of character as depicted by achievement in extracurricular or community involvement. Why do schools even care if you partake in such activities? There are at least four reasons for this. First, business is primarily a group-oriented activity. Business schools prefer leaders to loners. Group participation in a non-business environment mirrors teamwork within a business organization. Second, by showing a certain level of leadership or achievement in one single area of your life, it is believed that you could, by analogy, achieve a similarly high level of leadership or achievement in another area (positive transference). Your ability to excel in an extracurricular activity, etc. is interpreted as an indication of your ability to succeed in other areas of your life, including business. Third, you might say that schools are interested in interesting people. "Would I like to spend four hours with this person while stuck at the airport?" Fourth, you might say that schools are interested in all-round individuals. This includes the idea of balance. If a person has a number of outside interests (e.g., sports and hobbies), these hobbies and interests act as a buffer should the person have a bad day on the job, or worse yet, suffer a life-rendering trauma.

You are encouraged to judiciously develop this area of your application. It is highly recommended, in the absence of having a solid record of extracurricular activities, that you go out and join an organization or volunteer your time to a worthy organization. It might seem opportunistic to run out and join an organization just because you are prompted to do so by the need to strengthen your business school application. On a practical note, however, some evidence of involvement is better than no evidence of involvement. And who knows, you may become a volunteer junky and thank the business school application process for getting you started!

There exists a type of trade-off between recent involvement and past involvement. A candidate who was heavily involved in college activities, for example, needs less recent involvement; someone without much collegiate involvement would benefit from evidence of recent involvement.

Two professional organizations specializing in personal development through public speaking which are easy to join and exist worldwide are *Dale Carnegie* and *Toastmasters International*.

THREE TIPS FOR PRESENTING EXTRACURRICULARS

Tip #80: Mention why you feel an extracurricular entry is significant.

A key to presenting your extracurricular activities is your ability to wow the reviewer with your insights and personal commentary. You should think in terms of *why* a special achievement is important or significant regardless of whether a school specifically asks for a reason in the application. The "story" behind an award, extracurricular collegiate activity, or community service project is often as important as the actual accomplishment itself. Do not simply state your accomplishment on a single line, place a date beside it, and expect the reader to know exactly what it means. For example, if you were a member of the Oklahoma State Swim Team, explain what it means to you, why you feel it is significant, what you have learned, or perhaps why it is important to your future success in business school and/or your business career.

Adding summaries allows a person's record of extracurricular activities and community service to become one-of-a-kind.

In the sample presentation that follows on the next page, Masumi captures her personal comments under the heading of "thoughts"; the next candidate, Bill, presents a general summary of each activity and then follows up with personal blurbs enclosed by quotation marks.

In terms of drafting your presentation, you can choose to use either a portrait (vertical) format or a landscape (horizontal) format as presented in the exhibits that follow.

✍ Tip #81: Present hobbies and interests in lieu of extracurricular activities.

Occasionally schools will even ask you to list your hobbies and interests. The difference between a *hobby and interest* and an *extracurricular* is that an extracurricular takes place in a structured or designated environment and requires a fixed or going commitment of time on the part of the individual. Exhibit 9–3 provides a sample "hobbies and interests" presentation for candidate "Angel". As is the case with your extracurricular presentation, do not just list your hobbies and interests—personalize them, embellish them, articulate what makes them special for you.

When hobbies and interests are not asked for, and you are struggling to find entries to "fill up" your extracurricular presentation, why not list and elaborate on a few of your hobbies and interests in lieu of extracurriculars. The entry titled *Graphology – Handwriting Analysis* (Exhibit 9–1) was chosen to give you an idea of how to elaborate on a hobby and interest, by presenting it alongside extracurriculars in order to make your presentation look more substantial.

✍ Tip #82: If you have no extracurricular activities to speak of, then try presenting your part-time work experiences while in college as a substitute for your extracurricular involvement.

If you really do not have any extracurricular activities to speak of, but you chose or found it necessary to work during your free time while attending college or university, then present your work record to help the reviewer understand why you are not listing extracurriculars in your application. Refer to "Vivian's" presentation, Exhibit 9–4.

SAMPLE PRESENTATIONS

Candidate's biography: Masumi is female, Japanese, educated in Australia

Exhibit 9–1   Sample extracurricular presentation: Masumi

LANGUAGE STUDENT

International educational exchange: *Korean language student,*
                                          AIFS exchange program

Place: Yonsei University, South Korea   Date: August 1992 to June 1993

Activity: Studied (full-time) as an exchange student and lived in Korea at Yonsei University's foreign dormitory along with 150 international students.

* Thoughts: My language studies have allowed me to converse in Korean which helps me do business more efficiently and to understand Korean culture. Learning to speak Korean, however, is only the tip of the iceberg. Direct communication is important but the ability to understand what Korean people think is more critical. In becoming fluent in Korean, I started to gain a sixth sense about what Korean people were thinking before they could even speak. In business negotiations this has translated to a real advantage.

RAFTING GUIDE

Leadership and teamwork: *White Water rafting guide,*
                                           ultimate descents

Place: Katmandu, Nepal   Date: July 1992 to August 1992

Activity: Acted as a local guide (35 hours per week) for tourist groups of up to 50 persons making a three-day journey down the Karnali River in Nepal; responsible for the safety of one raft of eight persons; helped organize camp sites, tents, and supplies.

* Thoughts: Successful guide work requires not only careful preparation of supplies and improvization (you never can plan for everything) but also good people skills to combat those few "crazies" who disregard safety rules. Rafting is one of the best ways to get to know people. The challenges of the rapids help get everyone to work as a team and overcome obstacles. (Try getting back into an overturned raft by yourself.) It comes down to forcing people to have a common goal – and a great time.

Exhibit 9–1 *(cont'd)*

VOLUNTEER

Community service: *Volunteer for disabled children*

Place: Melbourne, Australia   Date: January 1990 to March 1991

Activity: Worked ten hours per week while at university; helped two disabled children; one 11-year-old orphaned boy; one retarded 9-year-old girl. Received a certificate from *Collins Institute* in appreciation of time and services given.

*Thoughts: My time spent volunteering allowed me to make some concrete contributions to less fortunate people and to re-evaluate my own beliefs about my personal limitations. One aspect of my volunteer work struck me in an unexpected way. I remember talking to Steven, the 11-year-old orphan, about the untold opportunities he had ahead of him, when I suddenly realized that there was not a single thing that I had said to him that could not apply equally to me. Personal impediments, like handicaps, are relative.

GRAPHOLOGY

Hobbies and interests: *Handwriting analysis*

Place: Melbourne, Australia   Date: Plans to start a 16-month certification course.

Activity: Learning to analyze handwriting for the purpose of revealing a person's personality and character traits.

*Thoughts: Graphology requires that a person be analytically minded and requires deciphering a number of details in handwritten script – writing slant, impression, size, etc. – as well as weighing the details relative to one another in order to judge, in context, what a writing sample is really telling you. My interest in graphology is purely avocational but I would like to advance my learning by taking a full IGAS (International Graphoanalysis Society) course by correspondence and obtain certification.

* Author's note: Look how much more meaningful the entries become when this candidate adds her thoughts.

Candidate's biography: Bill is male, American, educated in the U.S.

Exhibit 9–2 Sample extracurricular presentation: Bill

Activity	Location/dates/hours	Description and summary of what I have learned
TENNIS *3X participant,* *National Junior Tennis* *Championships* *(Awards and recognition)*	While residing in Sarasota, Florida 1995, 1996, 1997 Time: Daily practices and frequent tournament travel throughout the U.S.	**Description:** • participated three straight years in the U.S. National Junior Tennis Championships; • ranked number 4 in Florida and number 21 in the Atlantic States. **Summary:** Tennis taught me two important things: • be persistent and never give up; • the importance of training and conditioning. * "I found that the secret to winning close matches is actually the ability to reduce an important match down to its smallest components. A set is a series of *games*, a game is a series of *points*, and points are reduced to individual *strokes*. The closer a match becomes, the more important it is to concentrate on the smallest details and forget about winning the match."
DEBATE *Varsity team member* *(Extracurricular activity)*	Arizona State University September 1998 to May 1999 Time: Seven to ten hours per week excluding library research and occasional weekend travel	**Description:** • competed in inter-collegiate NDT debate and participated in individual speaking events; won two regional debate tournaments – Pomona and West Coast Challenge. **Summary:** Debate taught me four things: • to organize and defend coherent arguments; • to speak under pressure; • to develop excellent research skills; • to formulate strategies for beating tournament competitors. * "My time spent in debate taught me to develop affirmative and negative briefs to support and defend the resolution at hand. I learned to be ever mindful of the importance of anticipating both sides of an argument. For every argument there is an equal and opposite argument. It is here that I gained my first real insights into an old tenet of philosophy: 'Only through contrast do we have awareness.'"

Exhibit 9–2 *(cont'd)*

Activity	Location/dates/hours	Description and summary of what I have learned
BETA THETA PI SOCIAL FRATERNITY *Alumni liaison* (Extracurricular involvement)	Arizona State University September 1999 to May 2000 Time: Fifteen hours per week	**Description:** • acted as alumni liaison and was present at all meetings to schedule events both within the fraternity and for off-campus venues. **Summary:** My days spent working with members of my college fraternity have helped me work within large corporate organizations. Large companies frequently have unwritten rules ("do's and don'ts") based on a tier system of bosses and workers and the fraternity gave me a head start in understanding how to maintain favorable protocol with older and newer members alike. *"My early involvement with my fraternity, however, brought me frustration. I remember wanting to take charge to organize and 'fix things'. But in the end, it was the fraternity that taught me to relax, be spontaneous, and accept chaotic circumstances. As a businessperson, I see the benefit of approaching every situation as if it can be solved – it can be fixed. But outside of business, I also see the merit in learning to live naturally without always finding definitive solutions."
CPA CREDENTIAL *Arizona State Board of Accountancy* (Awards and recognition)	Phoenix, Arizona August 2002 Time: Weekly study including eight hours per week attending *Daubermann Chaykin CPA Review*	**Description:** • passed all four parts of the CPA exam – Audit, Law, Financial, and Managerial Accounting; only 15 percent of candidates pass all four parts on their first try. **Summary:** Passing the CPA exam is testimony of my ability to work with large amounts of information. I followed a rigorous, systematic study schedule. I came away seeing the advantages of strong theory as the driving force behind understanding practical, on-the-job problems. *"The key to passing the CPA exam was using a variety of learning tools – books, tapes, and videos. Besides mnemonics, I really like learning with the help of anecdotes whenever possible. How is this for differentiating between gift and inheritance tax: "Your uncle is on his death bed ... he says you can have his house ... do you say 'yes' and accept it and incur gift tax now or say 'no' and wait to inherit it but be subject to inheritance tax?"

* Author's note: Again, notice how the addition of the above blurbs captures the candidate's insightfulness.

The presentation below is a good example of how a candidate can create "energy on paper". Her genuine excitement about her activities is contagious.

Exhibit 9-3 Sample hobbies and interests presentation: Angel

INTERESTS – Each activity I choose to engage in gives me a different kind of satisfaction. The common thread is comradeship. I enjoy spending time with friends and consider myself an outgoing individual. Through these activities, I make new friends and form stronger bonds with old ones.

Scuba Diving – "Serene" is the word I would use to describe the underwater experience. It is so quiet yet so full of life. It is a world so close to us yet so mysterious. Diving allows me to travel beyond land, a world three times expanded. (Certified Advanced Open Water Diver by PADI in 2000.)

Culinary – Having lived in New York, I really enjoy fine food. I took a professional course at Peter Gump Culinary School In 1997 because I wanted to be able to tell the ingredients, herbs and spices that made those beautifully garnished dishes so good to taste. Knowing the culinary arts makes me appreciate not only the taste of my food more but also the effort behind it.

Photography – I started photography in 1993, and received a Silver Key from Boston Globe Scholastic Award in the same year. For me, photography is a means of showing the world in a personal perspective, from the subject I pick to the way I choose to frame it. When I find people who like my work, it is like finding a friend who shares the same "view".

Dancing – I love dancing, whether it is Ballet, Jazz, Ballroom, or Folk Dance. I love it because it combines art, music, rhythm, and above all it tells stories. When I dance, I forget my nationality, my age, my sex, and totally immerse myself into the music, using my body to express all the non-spoken feelings. (Received a Commended Award at the 26th Schools Dance Festival in 1990.)

French Language – I studied French since I was 13 years old for 6 years, of which I received 5 academic awards. I had a great teacher who taught me not only the language, but also the culture; that is what interests me most. Through a French film and theatre class, I learned a lot of things that I identified myself with, and the most important of all is the passion for life.

Outdoor Activities – Rock climbing and trekking are two of my favorite outdoor activities. My senses are enhanced: breathing the fresh air, feeling the sunshine upon my skin, stepping on earth and not concrete, hugging a tree or a rock, and being at awe with the power and beauty that nature inspires. (Received a Bronze Level in Expedition from the Duke of Edinburgh Award Scheme in 1990.)

TRAVEL – I have visited or lived in or worked in the following places:

North America: United States, Canada, and Mexico.
Europe: England, France, Italy, Switzerland, Denmark, Sweden, and Norway.
Asia and others: China, Japan, Singapore, Taiwan, South Korea, Thailand, Indonesia, Malaysia, Maldives, and Australia.

Candidate's biography: Vivian is female, Hungarian-American, educated in the U.S.

Exhibit 9–4 Sample presentation: Work record in lieu of extracurriculars

EXTRACURRICULAR ACTIVITIES IN COLLEGE/UNIVERSITY

While in college, I chose to pursue a variety of work experiences in lieu of more in-depth involvement in extracurricular activities available on the Boston University campus.

Dates	Employer/activity	Location	Duties	Hours/Week
9/90 – 12/90	Allied Irish Bank (Part of BU's London Internship Program)	London, U.K.	Credit analyst	24 hrs/wk
6/90 – 8/90	Mrs Miller's Muffins	Martha's Vineyard, MA, U.S.	Waitress/ cashier	30 hrs/wk
1/90 – 5/90	Smith Barney, Harris & Upham	Boston, MA, U.S.	Intern	8 hrs/wk
9/89 – 1/90	Pierre Deux, French lifestyle store	Boston, MA, U.S.	Salesperson	10–15 hrs/wk
7/89 – 8/89	*Interview Magazine*	New York, NY, U.S.	Editorial intern	40 hrs/wk
2/89 – 6/89	Houghton Mifflin Publishers	Boston, MA, U.S.	Intern	10 hrs/wk
6/88 – 7/88	*Madame Figaro*, magazine	Paris, France	Editorial intern	30 hrs/wk
1/88 – 1/89	*Boston Magazine*	Boston, MA, U.S.	Editorial intern	12 hrs/wk
9/87 – 12/87	Coffee Connection	Boston, MA, U.S.	Waitress/ cashier	8–10 hrs/wk

CHAPTER 10
Packaging Your MBA Essays and Application

"A product that looks good is worth something."

Merchant's adage

READABILITY TIPS AND TOOLS

Tip #83: Proof read your essay and application materials.

Spelling, punctuation, and grammar checks are wonderful tools but they are not infallible. Let's review a few things about punctuation and spelling that are often overlooked. There are two types of English: American English and British English. Each system has its own peculiarities. First is spelling and second is punctuation. Be consistent. Generally the place of your undergraduate institution will determine whether you are writing based on the rules of the U.K. or U.S. For example, if you attended Cambridge University it is obvious you'll be using words such as "summarise" and "favour" and "travelling". If you attended Boston University you will be using words such as "summarize" and "favor" and "traveling". Try not to commingle the systems. For your reference, here is a succinct list to summarize spelling differences.

Exhibit 10-1 Spelling: American English vs. British English

American		British	
-e	encyclopedia, fetus	-ae, -oe	encyclopaedia, foetus
-a	gage	-au	gauge
-s	license	-c	licence
-k	disk	-c	disc
-no "e"	judgment, acknowledgment	-e	judgement, acknowledgement
-in	inquiry	-en	enquiry
-ize	summarize, organization	-ise	summarise, organisation
-l	traveled, traveling	-ll	travelled, travelling
-og	catalog	-ogue	catalogue
-o	mold, smolder	-ou	mould, smoulder
-or	color, neighbor	-our	colour, neighbour
-m	program	-mme	programme
-ck	check	-que	cheque
-er	center, meter	-re	centre, metre
-no "s"	math	-s	maths
-ction	connection, inflection	-xion	connexion, inflexion

PUNCTUATION: AMERICAN ENGLISH VS. BRITISH ENGLISH

The following serves to highlight some of major differences in punctuation.

(A) = American English; (B) = British English

Abbreviations
(A) Agassi vs. Sampras
(B) Agassi v. Sampras

(A) Mr. / Mrs. / Ms.
(B) Mr / Mrs / Ms

Note: Periods appear after salutations in American English but not in British English.

Apostrophes
(A) Research was carried out in the 1970's.
(B) Research was carried out in the 1970s.

Note: Americans use an apostrophe between the zero and the "s"; the British do not use an apostrophe between the zero and the "s".

Colons
(A) We found the place easily: Your directions were perfect.
(B) We found the place easily: your directions were perfect.

Note: Americans capitalize the first word after a colon. The British prefer not to capitalize the first word that follows the colon even if what follows is a full sentence.

Commas
(A) She likes the sun, sand, and sea.
(B) She likes the sun, sand and sea.

Note: Americans use a comma before the "and" when listing a series of items. The British do not use a comma before the "and" when listing a series of items.

Quotation Marks
(A) Our boss said, "The customer is never wrong."
(B) Our boss said, 'The customer is never wrong.'

Note: Americans use double quotation marks for quotes. The British typically use single quotations marks for quotes.

☞ **Tip #84: Review readability tools: addendums, bolds, bullets, dashes, enumeration, headings and headlines, indentations, italics, and short sentences.**

Addendums

Adding addendums to your essays may be used to further describe an aspect of your personal or professional background but should be limited to a single page in length. Alternatively, addendum-type information could be included at the end of your application essays as part of an optional essay question in response to the question, "Is there anything else you would like the admissions committee to know?" One of the major purposes of an addendum is to remove detail from the body of your essays and yet still make that information available to the reader.

In order to support his goal of entering the publishing business, this candidate felt it important to include the addendum below as an overview of the publishing industry.

Addendum – My Career Focus and the Publishing Industry

Summary

I would like to substantiate briefly my career focus by looking at the book publishing industry and drawing a link to general business demand. Many people when hearing the words "book publishing" immediately think of a famous author or writer but forget about the whole business dimension of the industry. For example, assuming that an author has written a book, who determines how many books to print (statistics), the mix between hard and soft covers (consumer marketing), which book stores should sell the book (distribution channels), how international rights will be dealt with (business law), the best advertising and promotion strategies (marketing), or even new venture arrangements (entrepreneurial finance)?

Major players and some market statistics

In the U.S., the book publishing marketplace is considered fragmented with over 20,000 companies involved in book publishing. However, in the *trade* book category, it is more concentrated, as can be seen by the presence of the big "five" publishers: Random House, Simon & Schuster, HarperCollins, Bantam Doubleday Dell (Bertelsmann Group), and Warner Books. In terms of size, most businesspersons do not realize that the book publishing industry (book sales) has been growing at a compounded annual rate of seven percent and is expected to grow at that rate for the *next* five years. This growth rate is comparable with other vibrant growth sectors. Americans are buying more books than ever before; they spent US$25 billion on books last year and US$1 billion on books on CD-ROMs.

Market dynamics and trends

There are three major trends in book publishing. One is the merging of the book publishing and movie businesses (e.g., Warner Books is part of Warner Bros.), the second is customization (i.e., tailored education on demand – in the home, on the job, and in institutions), the third is relationship management (e.g., selling an on-going relationship with the consumer).

Bolds

Bolds may be used to emphasize key words or phrases or help to divide an essay into parts. Bolding the occasional key word causes words to jump out at the reader, making the job of reading your writing easier. Underlining or capitalizing does basically the same job as bolding. Underlining was popular when typewriters were in vogue and bolding was not an option. With the advent of word processing, bolding has taken over. Be careful not to overuse bolding. You will not only dull the effect but also risk patronizing the reader. And remember the unwritten rule of publishing: Never use bolds, full-caps and underlines at the same time.

Bullets

Bullets are effective tools when paraphrasing information. They are excellent for presenting information in short phrases when formal sentences are not required. Bullets are commonly used when presenting resumes or employment records and/or presenting extracurricular activities. Bullets are not, however, recommended for use in the body of your essays.

Excerpt from a resume

PROFESSIONAL
EXPERIENCE _____

1993–present **BANK OF AMERICA**, Hartford, Connecticut
Associate and Financial Analyst
- Analyzed branch performance and devised new strategies to improve regional market share. Formulated a two-year marketing plan for two branches.
- Developed new commission system and assisted in implementation.
- Devised tax saving strategies and advised principal clients on investment portfolio compositions.

Dashes

Dashes can be used to vary the rhythm of a sentence, and to present ideas in a more dramatic way.

> Dartmouth College—the world's oldest MBA program—awarded its first MBA degree in 1900.

Or:

> Dartmouth College – the world's oldest MBA program – awarded its first MBA degree in 1900.

Note the difference between a hyphen (a hyphen joins words e.g., the word two-thirds) and a dash; a dash is longer than a hyphen and you should not use a hyphen when what you want is a dash. There are two types of dashes and it is your choice. The first is called "em dash" ("—") which is the longer of the two dashes and is used in the example above. The second is called "en dash" ("–") which is the shorter of the two dashes. Often the convention followed by writers is to leave spaces on both sides of an "en dash" but not to leave spaces on either side of an "em dash". When using *MS Word*, you can always find these under the pull down menu: *Insert, Symbols*, then *Special Characters*.

Enumeration

Enumerations involve the numbering of points. Listing items by number is more formal but very useful for ordering data.

> Given time constraints, I see three potential scenarios that would overcome such an impasse. I would play a different role in each scenario to facilitate timely competition. The three scenarios are:

(i)   We have the same solution.

(ii) We have different solutions.

(iii) We have no solution at all.

Vivian (Candidate #3) uses enumeration in her career goals type essay appearing in Chapter 3.

> I feel that my greatest long-term contributions working in this field will be measured by: (1) my ability to find ways to define and quantify in "dollars and cents" terms the benefits of ethics and corporate citizenship and (2) my ability to sell corporations on the proactive benefits of these programs as a means to market the company, products and employees.

Headings and Headlines

Headings and headlines may be especially useful in writing essays for business school as both devices help the reader obtain information very quickly. Headings are usually a couple of words in length and serve to *divide* information under common grouping or sections. Headings are used in Audrey's essay. For example, Audrey's shortened version of her Five Chinese Elements Essay appearing in Chapter 5: *Writing Optional Essay Entries* uses each of the five key words—*Metal, Wood, Water, Earth,* and *Fire* as underlined headings. When we read each section, we know what topic is being discussed.

The purpose of headlines is to *summarize* or pre-phrase information in order to capture the reader's attention. Refer to Tip #47.

Indentations

Indenting paragraphs is very much optional. The rule of thumb might be: Do not indent the paragraphs of short essays (essays of two or fewer pages) but it is okay to indent the paragraphs of longer essays (essays of three or more pages). Indenting paragraphs usually has the effect of making writing look more personable—more like a story.

Italics

Italics, like bolds, serve similar purposes. Think of using italics to highlight certain key words, especially those of contrast or illustration. For example, words of illustration commonly include: first, second, and third. Words of contrast often include: no, not, and don't. Be careful of overusing italics because they are tiring on the eye and will make the page look unduly busy.

> I grew up understanding work as the act of *filling* a position, not as a career that should be strategized and planned.

Short Sentences

There is power in short sentences and you should concentrate on using a few of these in your essays. Short sentences catch the eye and stand as if "bare naked" in front of the reader.

"I like beer. Beer explains more about me than anything in the world. Who am I? I am the beer man – at least that is what many of my close friends call me."

One tip that has some merit is the "topic sentence, one-line-rule". Topic sentences are effectively the first sentence of each paragraph you write. Concentrating on trying to keep most of your topic sentences to a single typed line in length will make it easier for the reader to grasp the main ideas in each of your paragraphs.

Tip #85: Consider "writing out" the masculine generic "he".

The masculine generic refers to the sole use of the pronoun "he" or "him" when referring to situations involving both genders. Avoid using "he" when referring to both "he or she"; likewise avoid using "him" when referring to both "him or her". Avoiding the masculine generic signals to the reader that you are sensitive in acknowledging both sexes. The simple fact is that greater than 50 percent of admissions personnel are female. Thus, it is not only politically correct but also politically astute to avoid using the masculine generic.

Consider the way the following sentences read from a female perspective.

Original: Today's chief executive must be extremely well rounded. *He* must not only be corporate and civic minded but also be internationally focused and entrepreneurially spirited.

There are essentially two ways to "fix" this.
Either write "he" or "she" (or "him" or "her"):

Today's chief executive must be extremely well rounded. *He* or *she* must not only be corporate and civic minded but also be internationally focused and entrepreneurially spirited.

Or put the sentence in the plural using "they" or "them":

Today's chief executives must be extremely well rounded. *They* must not only be corporate and civic minded but also be internationally focused and entrepreneurially spirited.

✍ Tip #86: Think in terms of a top-down expository writing style.

MBA essay writing is expository writing. The primary purpose of expository is to inform or persuade, not to entertain. Writing that exists to inform or explain should follow a top-down writing style. This means that we conclude at or near the top and then proceed to supply details. If the reverse occurs, inefficiency will also occur, because the reader will not be able to figure out the main point of our writing until the end and details therefore will be much harder to remember. Perhaps the best example of the top-down approach in action is the newspaper. Newspaper writers know that if a story is too long and needs to be cut, the editor will start at the bottom and work up. Simply this is where the least critical information is. Contrast this with the world of entertainment, or the creative world of fiction, where we enjoy and expect surprise endings. We would never want to go to a movie and be told at the very beginning what the whole movie was about. This is not the case in the world of expository writing—in the sub-world of MBA essay writing. Don't play, "I've got a secret" and leave the reader guessing.

Top-down writing ☺
(inverted pyramid style)

Bottom-down writing ☹
(pyramld style)

MOST IMPORTANT
NEXT MOST IMPORTANT
NEXT MOST IMPORTANT
NEXT MOST IMPORTANT

LEAST IMPORTANT
NEXT MOST IMPORTANT
NEXT MOST IMPORTANT
NEXT MOST IMPORTANT

✍ Tip #87: Focus your writing. Try not to discuss too many ideas at one time.

Remember: It is better to do "a lot with a little" than "a little with a lot." As a fairly reliable generalization, it is true that most MBA applicants make a similar mistake with essay content; they try to cover too many topics in a given essay, sacrificing depth of writing. Given the fact that essays have length limits, discussing too many things will inevitably lead to superficiality.

Take the following analogy. You have just spent a year traveling around the world. You arrive back to tell a bunch of your friends (over beers!) all about the trip. For three hours, you talk and talk. Your friends are totally amazed and you're totally exhausted. Some of your friends living overseas are not present but they want to hear of things as well. So you decide to write to them and inform them about the trip in one page. You could probably take one whole page to simply list all the towns and cities you've been to. But that would not be very interesting, would it? So you focus in on one of the most memorable, quintessential, intriguing, unexpected parts of the journey—the day you went to the market in Morocco. Your essay begins by referencing the vast terrain you traveled but quickly hones in on Morocco and voila, you spend your page describing, in detail, the market. From a writing standpoint this is where the seasoned writer is separated from an amateur. The seasoned writer knows of the impossible task at hand in trying to cover the whole trip in one page, so he or she focuses instead on one aspect (e.g., the market in Morocco) and, in taking a stand, a memorable writing piece is created.

Tip #88: Try the "for example" technique.

The following sentences were taken from application essays written by prospective business school students. The "original" of each is an example of vague writing although none are grammatically incorrect. One of the best tips to use to avoid vagueness in your writing and help ensure that you lend adequate support for the points you are making involves placing "for example" immediately after what you write.

EXAMPLE #1

Candidate's statement: "Growing up in both the East and West, I have experienced both Asian and Western points of view."

Reviewer's likely comment: "Do you mind telling me what these Asian and Western points of view are?"

EXAMPLE #2

Candidate's statement: "I am an energetic, loyal, creative, diligent, honest, strict, humorous, responsible, flexible, and ambitious person."

Reviewer's likely comment: "Do you care to develop your discussion by choosing two or three of these traits and supporting each with concrete examples?"

EXAMPLE #3

Candidate's statement: "Although ABC Company did not flourish, I still consider my effort a success because I was able to identify strengths and weaknesses in my overall business skills."

Reviewer's likely comment: "What were the strengths and weaknesses you were able to identify?"

EXAMPLE #4

Candidate's statement: "Not only did I develop important operational skills in running a business, but I experienced and witnessed the challenges that entrepreneurs face on a daily basis."

Reviewer's likely response: "What were these challenges?"

EXAMPLE #5

Candidate's statement: "Sleeping in cheap hostels and on Eurorail trains, I got a much better picture of life in Europe than tourists do from the windows of a moving bus."

Reviewer's likely response: "Prove it!"

As a matter of practicality, you will decide whether to leave "for example" in your essay or edit it out, particularly if you are looking for more seamless connections between ideas and support points.

Original:

The other side of integrity is an unyielding nature. Sometimes I wish I could entertain broader points of view especially those that directly attack my value system. It is important to hold to one's convictions and not be unduly persuaded by others.

Better:

The other side of integrity is an unyielding nature. Sometimes I wish I could entertain broader points of view especially those that directly attack my value system. For example, during one of our high school's fund raising brainstorming sessions, a member of the committee suggested organizing a rave party and donating profits to the school. Although I could see that an event like this would generate a sizable profit, I vetoed the idea based on two considerations: the first was its association with a rave party, which has strong drug related connotations, and the second, the inappropriateness of not informing the donors of our purpose.

Original:

My college education in Florida provided me with an incredible chance to develop myself. I pursued a rich choice of academic, athletic, professional, and social activities. At different times during my undergraduate education, I was a member of the Varsity Debate Team, Varsity Tennis Team, and a member of both a well-known professional business fraternity and a social fraternity.

Better:

My college education in Florida provided me with an incredible chance to develop myself. I pursued a rich choice of academic, athletic, professional, and social activities. At different times during my undergraduate education, I was a member of the Varsity Debate Team, Varsity Tennis Team, and a member of both a well-known professional business fraternity and a social fraternity. Using just a few words to summarize what each experience taught me: from debate, I learned to be organized and think ahead; from tennis, I learned to be persistent and not give up; and from my business and social fraternities, I learned to work in groups, work with rules, and value personality.

Original:

I grew up in a Maine farm family which was ethnically Scottish, but really your everyday New England household. I am thankful now for a stable, happy childhood. My parents gave me the best education and upbringing they could. They taught me to be caring and respectful of people and the environment. They taught me honesty, humility, and the silliness of pretense.

Better:

I grew up in a Maine farm family which was ethnically Scottish, but really your everyday New England household. I am thankful now for a stable, happy childhood. My parents gave me the best education and upbringing they could.

They took me to museums, libraries, and swimming and ballet lessons. They taught me to be caring and respectful of people and the environment. Often they taught by example: when I was four or five, my elder brothers and I accidentally lit a field on fire. Wind caught the flames and quickly it engulfed the field and came dangerously close to our house and barn. After the fire was put out, my parents felt our guilt and remorse and never mentioned it. We learned the mercy of compassion and forgiveness in addition to the foolishness of playing with matches in dry fields on windy days. My mother taught me honesty in a different way: when we stole balloons she made us return them and individually admit our guilt, apologize, and offer to pay from our birthday money (we didn't get allowances). The humility of facing that storekeeper (whose sweet disposition and insistence that we keep the balloons made my guilt worse) has stayed with me until this day.

Original:

In the international publishing arena, Asia is the biggest future international market for English books if population is used as a measure. English is arguably the most influential language in the world, based on the number of people who speak English and on expanding international usage in business and travel.

Better:

In the international publishing arena, Asia is the biggest future international market for English books if population is used as a measure. English is arguably the most influential language in the world, based on the number of people who speak English and on expanding international usage in business and travel. How "big" is Asia? In terms of population, three fifths of the world's people currently live in Asia and by the year 2010 some three fourths of the world's people will live in Asia – from the Middle East to India to China. I find this population statistic quite revealing: If, in the year 2010, we wanted to statistically sample four persons from all the world's people, here is what would happen. One would be from India, one would be from China, one more would be from somewhere else in Asia – perhaps the Middle East, Indonesia, Japan, or Russia. The last of the four persons would have to be chosen from *all* of North America, South America, Europe, Australia and Africa!

Original:

When I left college I had no idea how many times I would think back to the people, places, and situations during those formative years in my life. So many things I wondered about or worried about then, seem simple to understand in retrospect. I do regret missed opportunities. But seven years out of college, I am a different person. For me, the secret boils down to three words: action, meaning, and simplicity. First, I act on things by not letting them slip by. Second, I look for more meaning in the things I do. Third, I keep things simple by looking for overlooked solutions.

Better:

When I left college I had no idea how many times I would think back to the people, places, and situations during those formative years in my life. So many things I wondered about or worried about then, seem simple to understand in retrospect. I do regret missed opportunities. But seven years out of college, I am a different person. It all happened in a strange but seminal moment. One day, while visiting a local university pub in Tucson, I was sitting on a pub stool pondering a wooden plaque posted on the wall behind the bartender. On it were scrawled the letters: "I I T Y W Y B M A D". I looked at it for a while but couldn't figure out what it meant. The bar patron next to me, looked to be regular and I asked him. But he did not know. So I posed the question to the bartender.

"Hey, what do those letters stand for?" I asked.
"If I tell you, will you buy me a drink?" the bartender replied.
"No problem," I said. "Now tell me what it means."
"I already told you," the bartender said.

Then the bartender pointed to each of the letters and said, "If I tell you, will you buy me a drink?" (*IITYWYBMAD*)

It was not only funny but incredibly revealing. How could something that looked so baffling, be so simple? And moreover, how could that regular bar patron have never thought to ask such a question about a sign that he had probably stared at dozens of times?

Then it occurred to me how this situation showed the power of opportunity. In a broader sense, I too had overlooked situations just like these. I too had failed to venture that first guess on many other occasions, just to sit there like others. I was not getting as much meaning from my life because I was not fully awake and recognizing the things around me. I too had assumed that the solutions to many problems were complicated.

I made a silent vow to use this novel incident as my watchword and guide. For me, it has resulted in a three-pronged motto: action, meaning, and simplicity. First, I act on things by not letting them slip by. Second, I look for more meaning in the things I do. Third, I keep things simple by looking for overlooked solutions.

Although the above example is an involved one, it does not take a necessarily long or complicated example to make a memorable point. Try two more.

Original:

> I was brought up out of context – an English girl in a British colony. I went through 13 years of international school and my primary school had 28 nationalities.

Better:

> I was brought up out of context – an English girl in a British colony. I went through 13 years of international school and my primary school had 28 nationalities. I remember when my 4th year teacher had the brainchild of holding an 'International Day'. Everyone wore a traditional or national costume, and brought a dish of traditional cuisine. There is no real national costume for England, so I was dressed as an English Rose, and brought Yorkshire Parkin, a sweet ginger cake as my dish.

Original:

> As an undergraduate, I chose to attend Oxford. Established in the 1200's, it is England's oldest university and many ancient traditions are still alive.

Better:

> As an undergraduate, I chose to attend Oxford. Established in the 1200's, it is England's oldest university and many ancient traditions are still alive. An example of one of these traditions includes the verbal promise that every undergraduate must make upon formal admission to the university. This promise includes not bringing sheep into the library for fear of damaging the books!

APPENDICES

"If you don't like your ranking, just wait five minutes until another one comes round the corner."

Dean of leading American business school

APPENDIX I

SUMMARY OF MBA APPLICATION TIPS 1 TO 88

Chapter 1 – What are Schools *Really* Looking For?

Tip #1: Plan your attack—make a map and chart your progress.

Tip #2: Submit applications to "lesser" schools first.

Tip #3: Supply goals and vision.

Tip #4: Create optional or "blank question" entries.

Tip #5: Build your application around a theme.

Tip #6: Reality check—boil down the whole MBA process.

Tip #7: Think of your target audience.

Chapter 3 – Essay Writing Part I: The Classic MBA Essays

Tip #8: Make an outline for your "who are you?" essay.

Tip #9: Consider employing a "creative approach".

Tip #10: Consider writing a short introduction for your "who are you?" essay; alternatively you may choose to begin your essay with a summary or lead sentence.

Tip #11: Break your discussion into three or four major parts.

Tip #12: Choose specific, concrete examples to support what you say.

Tip #13: Consider the use of quotes and anecdotes.

Tip #14: Consider the appropriate use of readability tools and keep track of reader friendliness.

Tip #15: Make an outline for your "career goals" essay.

Tip #16: Consider writing a short introduction for your "career goals" essay; alternatively you may choose to begin your essay with a statement of your career goals.

Tip #17: Create "goal statements".

Tip #18: Create "vision statements".

Tip #19: Clarify your career path.

Tip #20: Break down your background and summarize key elements in the body of your essay.

Tip #21: Choose relevant examples and support them with specific details.

Tip #22: Test your "career goals" essay by viewing it as an argument in disguise.

Tip #23: Think first and foremost in terms of why you are suited to be a businessperson and what you think is the hallmark of a businessperson.

Tip #24: Mention (or imply) that an MBA is the missing link between where you are now and the future.

Tip #25: Mention academic reasons for wanting to do an MBA including the reason for your proposed major and/or minor in business school.

Tip #26: Mention the need to obtain cross-functional skills (a common example is a person who has expertise in finance and who wants to study marketing or vice-versa).

Tip #27: Evaluate other reasons for wanting an MBA including switching industries, being recognized for advancement purposes, pursuing work in a different geographic region, securing a hedge against job uncertainty, obtaining an important credential, gaining contacts, and making new friends.

Tip #28: Mention that a school has a talented, diverse student body, high-caliber faculty, and/or top-notch facilities, and/or strong alumni networks.

Tip #29: Mention academic specialties and special programs offered by the school which attract you to the school.

Tip #30: Mention specific courses which you would like to take and/or mention the names of a couple of professors whose courses you would like to enroll in.

Tip #31: Mention wanting to do some independent research and cite a proposed research topic.

Tip #32: Evaluate other reasons for wanting to attend a particular school including joint-degree programs, exchange programs, special leadership programs, teaching methods, class size, and geographic location.

Tip #33: Mention employment opportunities including what you would like to do with your summer internship opportunity (if applicable).

Tip #34: Mention extracurricular organizations you may want to join while attending business school.

Tip #35: Think in terms of how you might contribute to the school as an alumnus.

Tip #36: Employ a search engine—Google, Yahoo, Hotmail, AOL—and search for relevant and current information about a particular business school.

Tip #37: Consult a travel guidebook (e.g., Lonely Planet Publications) to gain more information about the city and the environment around where your chosen business school is located.

Chapter 4 – Essay Writing Part II: The *Other* MBA Essay Types

Tip #38: Break your background down into four parts including professional, educational, cultural background, and personal experience.

Tip #39: Find your "diversity trigger".

Tip #40: Use a workable structure and signpost your discussion.

Tip #41: Be honest. Don't try to outguess the admissions committee.

Tip #42: Summarize any discussion of personal weaknesses by showing how each is a strength in disguise or at least what you have learned as a result of struggling with your weaknesses.

Tip #43:   Break up your discussion of strengths and weaknesses by first discussing strengths and then discussing weaknesses.

Tip #44:   You may employ a "creative approach" to describe your strengths and weaknesses.

Tip #45:   Consider the "mix" and order of your accomplishments.

Tip #46:   Test your accomplishment by making sure it has the "wow factor!". Imagine yourself as the reader. Ask, "Is this difficult?...is this impressive?"

Tip #47:   Consider using "headlines" to summarize and highlight your accomplishment(s).

Tip #48:   Do not define "leadership" too narrowly.

Tip #49:   Make sure the reader can actually figure out what your difficult situation is. Don't wait until the end of the essay to summarize.

Tip #50:   Consider using quotes from people as a way to help the reader understand what you or other people actually felt.

Tip #51:   In terms of describing your difficult situation and addressing what you have learned from the situation, a good rule-of-thumb weighting is: "two-thirds—describing" and "one-third—what you've learned."

Tip #52:   Reveal as much of your character and personal strengths as possible—personal, professional, motivations, spiritual, emotional, intellectual, latent potential, insights, likes and dislikes. These essay questions invite (and expect) you to get fancy and take chances.

Tip #53:   Briefly summarize and directly answer the question at hand before getting fancy (and do it in two or three sentences).

Tip #54:   Consider scenario analysis.

Tip #55:   Signpost your discussion using enumeration.

Chapter 5 – Essay Writing Part III: Optional Essay Entries

Tip #56:   Readability is of paramount importance. Try to keep each entry to a single page. You must make every effort to help the committee get through your optional questions. Think of the reviewer as skimming through your additional information.

Tip #57:   View the optional area as having five possible uses. Determine which of the five uses or combination of these will best serve you.

Chapter 6 – Resume or Employment Record

Tip #58:   Use corporate descriptions, especially if your company or organization is not well-known.

Tip #59: Use bullet points to start each line of your resume when highlighting a description of your work experience and use an equal or greater number of bullet points when listing your most recent job experience, compared with previous jobs held.

Tip #60: Use verbs and consistent verb tenses to begin each line of the resume when highlighting your work experience (i.e., responsibilities and/or accomplishments).

Tip #61: Quantify your work-related accomplishments with number-based modifiers to avoid overly general descriptions.

Tip #62: Add "employment summaries" to explain what you found significant about each of your work experiences.

Tip #63: Review employment themes as the basis of writing meaningful "employment summaries".

Tip #64: Anticipate strengths and weaknesses in your employment record.

Chapter 7 – Letters of Recommendation

Tip #65: Prepare early by choosing your recommenders.

Tip #66: Write a statement of your career goals to communicate to your recommenders where you feel your career is heading.

Tip #67: Update your resume and/or employment record complete with summaries on what you feel you have learned or what you feel is significant about your experiences.

Tip #68: Send your resume and/or employment record along with a personal letter to each recommender.

Tip #69: If your recommender insists that you draft your own letter, then ask a friend to write it for you so as to disguise your writing style.

Tip #70: Think detail. The goal is to get the recommender to write in a specific and concrete manner, often highlighting one or two major work accomplishments, one or two distinguishing personal traits, or one or two major strengths or weaknesses.

Tip #71: Send a thank-you note (or email) to your recommenders.

Chapter 8 – Interviews

Tip #72: Review the school's brochure.

Tip #73: Be able to defend every line of your resume (or employment record).

Tip #74: Articulate your career goals and your vision statements.

Tip #75: Anticipate mock interview type questions.

Tip #76: Relax and be yourself.

Tip #77   Answer questions in a succinct manner. Don't waffle.

Tip #78:   Have questions for the interviewer.

Tip #79:   Send a thank-you letter (or email).

Chapter 9 – Presenting Your Extracurricular Activities/Awards and Recognition/Community Service

Tip #80:   Mention why you feel an extracurricular entry is significant.

Tip #81:   Present hobbies and interests in lieu of extracurricular activities.

Tip #82:   If you have no extracurricular activities to speak of, then try presenting your part-time work experiences while in college as a substitute for your extracurricular involvement.

Chapter 10 – Packaging Your MBA Essays and Application

Tip #83:   Proof read your essay and application materials.

Tip #84:   Review readability tools: addendums, bolds, bullets, dashes, enumeration, headings and headlines, indentations, italics, and short sentences.

Tip #85:   Consider "writing out" the masculine generic "he".

Tip #86:   Think in terms of a top-down expository writing style.

Tip #87:   Focus your writing. Try not to discuss too many ideas at one time.

Tip #88:   Try the "for example" technique.

APPENDIX II

GMAT AND MBA CONTACT INFORMATION

GMAT Exam

The GMAT CAT (Computer Adaptive Test) is offered on demand. For more information or to sign up on the Internet:

- *www.gmat.org*
- e-mail: *gmat@ets.org*

If you wish to call the U.S. and talk with an ETS (Educational Testing Service) representative:

- GMAT customer service:
  Tel: (609) 771-7330
  Fax: (609) 883-4349

GMAT Test Prep Courses

The Kaplan Educational Centers and The Princeton Review provide in-class courses with the goal of helping students score higher on the GMAT:

- Kaplan Educational Centers   *www.kaplan.com*
- The Princeton Review   *www.review.com*

MBA Forums

There are three organizations currently involved in putting together annual MBA forums in the U.S. and international locations. To determine the dates, cities, and venues applicable to you, check their websites.

- *www.gmac.com*
  Sponsor: GMAC (Graduate Management Admissions Council)
  Name of forum: "MBA Forum"

- *www.topmba.com*
  Sponsor: Topcareer.net
  Name of forum: "World MBA Tour"

- *www.thembatour.com*
  Sponsor: Linden Educational Services
  Name of forum: "The MBA Tour"

Current MBA Application Essay Questions

Schools change application essay questions frequently. For the purpose of applying to a particular business school, you should plan on downloading actual business school application packages from a school's website.

Scholarships and Financial Assistance

Graduate Management Admissions Council

A substantial amount of information regarding financial assistance for U.S. and international students can be found right on the GMAC website. As a rule, each country takes care of its own citizens and residents first. In the U.S., financial assistance is more limited for international students than for U.S. residents. Most business schools do offer some financial assistance to at least some international students; students should inquire with the schools they are applying to.

- *www.gmat.org*

National Association of Student Financial Aid Administration

Use this site to search the web for ideas and resources.

- *www.finaid.org*

SallieMae Loans

- *www.salliemae.com*

Consortium Graduate Study Management

The Consortium for Graduate Study in Management is a multi-university alliance working to facilitate the entry of minorities into managerial positions in business. The universities recruit college-trained African-American, Hispanic-American, and Native-American United States citizens and invite them to compete for merit-based fellowships for graduate study leading to a Master's Degree in Business.

- *www.cgsm.org*

General Business School Information and GMAT/MBA Services

The GMAC (Graduate Management Admissions Council) is a primary source for business school information.

- *www.gmac.com*

The following magazines feature business school news throughout the year:

- *www.businessweek.com*
- *www.usnews.com*
- *www.financialtimes.com (www.ft.com)*

Other sources (in alphabetical order):

The following is a sampling of all GMAT, MBA, and business school websites containing related information. On-line searches on *google.com*, for example, using words such as "business school", "mba" and "gmat" will yield collectively several million results.

- *www.accepted.com*
- *www.admissionsconsultants.com*
- *www.allbusinessshcools.com*
- *www.aol.com*
- *www.bschool.com*
- *www.bschoolessays.com*
- *www.campusaccess.com*
- *www.essayedge.com*
- *www.essaysolutions.com*
- *www.foreignmba.com*
- *www.google.com*
- *www.hotmail.com*
- *www.mba.com*
- *www.mbaessayadvantage.com*
- *www.mbaexchange.com*
- *www.mbaentry.com*
- *www.mba-experience.com*
- *www.topmba.com*
- *www.top10mba.com*
- *www.yahoo.com*
- *www.mbazone.com*
- *www.800score.com*

APPENDIX III

HOW TO GET THE MOST OUT OF YOUR BUSINESS SCHOOL EXPERIENCE

Computer Skills

There are three computer application skills that a prospective MBA student needs prior to attending business school. These include word-processing capabilities, spreadsheet capabilities, and graphic capabilities. Most students have proficiency in terms of word-processing capabilities prior to attending business school, but many are rusty in terms of the other two capabilities. Mastering the basics of a spreadsheet application, such as *Microsoft Excel*, is a must. For example, given the actual and projected hypothetical profit scenario below, a prospective student should be able to type these figures onto an Excel spreadsheet and create a basic line graph, or a pie chart, or bar chart, showing revenues, expenses, and profits.

Periods	1	2	3	4	5
Revenues	875	1,050	1,260	1,512	1,814
Expenses	450	495	545	599	659
Profits	3,324	3,545	3,806	4,113	4,476

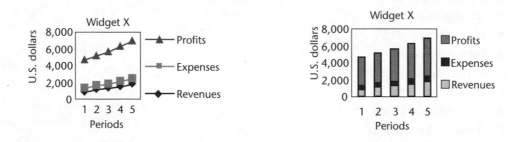

Mastering the basics of a graphic application, such as *Microsoft PowerPoint*, is very helpful. You may need to do a slide presentation and/or need to include clip art in your reports.

Quantitative Skills

The ability to familiarize yourself with key concepts covered in the core first-year courses can greatly assist you in getting a jump and not falling behind in your course work during first-year business school. Most first-year or core courses are quantitative in nature including Accounting, Economics, Finance, and Statistics; other first-year or core courses are qualitative in nature including Marketing and Management Organizational Behavior. A splendid book that gives you insight into all major areas in overview fashion is *The 10-Day MBA*, Silbiger, 1999, ISBN 0-7499-1401-7.

Books in the *Barron's Business Review Series* are recommended if you can stomach a more in-depth review. These are excellent books covering core topics including:

- *Accounting* – Eisen, 1993, ISBN 0-8120-1917-2,
- *Economics* – Wessels, 1993, ISBN 0-8120-1392-1,
- *Finance* – Groppelli and Nikbakht, 1995, ISBN 0-8120-1916-4,
- *Management* – Montana and Charnov, 1995, ISBN 0-8120-1549-5,
- *Marketing* – Sandhusen, 1993, ISBN 0-8120-1548-7, and
- *Business Statistics* – Downing and Clark, 1997, ISBN 0-8120-9658-4.

Barron's also publishes another series called *Barron's Business Library Series* which provides in-depth coverage of more specific topics such as purchasing or international marketing but books in this series are more applicable as supplementary reading while at business school rather than for preparation prior to attending business school. For more information in locating these books, try *www.barronseduc.com*.

Writing and Speaking Skills

Business school is not a haven for the vocally timid. Class participation may constitute 50 percent of your final grade in a given course. Your fellow classmates will compete with you for "air time". Professors may randomly call on you especially if you are not contributing to in-class discussion. It is hard to hide behind a large nametag placed conspicuously in front of you. Not only must you have courage but you must also have clear thoughts. You should endeavor to come across as confident and coherent. Therefore before starting business school make sure you can stand before a room of say 30 to 50 people and give a speech without trembling. Two organizations that specialize in building personal effectiveness through improved public speaking are Dale Carnegie and Toastmasters International. If applicable, plan to take a Dale Carnegie Public Speaking Course before attending business school or join Toastmasters even if it is only for a few months before attending business school.

Perhaps the best all-round tip for ease in presenting information involves using enumerations. Take your topic, break it into three to five points and say, "The purpose of this document (speech) is to summarize several reasons why Plan ABC makes sense. First..., second..., third..., moreover..., lastly...."

Improving writing skills is usually a long-term endeavor. One small reference book that has withstood the test of time in the American arena is *The Elements of Style*, fourth edition, Strunk, Jr. and White, 1999, ISBN 0-205-30902. If building vocabulary is your objective, the classic is: *30 Days to a More Powerful Vocabulary*, Funk and Lewis, 1993, ISBN 067174349. Another vocabulary book that merits recommendation is *Word Smart*, Robinson, 1993, ISBN 0679745890.

Case Study Skills

Most business schools use a hybrid between lecture and case study method. Certain business schools, such as Harvard Business School and The University of Virginia (Darden), rely almost exclusively on the case study method. The goal of case study work is to help students see broad themes across a number of unique business situations. You are given a case that contains background information about a business or venture, and which requires a management decision in order for the company or venture to proceed forward. The discussion is centered on the question: "What would you do?" From an academic standpoint, success in case study work results from two complementary aptitudes: inductive and deductive thinking. Whereas the study of new and unfamiliar cases requires seeing the details before shaping them into a more complete picture (inductive thinking), the recalling of previous but important related cases requires seeing the whole picture before engaging in details (deductive thinking). Students who have studied science, engineering, or law generally have an advantage in terms of their inductive thinking capability whereas students who have studied political science, philosophy, or business generally have an advantage in terms of their deductive thinking capability.

People and Networking Skills

It has been said that there are three reasons why a person goes to business school: (1) knowledge, (2) credentials, and (3) contacts. Many of your classmates will achieve substantial positions in business within 10 to 15 years from the time of leaving business school. Your ability to make friends and keep in touch will pay rich dividends—tangible and intangible. Certain classmates will become your best friends but remembering personal information about many others will not be easy.

Because of the strange, interconnected nature of business itself, you may have future need to contact a number of your business school classmates, some of whom you thought had totally different career paths and personal outlooks at the time of business school. Your ability to remember personal details will help cement future ties. Any classmate or alumnus will be flattered if you remember things so long afterwards and they will certainly believe that you are sharp to be able to do so. To this end, consider creating a "recipe card" system. When you meet people during your first year at business school, privately write down information about them on 3" by 5" recipe cards. Note their hobbies, alma maters, hometowns, birthdays, names of parents or family members, and any other information you deem interesting or relevant.

Job Search Skills

In reality, a lot of people go to business school not knowing what they *really* want to do with their careers (even if they claim to know so in their application). However, the better you know what you want to do with your career, the more you can get out of the business school experience. For example, if you pretty much know for sure that you want to work in venture capital, you have the advantage of joining relevant clubs, meeting other classmates with similar interests, securing relevant internships, tailoring academic course offerings, and doing independent research in this area. Make a point to find out what you *really* want to do; do not put it off. Ask classmates who may have already worked in your desired field. They will give you an insider's view, complementary but different from the one that you will read about in recruitment brochures or from the viewpoint that a recruiter will present in a less than completely candid sales pitch.

One worthwhile (and often overlooked) resource within the career services office is career and personality testing. Most tests are offered free of charge through the career services centers of major business schools. For example, the Myers-Briggs Indicator Test is well-known. This test comes complete with a written narrative based on the results of your test. With the help of a trained career services administrator, the results of a number of other such tests can indicate whether you are made for work in the world of high-strung banking or consultancy, work in the less quantitative world of corporate public relations, or work in the less profit motivated world of government.

Controlling Stress

Most stress in business school is precipitated by heavy workloads. Organization is key. If you are in need of a refresher course in time management try to get a copy of *How to Get Control of Your Time and Your Life*, Lakein, 1996, ISBN 0451-167724. The first source of stress is not finding time to do things you enjoy be it sports, hobbies, outside reading, etc. You may, during the first year, come to begrudge the amount of time business studies is taking from you. Putting time into your studies and endless group meetings will leave you with little time for yourself. Get creative. Given that there are some 100 waking hours in a week, you must carve out some time for yourself and not feel guilty. If you do not find time, things can become fanatical and frustrating.

You will most certainly feel guilty not keeping in touch with many of your friends. Tell your friends at the outset not to expect long email replies. But do plan on making a semi-annual news brief done in the form of a letter, to be sent out in December and June of each year.

Another major source of stress is falling behind in course work. Although everyone must set his or her own schedule, a good tip is to make a systematic review of your notes every Saturday morning. This will combat cramming. Another tip, used by a number of the very best students, entails making a course summary. Pretend that you are going to either teach the course next time or give your outline to another student. Your ability to try to summarize the course contents will force you to come to grips with major topics. Many students end up doing this anyway when making their own cheat sheets for cracking case study problems. But this same principle can be applied to course work. There is also a lot of satisfaction, confidence, and ownership gained from knowing that you completed a set of ten-page course summaries for each of your courses. Put it in your own handwriting to make it personal.

Finally, concentrate on picking good people for your study groups. Group work may constitute 50 percent of your total study time and 50 percent of your grade in some courses. "Bad study groups" occur when certain individuals either do not do their fair share of the work or are difficult to get along with in terms of their personalities. Likewise, you want to get off to a good start. Do more than your fair share of work and be cheerful and you will get a reputation as a good person to work with.

APPENDIX IV

EVALUATING YOUR MBA PROGRAMS

The following categories may be useful when evaluating the MBA schools/programs of your choice. You may want to assign a rating of 1 to 5, with 1 being the highest score and 5 being the lowest score.

Major categories	School A	School B	School C	School D	School E
Ranking or reputation					
Curriculum and academic specialties					
Teaching method and class size					
Location and living environment					
Job placement and employment opportunities					
Alumni and networks					
Financial cost					

APPENDIX V

APPLICATION TRACKING SHEETS

Application Deadline

The following charts are useful for keeping track of the schools you are applying to and their application deadlines.

Universities	Rank	Application downloaded	Fin. aid. information	1st round	Reply	2nd round	Reply	3rd round	Reply	Deposit required by

Letters of Recommendation and Others

The following charts are useful for keeping track of your transcript requests, interviews, GMAT scores, letters of recommendation, data information forms, and application essays.

Universities	Transcripts	GMAT taken	GMAT sent	1st recom.	Received (or sent)	2nd recom.	Received (or sent)	3rd recom.	Received (or sent)	Essays written	Interviews scheduled	Thank you card (or email) sent

APPENDIX VI

GMAT SCORES AT THE LEADING BUSINESS SCHOOLS

The chart below summarizes average GMAT scores at the leading business schools. TOEFL scores are also required for applicants who graduated from college or university in a non-English speaking country. Usually a minimum TOEFL score of 250 (computer test) or 600 (paper test) is required.

	Average GMAT score of entering students, fall 2002
U.S. Business Schools:	
American Graduate School of International Management (Thunderbird)	600
Berkeley (Haas), University of California–	703
Carnegie Mellon University	672
Chicago, University of	687
Columbia University	711
Cornell University (Johnson)	673
Dartmouth College (Amos Tuck)	695
Duke University (Fuqua)	701
Harvard Business School	705
Massachusetts Institute of Technology (Sloan)	707
Michigan–Ann Arbor, University of	681
New York University (Stern)	700
North Carolina–Chapel Hill (Kenan-Flagler), Univ. of	671
Northwestern University (Kellogg)	700
Pennsylvania (Wharton), University of	711
Stanford University	716
Texas–Austin (McCombs), University of	678
University of California–Los Angeles (Anderson)	699
Virginia (Darden), University of	683

	Average GMAT score of entering students
Yale University	698
Canadian Business Schools:	
McGill University	645
Queen's University	675
Toronto (Rotman), University of	674
Western Ontario (Ivey), University of	660
York University (Schulich)	650
European Business Schools:	
IESE [Spain]	660
IMD [Switzerland]	670
INSEAD [France]	690
London Business School [England]	690
Rotterdam School of Management (Erasmus) [Netherlands]	630
Australian Business Schools:	
Australian Graduate School of Management (AGSM)	635
Melbourne Business School (MBS)	620
Asia-Pacific Business Schools:	
Asian Institute of Management (AIM), Manila	665
Chinese University of Hong Kong (CUHK)	610
Chulalongkorn University (Sasin), Bangkok	540
Hong Kong University of Science and Technology (HKUST)	625
Indian Institute of Management, Ahmedabad (IIMA)	735
International University of Japan (IUJ), Japan	639
Nanyang Technological University (NTU), Singapore	642
National University of Singapore (NUS)	670
South African Business Schools:	
Cape Town, University of	590
The Wits Business School	580

APPENDIX VII

CONTACT INFORMATION FOR THE WORLD'S LEADING BUSINESS SCHOOLS

Contact information—mailing addresses, phone and fax numbers, email and websites for the world's leading graduate business programs:

U.S. Business Schools:
American Graduate School of International Management (Thunderbird)
Berkeley (Haas), University of California–
Carnegie Mellon University
Chicago, University of
Columbia University
Cornell University (Johnson)
Dartmouth College (Amos Tuck)
Duke University (Fuqua)
Harvard Business School
Massachusetts Institute of Technology (Sloan)
Michigan–Ann Arbor, University of
New York University (Stern)
North Carolina–Chapel Hill (Kenan-Flagler), University of
Northwestern University (Kellogg)
Pennsylvania (Wharton), University of
Stanford University
Texas–Austin (McCombs), University of
University of California–Los Angeles (Anderson)
Virginia (Darden), University of
Yale University

Canadian Business Schools:
McGill University
Queen's University
Toronto (Rotman), University of
Western Ontario (Ivey), University of
York University (Schulich)

European Business Schools:
IESE [Spain]
IMD [Switzerland]
INSEAD [France]
London Business School [England]
Rotterdam School of Management (Erasmus) [Netherlands]

Australian Business Schools:
Australian Graduate School of Management (AGSM)
Melbourne Business School (MBS)

Asia-Pacific Business Schools:
Asian Institute of Management (AIM), Manila
Chinese University of Hong Kong (CUHK)
Chulalongkorn University (Sasin), Bangkok
Hong Kong University of Science and Technology (HKUST)
Indian Institute of Management, Ahmedabad (IIMA)
International University of Japan (IUJ), Niigata
Nanyang Technological University (NTU), Singapore
National University of Singapore (NUS)

South African Business Schools:
Cape Town, University of
The Wits Business School

U.S. Business Schools:

X ■ **American Graduate School of International Management (Thunderbird)**
Thunderbird Graduate School
15249 North 59th Ave
Glendale, Arizona 85306-6000
Tel: (800) 848-9084
Tel: (602) 978-7100
Fax: (602) 439-5432
Email: admissions@thunderbird.edu
Website: www.thunderbird.edu

2Y-WE

■ **Berkeley (Haas), University of California–**
Haas School of Business
440 Student Services Wing
Berkeley, CA 94720
Tel: (510) 642-1405
Fax: (510) 643-6659
Email: mbaadms@haas.berkeley.edu
Website: www.haas.berkeley.edu

① MBA
② MFE   March /09

■ **Carnegie Mellon University**
Graduate School of Industrial Administration
5000 Forbes Ave
Posner Hall
Pittsburgh, PA 15213
Tel: (412) 268-2272
Fax: (412) 268-4209
Email: gsia-admissions@andrew.cmu.edu
Website: www.gsia.cmu.edu

① MBA
② MFSC

■ **Chicago, University of**
Graduate School of Business
6030 S. Ellis Ave.,
Chicago Illinois, USA 60637
Tel: (773) 702-7369
Fax: (773) 702-9085
Email: admissions@gsb.uchicago.edu
Website: www.gsb.uchicago.edu

MBA

■ **Columbia University**
Graduate School of Business
Office of Admissions
216 Uris Hall, 3022 Broadway
New York, NY 10027-7004
Tel: (212) 854-1961
Fax: (212) 662-6754
Email: gohermes@claven.gsb.columbia.edu
Website: www.gsb.columbia.edu

MBA   Jan 9

■ **Cornell University (Johnson)**   *MBA*   *Jan 9*
Johnson Graduate School of Management
111 Sage Hall,
Ithaca, NY 14853-4201
Tel: (800) 847-2082
Tel: (607) 255-4526
Fax: (607) 255-0065
Email: mba@cornell.edu
Website: www.johnson.cornell.edu

■ **Dartmouth College (Amos Tuck)**   *Jan 9*
Tuck School of Business at Dartmouth
100 Tuck Hall
Hanover, NH 03755-9000
Tel: (603) 646-3162
Fax: (603) 646-1441
Email: tuck.admissions@dartmouth.edu
Website: www.tuck.dartmouth.edu

■ **Duke University (Fuqua)**   *Jan 3*
The Fuqua School of Business
Towerview Road
Durham, NC 27708-0104
Tel: (919) 660-7705
Fax: (919) 681-8026
Email: admissions-info@fuqua.duke.edu
Website: www.fuqua.duke.edu

■ **Harvard Business School**   *Jan 3*
Graduate School of Business Administration
Soldiers Field Road
Boston, MA 02163
Tel: (617) 495-6127
Fax: (617) 496-9272
Email: admissions@hbs.edu
Website: www.hbs.edu

- ■ **Massachusetts Institute of Technology (Sloan)**
Sloan School of Management
50 Memorial Drive, Ste E52-101
Cambridge, MA 02142-1347
Tel: (617) 258-5434
Fax: (617) 253-6405
Email: mbaadmissions@sloan.mit.edu
Website: www.mitsloan.mit.edu

Jan 15

- ■ **Michigan–Ann Arbor, University of**
School of Business Administration
701 Tappan Street, Room 2260
Ann Arbor, MI 48109-1234
Tel: (734) 763-5796
Fax: (734) 763-7804
Email: umbsmba@umich.edu
Website: www.bus.umich.edu

TOEFL

- ■ **New York University (Stern)**
Stern School of Business
New York University
44 West 4th Street, Ste 10-160
New York, NY 10012-1126
Tel: (800) 272-7373
Tel: (212) 998-0660
Fax: (212) 995-4231
Email: sternmba@stern.nyu.edu
Website: www.stern.nyu.edu

Jan 15

- ■ **North Carolina–Chapel Hill (Kenan-Flagler), University of**
Kenan-Flagler Business School
McColl Building CB 3490
Chapel Hill, NC 27599-3490
Tel: (919) 962-3236
Fax: (919) 962-0898
Email: mba_info@unc.edu
Website: www.kenan-flagler.unc.edu

*2 yr. W.E.
Interview*

■ **Northwestern University (Kellogg)** *Jan 11* *interview*
Kellogg Graduate School of Management
Leverone Hall, 2001 Sheridan Road
Evanston, IL 60208-2001
Tel: (847) 491-3308
Fax: (847) 491-4960
Email: mbaadmissions@kellogg.nwu.edu
Website: www.kellogg.~~nwu~~.edu
northwestern

■ **Pennsylvania (Wharton), University of** *Jan 3*
Wharton MBA Program
420 Jon M Huntsman Hall
3730 Spruce Street
102 Vance Hall, 3733 Spruce St.
Philadelphia, PA 19104
Tel: (215) 898-3423
Fax: (215) 898-0120
Email: mba.admissions@wharton.upenn.edu
Website: www.wharton.upenn.edu

■ **Stanford University** *Jan 7*
Graduate School of Business
350 Memorial Way
Stanford, CA 94305-5015
Tel: (650) 723-2766
Fax: (650) 725-7831
Email: mba@gsb.stanford.edu
Website: www.gsb.stanford.edu

■ **Texas–Austin (McCombs), University of** *Feb 1*
McCombs School of Business
MBA Program Office, CBA 2.316
Austin, TX 78712-1170
Tel: (512) 471-7612
Fax: (512) 471-4131
Email: mccombsmba@bus.utexas.edu
Website: www.texasmba.bus.utexas.edu
www. mba. mccombs. utexas. edu

■ **University of California–Los Angeles (Anderson)** *Jan 2*
Anderson Graduate School of Management at UCLA
MBA Program
110 Westwood Plaza
Los Angeles, CA 90095
Tel: (310) 825-6944
Fax: (310) 825-8582
Email: mba.admissions@anderson.ucla.edu
Website: www.anderson.ucla.edu

■ **Virginia (Darden), University of** *Jan 3*
Darden Graduate School of Business Administration
University of Virginia
Charlottesville, VA 22906-6550
Tel: (434) 924-4809
Fax: (434) 243-5033
Email: darden@virginia.edu
Website: www.darden.virginia.edu

■ **Yale University** *Jan 9*
Yale School of Management
135 Prospect Street
Box 208200
New Haven, CT 06520-8200
Tel: (203) 432-5932
Fax: (203) 432-7004
Email: mba.admissions@yale.edu
Website: www.mba.yale.edu

Canadian Business Schools:

■ **McGill University**
MBA Program, Faculty of Management
1001 Sherbrooke Street West #300
Montreal, QC, Canada H3A 1G5
Tel: (514) 398-4066
Fax: (514) 398-2499
Email: mba.mgmt@mcgill.ca
Website: www.management.mcgill.ca

■ **Queen's University**
Queen's MBA for Science and Technology
Mackintosh-Corry Hall,
Kingston, Ontario
Canada K7L 3N6
Tel: (613) 533-2302
Fax: (613) 533-6281
Email: info@business.queensu.ca
Website: www.business.queensu.ca

■ **Toronto (Rotman), University of**
Faculty of Management
Joseph L. Rotman Centre for Management
University of Toronto
105 St. George Street
Toronto, Ontario
Canada M5S 3E6
Tel: (416) 978-4084
Fax: (416) 978-5812
Email: mba@rotman.utoronto.ca
Website: www.rotman.utoronto.ca

■ **Western Ontario (Ivey), University of**
Richard Ivey School of Business
115 Richmond Street North
London, Ontario
Canada N6A 3K7
Tel: (519) 661-3419
Fax: (519) 661-3431
Email: info@ivey.uwo.ca
Website: www.ivey.uwo.ca

■ **York University (Schulich)**
Schulich School of Business
4700 Keele Street
Toronto, Ontario
Canada M3J 1P3
Tel: (416) 736-5059
Fax: (416) 650-8174
Email: admissions@schulich.yorku.ca
Website: www.schulich.yorku.ca

European Business Schools:

- **IESE** Spain

  IESE Business School
  Avenida Pearson, 21
  Barcelona, Spain 08034
  Tel: (34 93) 253 4229
  Fax: (34 93) 253 4343
  Email: mbainfo@iese.edu
  Website: www.iese.edu

- **IMD** Switzerland

  MBA Admissions Office,
  Chemin de Bellerive 23,
  P.O. Box 915
  Lausanne, Switzerland CH-1001
  Tel: (41) 21/618 0298
  Fax: (41) 21/618 0615
  Email: mbainfo@imd.ch
  Website: www.imd.ch/mba

- **INSEAD** France/Singapore

  MBA Programme
  Boulevard de Constance,
  Fountainebleau, France 77300
  Tel: 33 (1) 60 724299
  Fax: 33 (1) 60 724141
  Email: mba.info@insead.edu
  Website: www.insead.mba

- **London Business School** England

  London Business School
  Sussex Place, Regents Park
  London, UK NW1 4SA
  Tel: (44 20) 7262-5050
  Fax: (44 20) 7724-7875
  Email: mbainfo@london.edu
  Website: www.london.edu

■ **Rotterdam School of Management (Erasmus)**   **Netherlands**
Rotterdam School of Management
Burgemeester Oudlaan 50
P.O. Box 1738
Rotterdam, Netherlands 3000 DR
Tel: +31 (0) 10 408 2222
Fax: +31 (0) 10 452 9509
Email: info@rsm.nl
Website: www.rsm.nl

Australian Business Schools:

■ **Australian Graduate School of Management (AGSM)**
AGSM School of Business
Sydney NSW 2052 Australia
Tel: (61-2) 9931-9225
Fax: (61-2) 9931-9231
Email: mba@agsm.edu.au
Website: www.agsm.edu.au

■ **Melbourne Business School (MBS)**
200 Leicester Street
Carlton, Victoria, Australia 3053
Tel: (61-3) 9349-8100
Fax: (61-3) 9349-8271
Email: enquiries@mbs.edu
Website: www.mbs.edu

Asia-Pacific Business Schools:

■ **Asian Institute of Management (AIM)**   **Philippines**
123 Paseo de Roxas St., Legaspi Village
1260 Makati City, Philippines
Tel: (63-2) 892-4011
Fax: (63-2) 893-7631
Email: admissions@aim.edu.ph
Website: www.aim.edu.ph

✗ ■ **Chinese University of Hong Kong (CUHK)**   **Hong Kong**
School of Management   3yr WE
Shatin, New Territories
Hong Kong, China
Tel: (852) 2609-7000
Fax: (852) 2603-5544
Email: cumba@cuhk.edu.hk
Website: www.cuhk.edu.hk/mba

■ **Chulalongkorn University (Sasin)**   **Thailand**
Sasin Graduate Institute of Business Administration
Sasa Patasala Building
Soi Chula 12
Phyathai Road
Bangkok 10330, Thailand
Tel: (66-2) 218-3850
Fax: (66-2) 216-1312
Email: sasin@chula.ac.th
Website: www.sasin.chula.ac.th

✗ ■ **Hong Kong University of Science and Technology (HKUST)**   **Hong Kong**
MBA/MSc Programs School of Business and Management
Clear Water Bay, Kowloon, Hong Kong
Tel: (852) 2358-7537   1Y - WE.
Fax: (852) 2705-9596
Email: mba@ust.hk
Website: www.bm.ust.hk/mba

■ **Indian Institute of Management, Ahmedabad (IIMA)**   **India**
Indian Institute of Management
Vastrapur, Ahmedabad 380 815
Gujarat, India
Tel: (91-79) 630-7241
Fax: (91-79) 630-6896
Email: admission@iimahd.ernet.in
Website: www.iimahd.ernet.in

■ **International University of Japan (IUJ)**   Japan
Office of Student Recruitment
Yamato-machi, Minami Uonuma-gun,
Niigata 949-7277 Japan
Tel: (81-25) 779-1104
Fax: (81-25) 779-1188
Email: info@iuj.ac.jp
Website: www.iuj.ac.jp

■ **Nanyang Technological University (NTU)**   Singapore
Nanyang Business School
50 Nanyang Avenue
Singapore 639798
Tel: (65) 6790-6183
Fax: (65) 6791-3561
Email: nbsmba@ntu.edu.sg
Website: www.nbs.ntu.edu.sg

■ **National University of Singapore (NUS)**   Singapore
The NUS Business School
FBA2, Level 5, Room 6
11 Law Link, Singapore 117592
Tel: (65) 6874-4799
Fax: (65) 6777-1296
Email: nusmba@nus.edu.sg
Website: www.fba.nus.edu.sg

South African Business Schools:

■ **Cape Town, University of**
The Graduate School of Business
Private Bag Rondebosch
South Africa 7700
Tel: (27 21) 406-1922
Fax: (27 21) 406-1070
Email: info@gsb.uct.ac.za
Website: www.gsb.uct.ac.za

- **The Wits Business School**
The Wits Business School
Johannesberg, South Africa
Tel: (27 11) 717-1000
Fax: (21 11) 339-7620
E-mail: reg@zeus.mgmt.wits.ac.za
Website: www.wits.ac.za

APPENDIX VIII

CURRENT BUSINESS SCHOOL RANKINGS

The dean of one of America's leading business schools has been quoted as saying, "If you don't like your ranking, then wait five minutes because there'll be another one around the corner." Since different rankings are based on different criteria, expect ratings to reflect different things. At present, there is even a U.S. organization that ranks the rankings. Business school rankings embody some truth and some vagary, so caution must be exercised. It is important to always factor in an element of probability and skepticism. Rankings can make business schools very self-conscious about public perception, and there is some humor to be found in the statement: "There are at least 20 schools in the top 10." Although rankings lead to some gamesmanship on the part of the business schools themselves, it does make business schools more consumer-oriented, by placing pressure on schools to address the needs of students, faculty, and corporate recruiters.

One thing that surveys cannot rank is the distinctive character each business school possesses. The intangible and unique flavor of a school in terms of its people, history, and atmosphere is what creates a lasting bond between student and school. Some of the distinctive flavor stems from differences in a school's academic specialties. For first-year U.S. business school students, business school jokes and amusing anecdotes are recounted almost to the point of nausea. For example:

> A new product is thrown onto a boardroom table around which are gathered several of the company's executives, each of whom graduated from a few of America's highly-regarded business schools. Each executive brings his or her own unique predispositions to the bargaining table. The story goes that the executives are trying to figure out how to proceed with the new "miracle" gadget. Present are graduates from Dartmouth, University of Chicago, Harvard, Wharton, and Northwestern Business Schools. The Dartmouth graduate wants to call a meeting in order to have all department members decide how to proceed further; the Chicago graduate instinctively picks up the object to figure out if it actually works; the Wharton graduate thinks first about how to raise financing for this venture; the Northwestern graduate considers doing a market study to see if a market really exists for the product. The Harvard graduate just sits back and wonders whether responsibility for the project should be delegated. After all, if things go awry he or she does not want to be responsible for the mess!

In the above anecdote, certain business school stereotypes are brought into play. The first is Dartmouth's reputation for producing team players. The second is Chicago's reputation for producing graduates with excellent technical and analytical skills. The third is Wharton's reputation for producing financiers. The fourth is Northwestern's reputation for producing marketers. And fifth is Harvard's reputation for producing politically astute executives. There may be some truth in any one of the stereotypes you come across—you will have to find out if it is really true and if it matters to you.

The Best B-Schools (U.S.), *BusinessWeek*, October 2002

The *BusinessWeek* (*www.businessweek.com*) ranking comes out every "even" year in October.

2002 Rank	School	2002 Rank	School
1	**NORTHWESTERN** (Kellogg) Evaston, Ill.	16	**UCLA** (Anderson) Los Angeles
2	**CHICAGO** Chicago	17	**USC** (Marshall) Los Angeles
3	**HARVARD** Boston	18	**UNC** (Kenan-Flagler) Chapel Hill, N.C.
4	**STANFORD** Stanford, Calif.	19	**CARNEGIE MELLON** Pittsburgh
5	**PENNSYLVANIA** (Wharton) Philadelphia	20	**INDIANA** (Kelly) Bloomington
6	**MIT** (Sloan) Cambridge, Mass.	21	**TEXAS** (McCombs) Austin
7	**COLUMBIA** New York	22	**EMORY** (Goizueta) Atlanta
8	**MICHIGAN** Ann Arbor	23	**MICHIGAN STATE** (Broad) E. Lansing
9	**DUKE** (Fuqua) Durham, N.C.	24	**WASHINGTON** (Olin) St. Louis
10	**DARTMOUTH** (Tuck) Hanover, N.H.	25	**MARYLAND** (Smith) College Park
11	**CORNELL** (Johnson) Ithaca, N.Y.	26	**PURDUE** (Krannert) W. Lafayette, Ind.
12	**VIRGINIA** (Darden) Charlottesville	27	**ROCHESTER** (Simon) Rochester, N.Y.
13	**UC BERKELEY** (Haas) Berkeley, Calif.	28	**VANDERBILT** (Owen) Nashville
14	**YALE** New Haven	29	**NOTRE DAME** (Mendoza) South Bend, Ind.
15	**NYU** (Stern) New York	30	**GEORGETOWN** (McDonough) D.C.

Area specific rankings (*BusinessWeek*):

Finance Skills	Marketing Skills	Global Scope	Technology	General Management
1. Chicago	1. Northwestern	1. Harvard	1. MIT	1. Harvard
2. Pennsylvania	2. Harvard	2. Pennsylvania	2. Carnegie Mellon	2. Northwestern
3. Columbia	3. Michigan	3. Chicago	3. Duke	3. Michigan
4. Harvard	4. Duke	4. Northwestern	4. Chicago	4. Pennsylvania
5. Michigan	5. Pennsylvania	5. Michigan	5. Michigan	5. Duke
6. Duke	6. Indiana	6. Columbia	6. Stanford	6. Virginia
7. Northwestern	7. Virginia	7. Duke	7. Pennsylvania	7. Dartmouth
8. NYU	8. Columbia	8. Virginia	8. Northwestern	8. Indiana
9. Virginia	9. Chicago	9. MIT	9. Harvard	9. Chicago
10. Indiana	10. Stanford	10. Thunderbird	10. Virginia	10. Stanford

The Top Schools From Canada and Europe, *BusinessWeek*, October 2002

1 **INSEAD** Fontainebleau, France
2 **QUEEN'S** Kingston, Canada
3 **IMD** Lausanne, Switzerland
4 **LONDON BUSINESS SCHOOL** London, England
5 **TORONTO** Toronto, Canada
6 **WESTERN ONTARIO** London, Canada
7 **ROTTERDAM** Rotterdam, Netherlands
8 **IESE** Barcelona, Spain
9 **HEC** Paris, France
10 **YORK** Toronto, Canada

America's Best Graduate Business Schools, *U.S. News & World Report*, April, 2003

The *U.S. News & World Report* (*www.usnews.com*) rankings arrive in the spring of each year.

Rank	School	Rank	School
1	Harvard Univrsity (MA)	42	Tulane University (Freeman) (LA)
2	Stanford University (CA)	42	University of Georgia (Terry)
2	University of Pennsylvania (Wharton)	42	University of Maryland–College Park (Smith)
4	MIT (Sloan)	45	Vanderbilt University (Owen) (TN)
4	Northwestern University (Kellogg) (IL)	46	University of California–Irvine
6	Columbia University (NY)	46	University of Wisconsin–Madison
7	Duke University (Fuqua) (NC)	48	Babson College (Qlin) (MA)
7	University of California–Berkeley (Haas)	49	University of Arizona (Eller)
9	University of Chicago	50	University of Pittsburgh (KAtz)
10	Dartmouth College (Tuck) (NH)	51	Georgia Institute of Tech (DuPree)
11	University of Virginia (Darden)	51	Rutgers–New Brunswick and Newark (NJ)
12	New York University (Stem)	51	Southern Methodist Univ (Cox) (TX)
13	University of Michigan–Ann Arbor	51	Texas A&M–College Station (Mays)
14	UC–LA (Anderson)	51	University of Oklahoma (PRice)
14	Yale University (CT)	56	Rensselaer Polytechnic Institute (Lally)
16	Cornell University (Johnson) (NY)	57	Clemson University (SC)
17	Carnegie Mellon University (PA)	57	DePaul University (Kellstadt) (IL)
17	University of Texas–Austin (McCombs)	59	College of William and Mary (VA)
19	Ohio State University (Fisher)0	60	University of Colorado–Boulder (Leeds)
20	Univ. of Southern California (Marshall)	61	Oklahoma State University
21	Emory University (Goizueta) (GA)	61	Univ of Massachusetts (Isenberg)
21	UNC–Chapel Hill (Kenan-Flagler)	63	Case Western Reserve (Weatherhead)
23	Indiana University–Bloomington (Kelley)	64	University of Miami (FL)
24	Georgetown (McDonough) (DC)	65	George Washington University (DC)
24	Purdue–West Lafayette (Krannert)	65	North Carolina State University
26	Univ of Minnesota–Twin Cities (Carlson)	65	SUNY–Albany
27	Rice University (Jones) (TX)	65	Syracuse University (NY)
27	University of Florida (Warrington)	65	University of alabama (Manderson)
29	Brigham Young Univ (Marriott) (UT)	70	Boston University
29	University of Iowa (Tippie)	70	CUNY Baruch College (Zicklin)
29	Notre Dame (Mendoza) (UN)	70	University of Missouri–Columbia
29	Washington Univ in St. Louis (Qlin)	70	University of Oregon (Lundquist)
33	Penn State–University Park (Smeal)	70	University of Southern Carolina (Moore)
33	University of Illinois–Urbana-Champaign	70	Virginia Tech (Pamplin)
35	University of California–Davis	76	Iowa State University
35	University of Washington	76	University of Connecticut
37	Arizona State (Carey)	78	Claremont Graduate School (Drucker)
37	Michigan State University (Broad)	78	Thunderbird Graduate School (AZ)
37	University of Rochester (Simon) (NY)	78	University of Tennessee–Knoxville
37	Wake Forest University (Babcock) (NC)	78	University of Texas–Dallas
41	Boston College (Carroll)	78	University of Utah (Eccles)

Asia's Top 25 Business Schools, *Asia Inc. Magazine*, August 2002

Asia Inc. (*www.asia-inc.com*) provides yearly rankings each fall.

1   Chinese University of Hong Kong
2   Indian Institute of Management, Ahmedabad
3   National University of Singapore Business School, Singapore
4   Hong Kong University of Science & Technology, Hong Kong
5   Asian Institute of Management, Philippines
6   Australian Graduate School of Management
6   University of Queensland Business School, Australia
8   University of Hong Kong, Faculty of Business & Economics, Hong Kong
9   Indian Institute of Management, Bangalore
10 Nanyang Technological University, Singapore
11 Melbourne Business School, Australia
11 Indian Institute of Management, Calcutta
13 China Europe International Business School (CEIBS), China
14 Chulalongkorn University, Sasin Graduate School of Management, Thailand
15 City University of Hong Kong
15 Chicago Graduate School of Business, Singapore
17 Yonsei University, South Korea
17 Monash University, Australia
17 Indian Institute of Management, Lucknow
20 International University of Japan
21 Macquarie Graduate School of Management, Australia
21 Asian Institute of Technology, Thailand
23 Peking University, Guanghua School of Management, China
23 National Institute of Development & Administration, Thailand
25 Lahore University of Management Sciences, Pakistan

MBA Rankings for Latin and South America, *AméricaEconomía*, September 2002

1   TEC de Monterrey (Monterrey), México
2   INCAE, Costa Rica
2   Universidad Católica de Chile, Chile
3   ITAM, México
4   Universidad Adolfo Ibáñez, Chile
5   Universidad de Chile–Tulane, Chile
6   Universidad de São Paulo, Brazil
7   Universidad de Chile, Chile
8   IAE, Argentina
9   IPADE, México
10 Coppead – UFRJ, Brazil

South Africa's Best MBAs, *Financial Mail* (www.fm.co.za), August 2002

1 Wits Business School
2 University of Cape Town
3 Unisa
4 University of Stellenbosch
5 Gordon Institute of Business Sciences
6 University of Pretoria
7 University of Natal
8 Henley
9 Rand Afrikaans University
10 Potchestroom Business School

The Top 100 Full-Time International MBA Programmes, *Financial Times*, January 2003

1 University of Pennsylvania: Wharton, U.S.
2 Harvard Business School, U.S.
3 Columbia Business School, U.S.
4 Stanford University GSB, U.S.
5 University of Chicago GSB, U.S.
6 Insead, France/Singapore
7 London Business School, U.K.
8 New York University: Stern, U.S.
9 Northwestern University: Kellogg, U.S.
10 MIT: Sloan, U.S.
11 Dartmouth College: Tuck, U.S.
12 Yale School of Management, U.S.
13 IMD, Switzerland
14 University of Virginia: Darden, U.S.
15 Duke University: Fuqua, U.S.
15 University of California at Berkeley: Haas, U.S.
17 Georgetown University: McDonough, U.S.
18 Iese Business School, Spain
19 Cornell University: Johnson, U.S.
20 University of California at Los Angeles: Anderson, U.S.
21 University of Toronto: Rotman, Canada
22 University of Western Ontario: Ivey, Canada
23 Carnegie Mellon University
23 University of North Carolina: Kenan-Flagler, U.S.
25 University of Michigan Business School, U.S.
26 Instituto de Empresa, Spain

26 York University: Schulich, Canada
28 Rotterdam School of Management, Netherlands
29 Emory University: Goizueta, U.S.
30 University of Cambridge: Judge, U.S.
31 University of Southern California: Marshall, U.S.
32 University of Texas at Austin: McCombs, U.S.
33 University of Maryland: Smith, U.S.
34 Warwick Business School, U.K.
35 University of Oxford: Said, U.K.
35 Vanderbilt University: Owen, U.S.
37 McGill University, Canada
38 University of Rochester: Simon, U.S.
39 Ohio State University: Fisher, U.S.
40 Queen's School of Business, Canada
40 Rice University: Jones, U.S.
40 University of California at Irvine, U.S.
43 SDA Bocconi, Italy
44 Manchester Business School, U.K.
45 Indiana University: Kelley, U.S.
45 University of South Carolina: Moore, U.S.
47 Purdue University: Krannert, U.S.
48 Pennsylvania State University: Smeal, U.S.
49 University of Illinois at Urbana-Champaign, U.S.
49 Washington University: Olin, U.S.
51 Brigham Young University: Marriott, U.S.
52 University of Iowa: Tippie, U.S.
53 Southern Methodist University: Cox, U.S.
54 Cranfield School of Management, U.K.
54 University of Notre Dame: Mendoza, U.S.
56 College of William & Mary, U.S.
57 Babson College: Olin, U.S.
57 Thunderbird, U.S.
59 Hong Kong University of Science and Technology, China
60 Michigan State University: Broad, U.S.
60 Virginia Tech: Pamplin, U.S.
62 Boston University, U.S.
62 HEC, France
64 Arizona State University, U.S.
64 Case Western Reserve: Weatherhead, U.S.
64 Melbourne Business School, Australia

64 Wake Forest University: Babcock, U.S.
68 City University Business School: Cass
69 Australian Graduate School of Management, Australia
69 Texas A&M: Mays, U.S.
69 University of Wisconsin-Madison, U.S.
72 University of Pittsburgh: Katz, U.S.
73 Edinburgh University Management School, U.K.
73 Universiteit Nyenrode, Netherlands
73 University of British Columbia, Canada
76 Tulane University: Freeman, U.S.
77 Chinese University of Hong Kong, China
78 Helsinki School of Economics, Finland
78 Imperial College Management School, U.K.
78 University of Georgia: Terry, U.S.
81 University of Minnesota: Carlson, U.S.
82 ESCP-EAP, France
83 Esade, Spain
83 Ipade, Mexico
85 Bradford School of Management/Nimbas, U.K./Netherlands/Germany
86 Trinity College Dublin, Ireland
86 University of Arizona: Eller, U.S.
88 IAE Management and Business School, Argentina
89 University College Dublin: Smurfit, Ireland
90 Ceibs, China
91 University of Bath School of Management, U.K.
92 ENPC School of International Management, France
93 University of Calgary: Haskayne, Canada
93 University of Washington Business School, U.S.
95 Ashridge, U.K.
95 Fordham University GBA, U.S.
95 University of Durham Business School, U.K.
98 Strathclyde GSB, U.K.
99 Coppead, Brazil
100 University of Alberta, Canada

On a Personal Note

It is perhaps strange to address the question, "Should I pursue an MBA/Is an MBA worth it?" at the back of the book as opposed to the beginning. However, for those who insist on going to a top business school this question has already been answered or is a mere afterthought. Although the answer below to the question above is a personal one, I believe there are many "incomplete" ways to analyze the question, so much so, that I have chosen to write a short response to address the question.

The most incomplete answer comes from analyzing the question only from a quantitative dimension. This involves evaluating the cost of a business program including tuition, books, housing, food, and other living and incidental expenses, and adding to this the opportunity cost of forgone wages (including two years' salary and benefits), and comparing all of this to the increase in salary you expect to receive post-MBA. The flaw in this approach is that it is terribly difficult to project the expected revenue to be received in your future working years. For example, a single idea gained during your MBA program could be, for you, a million-dollar idea; another idea could save you hundreds of thousands of dollars when making an important future business or personal decision.

The biggest flaw, of course, is that such an approach ignores qualitative considerations. These considerations include an increased feeling of self-confidence, sense of accomplishment, and personal fulfillment gained from completing your graduate education. Other qualitative reasons include the making of new friends, gaining of new contacts, the pursuing of an enriching academic experience, bolstering problem solving skills, honing of personal skills, and the ability to think and reason better both personally and professionally. As one MBA graduate remarked, "It's two years of learning to think outside the box."

A common deficiency in thinking about an MBA purely in quantitative terms is the inability to account for the "people factor". There is a certain strength gained when facing certain business or personal problems or opportunities, and being able to call, contact, or just think back to one or more business school classmates and recall their strengths, characteristics, and idiosyncrasies. What would they do in this situation? In the words of another business school graduate, "I never feel alone because I have a vast reservoir to draw upon."

There is some truth to the brash remark: "If you have to ask whether it is worth doing an MBA, you're not the right person to do one." However, one way to answer the question, "Should I pursue an MBA/Is an MBA worth it?" is to view the MBA in the broader light of all graduate degrees, in which the MBA is neither greater not lesser than any other graduate degree. Here, the belief is: "A young person should pursue an advanced education credential be it business, law, medicine, engineering, international relations, or the sciences because obtaining an advanced education credential is a great way to finish one's formal education." Stated from an opposite angle: "Pursue an MBA unless you have a good reason not to." Some good reasons for not doing so would include: (1) "I have a great job and to give it up to go to business school means risking not getting it back again", (2) "I have my own growing business and to leave to go to business school would entail the risk of losing it even if placed in the hands of another manager while I am at business school", and (3) "I have a family and leaving to go to business school would cause too much disruption and strain."

Perhaps the acid test for the question, "Should I do an MBA/Is an MBA worth it?" arises when asking business school graduates whether they would make the same decision again. Interestingly, a number of law school graduates answer "no" to the question of whether they would pursue a law degree (or a legal career) if they had to do things all over. However, extremely rare is the MBA graduate who says, "Boy, that was a dumb decision, I wouldn't do that again." Along the way you may meet a few arguably cynical MBA students who will tell you that an MBA is just a two-year job search. But even these graduates—throwing all other possible positive qualitative and quantitative factors to the wind—will answer "yes" to the question at hand, if for no other reason than the "credential factor".

About the Author

Brandon Royal is a graduate of the University of Chicago's Graduate School of Business and a Certified Public Accountant. In his role as Managing Director of Royal Publications in Hong Kong, he works as an education consultant, corporate trainer, and independent author. He also works concurrently for U.S.-based Kaplan Educational Centers—a Washington Post subsidiary and the oldest and largest test preparatory organization in the world—and, through his work as a GMAT test-prep instructor and admissions coach, has helped hundreds of applicants achieve acceptance at one or more of the world's leading programs. As one of Asia's most well-known admission specialists, Brandon has been an on-going speaker for the American Chamber of Commerce in Hong Kong, and has contributed to various news and TV programs including the *South China Morning Post* newspaper, the *Far Eastern Economic Review* and *Fortune (China)* magazines, and CNBC's *Smart Money* program. His authorship in the business school product line includes the companion book *Ace the GMAT* (Topscore Ltd, 2003; available on Amazon.com).

Brandon has an eclectic mix of marketing, accounting and finance, and entrepreneurial experience gained from having worked successfully across a wide range of industries including oil and gas, public accounting, education, and teaching and training. As a former joint-venture auditor for the Ernst and Young accounting group in Hong Kong, he audited client companies including Coca-Cola, McCormick Seasoning and Foodstuffs Company, and the Hilton and Holiday Inn Hotels in China. He has conducted training seminars for such well-known organizations as AT&T, ATKearney, Australian Society of CPAs, Bank of East Asia, Deloitte Touche Tohmatsu, Hongkong International Terminals (Hutchison Whampoa Group), Hong Kong University of Science and Technology, JP Morgan, Mast Industries, Merrill Lynch, and Pacific Century Insurance.

A Canadian by birth and a resident of Hong Kong, Brandon is an avid writer and traveler. He also enjoys running, golf, and tennis, and is a former three-time Canadian National Junior Tennis qualifier. In his own words, he is light-hearted but not long-winded: "I am an accountant by training, an anthropologist by disposition, a writer by choosing, and a bar patron by necessity."